ESSAYS IN JEWISH BIOGRAPHY

The publication of this book was made possible
in part by a gift of the
SOLIS-COHEN FAMILY FUND
in honor of
SOLOMON SOLIS-COHEN,
POET, SCIENTIST, PHYSICIAN
one of the founders of The Jewish Publication Society
and a friend of the author of this volume.

ESSAYS IN JEWISH BIOGRAPHY

by

ALEXANDER MARX

PHILADELPHIA

THE JEWISH PUBLICATION SOCIETY OF AMERICA

5708–1947

60

PRINTED IN THE UNITED STATES OF AMERICA
PRESS OF THE JEWISH PUBLICATION SOCIETY
PHILADELPHIA, PENNA.

Preface

THE twelve biographies included in this volume were not written according to a plan. Most of them were called forth by anniversaries of great men; others were intended as memorials to departed scholars whose names and achievements deserve to be retained in the minds of our own and future generations. Moreover, personal reasons also had a share in motivating my selection of each of these men, whose lives are here presented to a wider circle of readers.

The four mediaeval scholars discussed herein, though not statesmen who influenced the course of history, left a lasting impression on the development of Judaism. The works of Rashi have attracted me since my early youth. My Talmud teachers, as well as Professor Adolf Berliner, my first teacher in Jewish History, imbued me with admiration for Rashi's rare personality and I have, in the course of my talmudic studies, gained in admiration for his wonderful Commentary on the Talmud. My interest in Saadia was aroused by the greatness and originality of his work and the unusual story of his life. It was sustained by the continued discoveries of new material in the *Geniza* which changed and clarified the picture of this outstanding gaon. He was the pathfinder in a variety of fields which reached the culmination of their development in the works of that incomparable genius, Moses Maimonides. While the essays on these three intellectual giants were prepared in connection with their recent anniversaries, the paper on Rabbenu Gershom was written at the suggestion of Professor Louis Finkelstein for the Institute of Religious and Social Studies. It was difficult to get a clear picture of the

work of this eminent personality who stood at the thresh-
hold of the development of Judaism in northern Europe;
this essay therefore required more detailed research than
the others. It was not my aim to offer novel results in these
biographies, but I have tried to give a well-rounded picture
of the activity of the four towering scholars on the basis of
our present knowledge.

The eight modern scholars presented here have to a
greater or lesser extent helped to interpret Jewish life and
literature for our own day. In their case, too, I had a personal reason for selecting these men — in one way or
another, each of them either affected my own scholarly
career or was bound to me by ties of close friendship.
Steinschneider, Hoffmann and Schechter made immense
contributions to Jewish learning; Schechter, moreover,
has had a tremendous influence on the development of
Judaism in this country. The other five cannot rank with
these great figures and their epoch-making works, but
they also contributed their share in the furtherance of Jewish learning in America and their works constitute an
important part of the storehouse of our vast literature.
As their intimate friend, I felt that I could give a more
vivid account of their lives and of their works, many of
which were prepared almost under my eyes. These sketches
were written shortly after their deaths and I have striven
to gather all possible information about them.

Judge Mayer Sulzberger falls a little outside of the scope
of this volume. All his scholarly work was undertaken
during his late years. But it was Sulzberger who laid the
foundation for a great Jewish library in the United States
to serve as a basis for the development of Jewish learning
on this continent. The stimulus given to research in our
field by his rare vision and foresight should assure him a
prominent place in the history of Jewish scholarship in
this country. Similarly the brilliant and versatile scholar

and writer Joseph Jacobs, whose greatest merits lie perhaps in other fields, deserves grateful recollection in the annals of Jewish learning.

I was especially eager to set a literary monument to three of the men who, besides my revered father, had the greatest influence on my own development: my teachers David Hoffmann — later my father-in-law — and Moritz Steinschneider and my fatherly friend, Solomon Schechter. My contacts with them influenced my own work to a large extent. In this connection I may be permitted to express my indebtedness to another teacher, Professor Franz Ruehl of the University of Koenigsberg who taught me historical method, the principles of textual criticism and the method of preparing critical editions. The few necrologies on Hoffmann and the numerous articles published on Steinschneider's eightieth and ninetieth birthdays and the hundredth anniversary of his birth, though they throw light on various aspects of the activity and personality of these great masters and have been very helpful, by no means give a full account of their lives and works. In the bibliographical notes at the end of the volume I have recorded the sources on which I have drawn for these two essays and have given a selected literature for the other papers. Titles of books, throughout this volume, are generally given in English translation; the interested reader will find the original titles with the help of the bibliographical notes.

The essays on Rabbenu Gershom, Steinschneider and Hoffmann are published here for the first time; that on Hoffmann was prepared for the hundredth anniversary of his birth. The article on Steinschneider, the most extensive of all, was written for this volume to voice my feeling of personal indebtedness, and that of Jewish scholarship in general, towards this master-builder of the history of Jewish literature. The other nine essays have been printed before. Five of them were included in my *Studies in Jewish History and Booklore*, New York, 1944; but since that book was meant for a smaller circle of readers and its edition of 650 copies is entirely out of print, they are repeated here.

This book is due to a suggestion made some years ago to The Jewish Publication Society by my friend, Professor Shalom Spiegel. I am very grateful to him and to the authorities of The Society for publishing this volume. Miss Anna Kleban was helpful with the preparation of many of these essays when they first appeared. Dr. Solomon Grayzel made numerous valuable suggestions in revising these papers for publication. I want to express my special thanks to my wife for her help, her encouragement and her constructive criticism.

I have striven, so far as it is humanly possible, to present an objective picture of each of the ancient and modern scholars, not permitting my personal feelings of admiration or intimate friendship to blind my judgment. I hope that these biographies will find a friendly circle of readers and will serve, in spite of their simple and artless presentation, as a slight contribution to the study of Jewish history and the appreciation of some of our great scholars and sages.

ALEXANDER MARX

New York, December 1, 1947.

TABLE OF CONTENTS

		PAGE
PREFACE		vii–x
1	RAB SAADIA GAON	3–38
2	RABBENU GERSHOM, LIGHT OF THE EXILE	39–60
3	RASHI	61–86
4	MAIMONIDES	87–111
5	MORITZ STEINSCHNEIDER	112–184
6	DAVID HOFFMANN	185–222
7	MAYER SULZBERGER	223–228
8	SOLOMON SCHECHTER	229–250
9	THE JEWISH SCHOLARSHIP OF JOSEPH JACOBS	251–254
10	HENRY MALTER	255–264
11	MAX LEOPOLD MARGOLIS	265–279
12	ISRAEL FRIEDLAENDER THE SCHOLAR	280–289
BIBLIOGRAPHY		293–298

ESSAYS IN JEWISH BIOGRAPHY

1

Rab Saadia Gaon

OUTSIDE of Palestine no country has exerted a deeper influence on the development of Judaism than Babylonia. Jews had been settled there since the destruction of the first Temple. They had arranged for the return to the homeland under Cyrus; they had inspired and financed the later group which returned under Ezra's leadership and the trips of Nehemiah to strengthen the new Palestinian settlement. Only a small section of Babylonian Jewry, however, had taken an active part in the restoration of Palestine. The majority had remained in the new home where they had taken deep root and carried on their economic activities while looking to Eretz Yisrael for spiritual guidance. In the course of centuries, they developed a certain degree of intellectual life, undoubtedly establishing schools in which the Bible and the language of their fathers were cultivated. Advanced studies, however, could only be carried on in Palestine. It was for this reason that, shortly before the beginning of the Common Era, a man like Hillel left the land of his birth to acquire a deeper knowledge of Jewish law. More than a century later, Palestinian scholars, who emigrated from Palestine during the Bar Kochba uprisings against Rome, made efforts to transfer Jewish intellectual life to Babylonia. The schools they founded were at first only of local significance, but they laid the foundation for the great development of the following period.

Only with the codification of the Oral Law in an authoritative code, the Mishna, around the year 200, did it become possible to create a center of Jewish studies outside of the

Holy Land. Two of the greatest pupils of Rabbi Judah the Prince, the compiler of the Mishna, were to become the architects of the great Babylonian center. Rab and Samuel, who for years had studied in the academy of the great master, returned to their old home and established schools, thus giving a new impetus to Jewish learning in Babylonia. The one took over the older school of Nehardea and imbued it with a new spirit. The other founded an academy in Sura, a place where complete ignorance had prevailed. After the destruction of Nehardea, its school was transferred to Pumbedita, and the two sister academies of Sura and Pumbedita became the spiritual centers of Judaism for many centuries.

In these academies the Mishna was expounded and reinterpreted to fit the different economic conditions of Babylonia. In the course of three centuries, the academies created the gigantic work which was to become the cornerstone of Judaism for all time — the Babylonian Talmud.

When the creative spirit of these schools ceased to function, after the year 500, the Amoraim, the authors of the Talmud, were succeeded by two generations of Saboraim, who put the discussions of the academies during the preceding centuries into final form. They were the redactors of the Talmud.

A time of stagnation followed. The new heads of the academies, the geonim, devoted themselves to the study and interpretation of the great work; but only few traces of their activity during the next two centuries have been preserved.

In the middle of the eighth century, we first meet with a head of one of the academies who is more than a mere name to us — he is the blind Gaon Yehudai of Pumbedita, the author of the first code produced by the Babylonian schools. Rab Yehudai must have been a very great personality, for, although he presided over his academy for only three years, he exerted a deep influence on his contemporaries. The following generations limited their literary activity mainly to answering questions directed to them from Babylonia and from other countries. These geonic responsa contain the nucleus for the various branches of Jewish literature which developed in the following period. Originally very brief, these responsa sometimes grew to great length. The first text of the prayer book, composed by the Gaon Rab Amram at the request of the Spanish communities, was in its form nothing but a responsum.

The Babylonian Jews were a well organized group, guided in spiritual matters by the geonim. Politically, however, the exilarch, a scion of the royal family of Judah, ruled over them as an autonomous, recognized minority in the caliphate. He represented them at court, where the exilarch held a very high position. The office had flourished throughout the Persian period by appointment of successive Persian rulers, and later, after the Muhammedan conquest of Babylonia, was continued by the caliphs. After designation by the Jewish representatives, the exilarch was inducted into his office with great solemnity by the heads of the two academies.

Relations between the political and the spiritual heads of Jewry were not always pleasant. Our sources inform us of a number of bitter quarrels between the two. Even in the academies, peace and goodwill did not always prevail. Several times the academies were split between contenders for the Gaonate, and two opponents presided simultaneously over factions of the membership of the same school. Most of the geonim of both academies belonged to the same few leading families which opposed the election of anyone from the outside. Sherira Gaon, the historian of the academies, refers disdainfully to one of his predecessors, Aaron ben Joseph ha-Kohen, i. e., Kalaf ben Sarjado, of whom I shall have to speak later. Sherira states that originally Aaron did not belong to the scholars of the academy, but was the son of a merchant.

During the five centuries of the geonic period, only one of the heads of the academies was not a native Babylonian. Rab Saadia ben Joseph al-Fayyumi, — i. e., from the Egyptian district of Fayyum — had come to Babylonia as a recognized scholar. The mere fact that such a man attained this outstanding position which made him one of the world-leaders of Jewry is sufficient to indicate that we are dealing here with a towering personality, a man of such outstanding qualifications that all notions of local pride, of petty objections, were silenced by his merits. What the particular merits were which brought to him this unique distinction, we shall discuss later.

We now turn to the life of this greatest and most original of the geonim, the pioneer in so many fields of Jewish literature, the thousandth anniversary of whose death was commemorated in 1942.

The discoveries of the last fifty years in the treasures of the *Geniza* have enormously enriched our knowledge of the life and works of our hero. The *Geniza* was a room in an ancient synagogue at Cairo into which, for a thousand years, discarded books and documents in Hebrew characters had been dumped. Although there are still a great many gaps in the information we have gleaned — and further researches in the scattered documents of the Cairo treasure trove may help to fill some of these gaps — we can draw today a much fuller picture of Saadia's life and activity than was possible in the last century. Even the date of his birth was wrongly transmitted by an early historian, so that the millennium of his birth was celebrated ten years too late — in 1892. We know now that Saadia was born in 882, between the 27th of June and the 5th of

July, and died in the night between Sunday and Monday, May 16, 942, about 2 o'clock in the morning. This information we owe to his two sons who, eleven years after his death, compiled a list of his works in which they also gave the date of his death and a statement that he died some forty days before his sixtieth birthday.

Saadia was a man of strong convictions as well as of a pugnacious nature and was often involved in controversies. Some of the data on his personal life are derived from remarks made by his opponents in bitter attacks on his personality. From such sources we gather that his native place was Dilaz in the Fayyum and that his father followed him to Palestine and died in Jaffa. In order to disparage him, his opponents claimed that his father was a butcher, a barber, and even a muezzin in a mosque! While Saadia claims descent from Shelah, the son of Juda, his enemies maintained that he was descended from converts. Sherira, in the epistle in which he traces the history of the oral tradition, refers to Saadia's father as a scholar, and there is thus good reason to disregard the charges of evil-tongued adversaries.

Saadia was reared in Egypt, where he received his education. There he started his literary activity and gathered a group of pupils around him. We conclude from this that the Muhammedan conquest had greatly improved the condition of the Jews in Egypt, too, and had caused a revival of spiritual activity after the oppression by the Church.

About the teachers who inspired the young genius to devote his great gifts to the furthering of Jewish learning, we know nothing. The Arabic historian Masudi mentions the name of the Tiberias scholar, Abu Kathir Yahya al-Katib, as Saadia's teacher. But Saadia probably came under his influence at a later period, when he had emigrated to Palestine.

We know that at the age of twenty Saadia composed his dictionary, *Agron*, which he later revised, and that at the age of twenty-three he inaugurated his polemical writings with a refutation of the work of Anan, the founder of Karaism.

Again our sources do not permit us to state whether the sectarian movement of the Karaites, which at that time had its center in Palestine, had spread to Egypt. Possibly Saadia had become acquainted with Anan's work and considered it necessary to write against it, although Karaism had not as yet extended its influence to his homeland.

The Egyptian period of Saadia's life is shrouded in darkness. We cannot tell when he left Egypt for Palestine. The only allusion to a definite date is found in a letter to his pupils whom he left in Egypt. In this letter, written in 921 or 922, he says that he had not heard from them for six and a half years and that he was separated for this length of time from his wife and children. Accordingly, it is stated that he left Egypt in 915. But a description is extant of a trip through Palestine and Syria by a young man in his early twenties, which Schechter thought might possibly have been written by Saadia. If that hypothesis is correct, we should have to conclude that Saadia left his home about ten years earlier and perhaps returned again to Egypt. However that may be, we may assume that there was no challenge to his abilities in Egypt, and that he decided to turn to one of the centers of Jewish spiritual life to find for himself a wider sphere of activity. But success was slow in coming.

What his activities were in the various cities of Palestine and Syria that he visited, and how long he stayed there, we cannot tell. As stated above, he probably enjoyed for some time the instruction of a scholar at Tiberias, but the Palestinian academy did not offer an opening to the gifted foreigner. There, as in Babylonia, all the important positions were held by the members of a few families. Undoubtedly, he wrote some books during these years and made a name for himself. Only thus can we understand his being in correspondence with one of the Babylonian geonim, R. Judah, the head of the Pumbedita academy, who died in 917.

A recently discovered responsum of Sherira Gaon mentions the questions which Saadia, while still in Palestine, directed to this Gaon Judah, Sherira's grandfather. One of these questions dealt with a point of the Jewish calendar which was to play a decisive part in Saadia's life.

The announcement of the new moon and the determination of the date of the holidays was an ancient privilege which the Palestinian schools maintained for many centuries. Though it is generally assumed that the calendar was published in the middle of the fourth century by Hillel II, it seems that it was not automatically followed without official announcement by the Palestinian authorities. As late as 835, a Babylonian exilarch expressly stated in a letter that, in the interest of the unity of Israel, he, the geonim, the scholars and the public at large follow the calendar announcement of the Palestinian scholars. About the same time, it seems, the Babylonian schools sent a group of scholars to Palestine to study and discuss the problem of determining the calendar and, probably soon afterwards, they emancipated themselves from the ancient custom of relying on Palestine for the calendrical announcement. Yet less than a century later the Babylonian scholars already claimed that even the oldest among them did not recollect that they had ever waited for Palestinian guidance in this matter. At the time, however, there was no difference between the two countries as to the dates of the holidays.

A new situation arose when an energetic head of the

Palestinian schools, Aaron ben Meir, a scholar or high standing, decided to announce a rule which would prevent the postponement for two days of Passover and New Year in the year 921. The Babylonian academies refused to recognize this rule.

Ben Meir hoped to be able to carry his point, and he made careful preparations to do so. He had been having great difficulties with the Karaites. This sect which denied the authority of the Oral Law had grown very powerful in Jerusalem. To gain the support of the central government, Ben Meir traveled to Bagdad and obtained the assistance of Aaron ben Amram, one of the great bankers at the court of the caliph. Through the banker's influence, he succeeded in getting a favorable decree against the Karaites.

The exilarch, David ben Zakkai, probably did not cooperate with him and kept aloof. Ben Meir, however, made contacts with the head of the school of Pumbedita, Rab Mebasser, who had been appointed by the members of his school in 917 after the death of Saadia's above-mentioned correspondent, the Gaon Rab Judah. There had been a bitter quarrel between the previous exilarch, Ukba, a cousin of his successor, and the academies. Ukba had been removed from his position and exiled from the country. Rab Mebasser and the members of the Pumbedita academy were afraid to see his cousin, David ben Zakkai, take his place, and refused him recognition. The exilarch thereupon appointed one of his adherents, Rab Kohen Tsedek, counter-gaon of Pumbedita. But only a smaller group of the scholars recognized the new appointee.

During his stay in Bagdad, Ben Meir made contact with the Gaon Mebasser and his partisans, and on his return promulgated a decree of excommunication against the exilarch and his appointee, Kohen Tsedek. He was confident that these friends he had made in Bagdad would support him in his calendar scheme, which, he claimed, was not to institute a reform, but to follow ancient tradition. He proceeded to make his announcement and it caused a split in Jewry.

A Christian Syrian chronicler of the eleventh century records that in 921 the Western (Palestinian) Jews started their New Year on Tuesday; those of the East (Babylonians) on Thursday. This statement, first brought to the attention of Jewish scholars by Dr. Cyrus Adler, as well as a remark of a Karaite zealot of the tenth century about a controversy on the calendar in Saadia's time, can be properly understood now on the basis of the documents which were brought to light from the treasures of the *Geniza.*

In the summer of 921, Ben Meir sent circular letters to various countries, stating that in the fall of that year the months of Marheshvan and Kislev would have only 29 days, while according to the Babylonian calculation they would be full months of 30 days. At the annual solemn convocation which took place on Hosh'ana Rabba on Mount Olivet, he ordered his son to make a public announcement to that effect. Thus the struggle between Palestine and Babylonia was started..

Saadia was traveling that summer from Aleppo to Bagdad. He heard rumors of Ben Meir's plans and sent him letters advising him that he was mistaken in his method of fixing the calendar and urging him to desist from his plan. When Saadia arrived in Bagdad, he learned that he had been wrong in his assumption that Ben Meir would accept his reasons and give up his new plan. The exilarch and the heads of the academies thereupon issued letters denouncing Ben Meir's proceedings and insisting that their calculation of the calendar be followed. Neither side was ready to yield, and thus the Passover and the following New Year's Day were observed on different days by the adherents of the contending parties. How far the influence of the two sides extended we cannot tell, but we learn from the above-mentioned Karaite that both sides had adherents in Palestine as well as in Babylonia.

Saadia seems to have become the leader of the Babylonian party immediately upon his arrival. Of a militant nature and powerful personality, his great superiority over the other participants was evidenced at once, and they recognized him as the natural champion of their cause.

It was of the utmost importance to create a united front in Babylonia, and the exilarch was prevailed upon to make peace with the rebellious faction of the Pumbedita academy. While his appointee, Kohen Tsedek, retained his income and title, the exilarch, David ben Zakkai, now recognized Rab Mebasser, the choice of the members of the academy. The majority of the academy had joined him from the beginning, and their number probably increased in consequence of the exilarch's recognition, only a few adherents remaining faithful to his opponent.

Ben Meir resented the change of mind of his former partisans. He pleaded with them; he voiced bitter recriminations; but to no avail.

Only a small part of the writings of the contending parties has been discovered so far, but we get a general picture of the course of the controversy. The details of the struggle are too technical to be presented in a popular essay. What interests us in particular is the part Saadia played in this fight and the influence it had on his life.

Naturally it was his task to see to it that his old home, Egypt, should side with the Babylonian authorities. Some letters of his to his former pupils in Egypt have been preserved. In two of them he urges these pupils to take steps so that Passover should be observed in Egypt on the right days and that they should not eat leaven on the holidays. The first letter was evidently written towards the end of the year 921 and included a proclamation by the exilarch

and the heads of the academies. This is the letter already
mentioned, in which he tells them that he has not heard
from them directly for six and a half years. In the second
letter, written in the beginning of 922, he emphasizes that
in Babylonia all the scholars stand together and maintain
the same point of view on the calendar question. By that
time unity had been restored in the academies.

A third letter of Saadia to Egypt, in Arabic and evidently to the same pupils, is dated Friday, January 3, 922.
They had written that Egyptian Jewry had followed Ben
Meir's calendar. Saadia implores them to change their
attitude and not to cause him further mortification.

The controversy raged for some time and both sides
sent appeals to the Jewries in and outside their countries
for support. Direct communications between Ben Meir
and his opponents seem to have ceased after a while and,
as far as we can judge, unity was restored in Israel after
two years. Babylonia prevailed over Palestine.

Saadia undoubtedly had the lion's share in this triumph.
It brought him at last an adequate position and ended
the years of his restless wanderings. For shortly after his
arrival in Babylonia, he was rewarded for his energetic
stand by an appointment to a high post in one of the
academies.

He signs the first letter to his Egyptian pupils, the one
written towards the end of 921, "Said ben Josef, Ras al-
Kal." Five or six months later, in Tammuz 922, he signs
one of the documents on the controversy as "Saadia ben
Josef, *Alluf*." *Alluf*, or *Resh Kalla*, was a title given to the
first seven members of the academy after the gaon and the
ab-bet-din. Which of the two academies honored itself
by adding this new member to its staff cannot be determined. Thenceforth Saadia was an outstanding member
in a most exclusive group of scholars in one of those ancient

schools which were reluctant to admit an outsider into their midst.

After the conclusion of the controversy, Saadia, at the request of the exilarch, recorded the facts for future generations in a book called *Book of Festivals*. Only fragments of this book have been preserved and contribute to the reconstruction of this interesting chapter of Jewish history.

We may assume that in the following years Saadia devoted himself to teaching in the academy and to literary pursuits. We hear that one of the powerful court-bankers, Sahl ben Natira, became his pupil.

Two of Saadia's poetical compositions bear his name in the acrostics, with the title *Alluf* and *Resh Kalla* respectively, and must have been composed in the years following his settlement in Babylonia.

His most comprehensive work against the Karaites was written in 926. Many other works for which we lack such indications undoubtedly came from the pen of the indefatigable scholar during the years he was a *Resh Kalla* at one of the academies.

But Saadia was destined for a much greater distinction. By his valiant and successful fight against Ben Meir, he had placed the exilarch under deep obligation. This brought him, a few years later, the fulfillment of an ambition of which he might hardly have dared to dream.

The Academy of Sura, founded by Rab in the third century, which for centuries had enjoyed considerable privileges over the rival Academy of Pumbedita, had fallen into a very precarious state. Perhaps it was the fact that the Academy of Pumbedita, though retaining its name, had been transferred to Bagdad, the capital of the Caliphate. This may have given it new prestige and attracted the best scholars, even from the rival academy. At any rate, Sura had declined to such an extent that serious consideration was being given to closing the famous seat of learning and merely maintaining its name by appointing a member of the Pumbedita school as titular Gaon of Sura, a gaon *in partibus*. But the man designated for this distinction, an uncle of the later Gaon Sherira, died before the plan was carried out. His sudden death was taken as an omen that this step was wrong. A new gaon, therefore, was to be appointed who should be able to restore the old luster of Sura. The exilarch first turned to one of the scholars of Sura who had been instrumental in terminating the fight between Rab Mebasser of Pumbedita, the leader of the opposition, and the exilarch, David ben Zakkai. But this old scholar, Nissi al-Naharwani, a blind man, did not feel equal to the arduous task and refused the honor.

Thereupon the exilarch asked his advice as to which of two other candidates was preferable. One of these was Tsemah ben Shahin, a descendant of Babylonian scholars. The other was none other than Saadia. Nissi, though recognizing the eminence of Saadia, advised against him, for, although a scholar of outstanding merit, he was difficult to get along with. His great learning and piety would never permit Saadia to take personal considerations into account.

But the exilarch had made up his mind beforehand that Saadia was the only person who could be expected to restore the Sura academy to its ancient glory, and he determined to appoint him. The objection of the wise old scholar, however, made an impression on him and, before appointing Saadia, he exacted a formal promise from him never to oppose him, conspire against him, or join a counter-exilarch. He claimed later that Saadia accepted these conditions and confirmed them by an oath. It is to the credit of David that, in spite of the warning, he made the choice which in his judgment was the only proper one in the interests of the academy.

Saadia must have been deeply gratified with this appointment to the highest and most dignified office to which a Jewish scholar of that time could aspire. To fill the position which Rab, the greatest Babylonian leader, the founder of Jewish learning in that country, had created seven centuries before, must have given him the greatest satisfaction possible. The appointment was probably unexpected, for he applied to it the verse, "And Hezekiah rejoiced, and all the people, because of that which God had prepared for the people; for the thing was done suddenly" (II Chron. 29.36). The passage occurs in one of the two letters announcing his election to his friends in Egypt.

Of the first of these letters only the beginning and the end have been preserved. He asks the Egyptians to turn to him for any support they may need from the Bagdad government. He will present their wishes to the court-bankers, the sons of Netira and of Aaron, who will ask the ruling powers to grant their requests. He is aware of the great responsibility that has been placed upon him. He is anxious to hear from his pupils regularly, for there cannot be a king without a people and there is no honor for scholars without pupils.

In this "letter of good tidings" he promises a second "letter of warning and advice." This one also has been discovered in recent times, although not in the *Geniza*. Here he speaks of the sessions of the academy over which he had presided and of the prayers he directed to the Lord for the remnant of Israel. The letter contains thirty short paragraphs addressing the readers as "Sons of Israel." He urges them to watch and reprove one another, to fulfil every *mitsva* wholeheartedly. He exhorts them to expect the redemption every day. He asks them, possibly in view of the Karaite attacks, to maintain every part of the Oral Law.

For two years Saadia devoted his tremendous energy and his great gifts to the re-establishment of the Sura academy and injected new life into the old school. The relations between the gaon and the exilarch were most friendly. How the head of the rival school of Pumbedita felt about the newcomer who outshone him and restored its old privileges to the Sura academy, we cannot tell. But we may assume that there were many who envied the outsider, and some who would have preferred the Sura school to decay so as to bring about a merger between the two institutions.

The harmony between Saadia and David ben Zakkai came to an abrupt end in 930 or thereabouts. As Nissi had foreseen, the two strong and unbending personalities were bound to clash sooner or later; and the occasion came more quickly than expected.

Certain decisions by the exilarch in important civil matters required endorsement by the two geonim. By chance, one such decision by David ben Zakkai, with Saadia's endorsement, has been preserved. A similar case caused the clash between the two men. About the year 930, the exilarch was asked to decide on the distribution of an inheritance, estimated to amount to 70,000 gold pieces, of which he, possibly in his official capacity, was to receive ten percent. He rendered his opinion and asked the parties to submit it to the geonim for their approval. Saadia did not agree with some points; however, he did not want to raise any questions and asked the men to submit the document to his older colleague, the Pumbedita gaon, Rab Kohen Tsedek, who signed it without hesitation. When it was returned to him, he tried to avoid a quarrel by saying that one endorsement was sufficient. But the people insisted that he should give the reason for his refusal and, after being repeatedly adjured to reveal his opinion, he finally had to explain his objections. The exilarch naturally was

incensed over this action and sent his son to tell Saadia:
"Don't be a fool; sign the document." The young man
politely urged him to avoid a quarrel. The gaon replied
that one must show no respect to a person in matters of
law. The young man was repeatedly sent to and fro, and
in the end he lost patience and threatened the gaon with
physical force. Thereupon Saadia's adherents unceremo-
niously threw the son of the exilarch out of the house.
The exilarch now put the gaon under excommunication
and appointed in his place Joseph ben Jacob ibn Satia,
a more pliable man, a scholar of no consequence, but a
descendant of geonim. Saadia's fighting spirit was now
aroused. He was not a man to yield easily to a powerful
opponent. He in turn excommunicated the exilarch and
appointed the latter's brother, Hasan, or as they called
him in Hebrew, Josiah, as a counter-exilarch. Thus began
the battle between the two headstrong leaders, the issue of
which remained in doubt for several years.

Besides the gaon and the exilarch, a third power had
developed in Bagdad during the tenth century — the
court-bankers. Two rich and powerful merchants, Joseph
ben Phineas and Aaron ben Amram, both from the Persian
province Ahwaz, had joined forces and founded a firm
which exerted great power and influence at the court of
the caliph. Arabic sources, which have been investigated
recently by Dr. Walter Fischel, supplement our information
and shed much light on that period. The two bankers are
mentioned for the first time in 908, when they had business
dealings with one of the viziers. In 912 or 913, they were
officially appointed court-bankers and for many years they
carried on large scale operations. Their names occur in the
records till 924, and we are informed that they retained
their position until their deaths. Their clients were mainly
high officials and viziers. One of the latter had deposited
with one of these bankers not less than 160,000 dinars by

the time he was deposed. These were public funds which the vizier had turned over to his own secret account, and the Caliph al-Muktadir compelled the bankers to return the money to the royal treasury. The bankers were employed to transfer money from one place to another by means of letters of credit, thus avoiding the risk of robbery which the transport of large sums to distant places would involve. By this method the taxes from the provinces were transmitted to the capital. Sometimes the bankers had to make large advances to the payrolls of the army, or for other urgent needs. They were reimbursed by income from the taxes. For a period of sixteen years the firm advanced loans of 10,000 dinars on letters of credit for taxes which were not yet due, and they received a monthly interest of 2,500 dirhams. Once they were compelled to make an advance of 150,000 dirhams a month under duress by one of the viziers.

These bankers were deeply interested in the welfare of their coreligionists and seem to have been particularly concerned with the affairs of the academies. It was through their good offices and international connections that the contributions collected abroad, in the various communities of Northern Africa, Spain, and elsewhere, for the sustenance of the Babylonian schools were transferred to Bagdad. In all likelihood, they also transmitted the correspondence between the geonim and these foreign Jewish centers.

We can well imagine that these men, because of their daily contacts with the highest government officials, had greater influence and that their opinions carried more weight than the word of the official head of the Babylonian Jewry, the exilarch, in spite of the august rank of the latter at court.

It was the support of these bankers which had enabled the geonim to succeed in their fight against the previous exilarch, Ukba, and to have him banished from the caliphate. One of these bankers, Aaron ben Amram, had lent his support to Ben Meir and procured for him a favorable decree against the Karaites. He had, at least for some time, supported him in his calendar scheme. Ben Meir in his letters repeatedly refers to this support.

By the time Saadia had been elevated to the gaonate, the two founders of the firm were no longer among the living. But some years before they passed away, they had taken into the firm Natira, the son-in-law of Joseph ben Phineas, the one partner, and the sons of Aaron ben Amram, the second partner. Natira must have passed away before his father-in-law and was succeeded by his two sons who carried on the business with their grandfather. The sons of Natira and the sons of Aaron enjoyed the same influence which had been exerted by their father and grandfather. During the crisis produced by the quarrel between the gaon and the exilarch, they were divided in their sympathies.

The sons of Natira were staunch adherents of Saadia. One of them had been, or still was, his pupil and the proud owner of copies of Saadia's literary works, while their partners favored Saadia's opponents. The daughter of one of the latter was married to a scholarly man, Kalaf ibn Sarjado (in Hebrew — Aaron ben Joseph ha-Kohen). Kalaf was not a member of the old families from which the dignitaries of the academy were commonly chosen, but a newcomer, a member of a rich merchant family whom the Gaon Mebasser had appointed to a high place in his academy, perhaps to gain influential support in his fight against David ben Zakkai. As a matter of fact, Aaron ben Amram, one of the court-bankers, had sided with him. Kalaf was a scholar of standing and a man of burning ambition who was intensely jealous of the foreign scholar who had attained so high a rank. He spent a fortune to have Saadia deposed and published a very scurrilous pamphlet against him. An abstract of this pamphlet has been preserved in a work of a Karaite who gloats over these undignified squabbles among his Rabbanite opponents.

Because of the division between the partners in the bank, and because they could not afford to work at cross-purposes at court, they refrained from using their influence. The two opponents thus had to carry on their fight without political support. An Arabic writer tells us that the quarrel was once considered by the state council, but, since he does not mention the result, we may assume that the government also washed its hands of these internal Jewish affairs.

The documents pertaining to this controversy, which came down to us, are in a very fragmentary form and do not permit a clear view of its various stages. We are not even properly informed about the charges of the two sides. In Kalaf's pasquil Saadia is charged with having taken bribes in law suits which came before him, and it is likely that the same charge was raised by the other party against the exilarch. We are told that Saadia appealed to high officials and bribed them on a Sabbath, as witnessed by many Jews of Bagdad. In this connection he also was held responsible for the fact that many Jews suffered corporal punishment on Sabbaths and Holy Days.

In the beginning it seemed as if Saadia would triumph over his powerful opponent. He published an intensely interesting document, his "Open Book" (*Sefer ha-Galui*) which unfortunately has been lost; only a few fragments of it have been recovered in recent years, but these are very revealing. Of the seven chapters, the third, according to Saadia's statement, describes the misfortune which befalls a people ruled by a despot (like the exilarch); the fourth states that God sends to every generation a sage whom He inspires and enlightens to lead the people in the right path. He points to his own providential mission as leader and defender of the Jewish faith. In the sixth chapter, he gives an account of his sufferings at the hands of his unjust enemies. The final section of the book is meant as a warning to his opponents, since, as he points out, the Bible teaches us that the wicked who oppress the innocent are severely punished.

This book, written in poetic form, was provided with vowels and accents, a point for which his opponents attacked him as placing his work on a par with biblical books. It was by no means merely a polemical pamphlet. The other chapters of the book deal with general subjects, and even those mentioned above contain much more than attacks on the exilarch and his adherents. But Saadia's tone must have been very sharp. He makes bad puns on the names of his leading opponents, calling, e. g., Kalaf, *Keleb met*, the "dead dog." It is evident that, when he published this work, Saadia felt sure of the downfall of his enemies and had faith in his own victory.

His attack called for a rejoinder, and it was Kalaf ben Sarjado who undertook this task in a scandalous document which, to quote D. S. Margoliouth, "in virulence and obscenity exceeds anything of the sort I have ever seen." As I said before, we owe the preservation of these filthy charges against the great gaon to a Karaite opponent of Saadia who did a service to historical research, although that was far removed from his thoughts. It has been suggested that he may have garbled the original text. If he intended to besmirch the memory of the greatest foe of Karaism, he did not succeed. It is the enemies of Saadia who appear in a most unfavorable light.

Saadia answered again in a new edition of his "Open Book" to which he added an Arabic translation and a lengthy introduction, also in Arabic, wherein he outlines the contents of the entire work.

For a number of years, Babylonian Jewry was split: there were two exilarchs and two geonim of Sura, both of whom had their adherents and both of whom claimed to be the only rightful incumbents of their respective offices. Such a condition had existed before, and it certainly did not help to raise the standard of the exilarchate and gaonate. Nobody could foresee how long this struggle would last and how it would end, when conditions were changed by the murder of the Caliph al-Muktadir in a rebellion in October 932. His brother, Al-Kahir, succeeded him, but was in turn overthrown by the army which, after a year and a half, placed the son of a former caliph, Al-Radi, on the throne in 934.

It seems that the sons of Natira, Saadia's strongest supporters, lost their influence in the course of these events and returned to Ahwaz. Now there was no reason why their former partners should not use their power in the interest of David ben Zakkai and his devoted adherent, Kalaf, a member of their family. Hasan, the counter-exilarch, was banished to a remote province, and Saadia had to retire and even go into hiding for some time. But he must have retained many prominent and influential men among his adherents, while he lived as a private man in Bagdad, pursuing his literary plans and enriching Jewish literature with many more important works.

His life was not to end in eclipse. Even in the darkest hour, he was not without influence and many people looked up to him as their leader. By a curious trick of fate, it was a litigation which was to bring about his rehabilitation, just as a litigation had been the cause of his removal.

Two men decided to have their dispute arbitrated by judges of their choice: one chose the exilarch, the other chose Saadia. The exilarch was greatly incensed over this. In his formal excommunication of Saadia, David ben Zakkai had declared that anyone who would appear before the deposed gaon in a litigation, would direct a legal question to him, or would recognize him in any other way, should likewise be excommunicated. He therefore saw in this choice by one of the litigants a defiance which he bitterly resented. Accordingly, he had the recalcitrant apprehended by his guards and badly manhandled. This proceeding aroused general resentment in Bagdad, since any man not belonging to the exilarch's jurisdiction had the right to choose whomever he pleased. A group of notables approached the banker Bishr ben Aaron, father-in-law of Kalaf ben Sarjado, and urged him to bring to an end the long struggle for which his son-in-law was largely responsible. Bishr, who evidently had retained his influence at court, was prevailed upon to take the matter up. He invited the leaders of Jewry to his house, summoned the exilarch, and told him plainly that the people were tired of the protracted struggle and that he had to make peace with Saadia.

We may assume that David, on his part, was tired of the drawn-out quarrel which evidently, as he must have realized, did not strengthen his position. We hear, for instance, that his son was once shown scant regard when on a mission from his father to a province under his jurisdiction. Through his influence at court, the exilarch took bitter revenge on these opponents who were, perhaps, partisans of Saadia. Such events must have convinced him that it was in his own interest to end these internecine fights. Thus the request of the notables of Bagdad found a willing ear. Saadia, who was approached next, certainly had been made to feel that it was to his advantage to come to terms with his powerful opponent.

Bishr brought the two men to different rooms of his residence and acted as the go-between to arrange the terms of reconciliation. When an agreement had been reached — it is noteworthy that neither of them was asked to take the first step in approaching the other — they came forward, embraced and made peace with each other. This took place on the Fast of Esther, and Bishr wished to crown his efforts by having both as his guests at the reading of the *Megilla* and at the succeeding Purim festivities. But they refused and decided that one of them should be the guest of the other. In the spirit of Purim, the matter was settled by drawing lots. Saadia, accordingly, was for two days the exilarch's guest, and the old friendly relations between them were fully restored.

As far as Saadia's position was concerned, he was reinstated as gaon of the Sura academy, while Joseph ben Jacob retained his income and was designated as Saadia's successor — just as had happened previously in the Pumbedita academy when David ben Zakkai had made his peace with Rab Mebasser, and Rab Kohen Tsedek had to yield his place, retaining his income.

For about five years longer, Saadia adorned the gaonate of the Sura academy, and gave it new luster. But that was too short a time to re-establish it permanently. A few years after Saadia's death, his insignificant successor gave up the struggle against the rival academy which now was presided over by Kalaf ben Sarjado, Saadia's bitter opponent, who, Sherira tells us, had by force and intimidation finally attained the goal of his ambition. The gates of the Sura academy were closed for half a century, not to be reopened until about the end of the tenth century. The third gaon, after its reopening, was Saadia's second son, Dosa (1013–1017).

To return to Saadia, we know very little about his activity after his restoration to his position. There is only one interesting and characteristic record: David ben Zakkai died some time after the reconciliation, and his son and successor, the man who had threatened Saadia with physical violence, followed him to the grave seven months later, leaving a young son of twelve. Saadia took upon himself the education of the child of his former enemies and befriended him in every way.

This is the life story of the great leader of the Sura academy as far as we can reconstruct it from the documents discovered in the *Geniza* and from the all too brief remarks of the Gaon Sherira who, as a young man, had been an eyewitness to the events. Fortunately, we have a fuller account from the pen of another eyewitness, a certain Nathan ha-Kohen ben Isaac ha-Babli.

There are, however, certain inaccuracies in the latter's account of the quarrel between David ben Zakkai and the Pumbedita academy and some contradictions between his report and that of Sherira. We are therefore not absolutely sure that he is correct in all the details. But we are grateful to him for the picture of the active and eventful life of the greatest of the geonim — a fuller picture than we have of any other head of these academies. The documents of the *Geniza*, which have yielded so much information in the course of the last fifty years, may perhaps in time clarify some further points.

The space devoted to the interesting life story of Saadia is justified by the tremendous contributions he made to many fields of learning. Both quantitatively and qualitatively, his literary work is astounding. We can place him side by side with Maimonides. In several fields, the latter brought to fruition what Saadia Gaon had started; and without his pioneer work, Maimonides might not have been able to accomplish what he did. Saadia, moreover, was more versatile in his activity than the later sage of Cairo.

Abraham ibn Ezra characterized Saadia aptly as "the first speaker in every field" among the Jewish mediaeval scholars, a characterization which is by no means to be taken merely chronologically. Saadia's work was epoch-making in the true sense of the word — in his work on Hebrew grammar and exegesis; in his translation of the Bible into Arabic; in his study of the Hebrew calendar;

in his defense of tradition against the onslaughts of the sectarian Karaites as well as against Hiwi, the sceptic and early Bible critic of Balk.

Even in the subject of Halaka, to which his predecessors in the gaonate had devoted their literary and teaching activity almost exclusively, we find him hewing new paths and making original contributions of the first order.

To the modern mediaevalist, his first serious effort to reconcile religious tradition with the philosophy of his time, is of the greatest interest. It was granted to few scholars to be pathfinders in so many subjects, and we cannot but admire the originality, profundity and lasting quality of the work accomplished by this genius as these characteristics are reflected even in the incomplete form in which many of his important works have come down to us. How he could find the time, during his full and active life and during his extended travels, to write so much is hard to understand, the more so if we remember that he also had to devote a great deal of time to practical affairs.

To do justice to his important original contributions to learning would require more space than we have devoted to the sketch of his life. I must therefore limit myself to a very brief outline of his literary activity in all fields of Jewish learning.

Hebrew philology did not exist before Saadia. Only crude beginnings can be discerned in the work of the Masorites. Saadia was the first to realize the necessity of investigating the phenomena of the language in order to reach a clear understanding of its literature. Only little of his twelve *Books on the Language* or the *Book on the Elegance of the Language of the Hebrews* has been published, though a considerable fragment was discovered half a century ago. Of his dictionary, *Agron*, which he composed at the age of 20, a few specimens have appeared, aside from the incomplete introduction. We see that this earliest attempt at writing a Hebrew grammar was comprehensive in its scope and dealt with many of the linguistic phenomena in a systematic way.

Naturally, Saadia's philological insight must not be measured by comparison with his great successors in Spain. Its shortcomings are considerable, but his conscious effort to get behind the formation of the language is remarkable. His dictionary, again the first in the field, is very brief and contains also a part arranged by the end letters. One of its purposes was evidently to serve as an aid to the poet who wished to arrange his verses with acrostics and rhymes as Saadia did himself. A short treatise on seventy (actually ninety) hapax-legomena in the Bible is remarkable as the earliest tentative trial of comparative linguistics. He applied the later Hebrew of the Mishna and the Aramaic to the interpretation of biblical Hebrew.

More important is Saadia's contribution to the understanding of the Bible. Here the attacks of the Karaites against the rabbinic interpretation may have given him the impetus. His lengthy commentary on the first part of Genesis, on Exodus and Leviticus, which seems to have been one of his early works, contains linguistic, philosophic and halakic discussions as well as attacks on the Karaites. Only fragments and quotations of this work have reached us. We know even less about his glosses on the whole Pentateuch to which he gave the title *Garden Flowers* and his *Questions and Solutions* on the same book.

Of far greater significance is his translation of the Pentateuch, which was printed in the first Jewish polyglot (Constantinople, 1546), together with the Aramaic Targum and a Persian translation. It became the standard Arabic translation for the Jews and even the basis of the Arabic translation of the Samaritans. The Jews of Yemen use it

in their services to this day and, at the end of the last
century, they published an edition in Jerusalem. This
monumental work, the first translation from Hebrew
into Arabic, aimed simply to give a clear rendition of
the text. It is a free translation, not a paraphrase, but
it sometimes contains additions of single words and tries to
bring the parts of the verses, and occasionally the verses of
a section, into a syntactic context which enables the reader
to get a picture of the content, although it loses thereby
some of the color of the text.

Under the influence of the Aramaic Targum, the authoritative interpretation of the old synagogue, Saadia avoided
anthropomorphic terms and expressions. It was his purpose
to show that there is nothing in the Bible which is uncertain
and which we do not understand. Therefore he did not
hesitate to render technical words with definite Arabic
terms, although he had no tradition as to their meaning.
He also identified geographical names of the Bible with
Arabic ones which were known to his readers, identifications which often have no real basis. Curiously, he sometimes used Arabic words which phonetically resemble the
Hebrew ones, although they do not have the same meaning
in Arabic.

It seems that Saadia wrote this translation in Arabic
characters in order to make the Bible available to Muham-
medans as well as to Jews, although in general he wrote all
his Arabic works in Hebrew characters, as the Jews were
wont to do in Arabic speaking countries. However, the few
manuscripts of the translation in Arabic characters which
have come down to us, do not contain his original text
but are later revisions by other hands. None of our texts
offers a faithful reproduction of Saadia's version.

The Jews immediately transcribed the work into the
more familiar characters, and the very numerous manuscripts in this form are closer to the authentic work of the

gaon. Besides the Pentateuch, we have his translation of Isaiah, Psalms, Job, Proverbs, Daniel, Esther, Lamentations, and perhaps Canticles as well as fragments of Samuel and Ezekiel. To Esther he added a translation of *Megillat Bene Hashmonai* with an introduction. Some of these books are accompanied by shorter or longer commentaries and provided with introductions.

To the Minor Prophets he composed a commentary in the form of questions. His interpretation of the Books of Kings is mentioned in a book list, but not in the list of his works. It is curious that Hebrew commentaries on Daniel and Ezra were published under Saadia's name, though they are undoubtedly not his work. Perhaps a later man by the same name is responsible for them.

The calendar was a subject in which Saadia was deeply interested. In his polemics against the Karaites, he deals again and again with questions pertaining to the calendar and, as I have already stated, he carried on a correspondence on this subject with the gaon of Pumbedita before 917. The objections of the Karaites to the Jewish method of calculating the calendar may have given him the impetus to take up this study and thus he was especially well prepared to defend the method of these calculations by the Babylonian academies against the attack of Ben Meir which I have discussed at length. A special work dealing with the calendar is recorded, but since nothing of it has come down to us, we cannot determine its character. Whether his *Kitab al-Aflak* ("Book of the Spheres" or "Heavenly Bodies," or "Astronomy"), which is recorded in book lists of the *Geniza*, refers to this subject, also must remain doubtful.

Polemical works by the great gaon fill an important part of his literary activity and are particularly characteristic of his fighting nature. The centuries preceding our author were filled with religious unrest. Numerous sects arose in the East and, while most of them were of ephemeral character, they inaugurated a movement which finally led to the rise of Karaism, a sect which was founded in the second half of the eighth century and is still in existence. Like the other movements that preceded it, it was directed against the authority of official rabbinic Judaism and threatened to undermine and overthrow it. Curiously, the earlier geonim, as far as we know, paid no attention whatever to these opponents, and we have only a single reference to them in a geonic work of the ninth century.

Saadia was the first to realize the dangers inherent in the movement, and as a young man of twenty-three he already wrote against the Karaites. He devoted numerous works to the subject during the four decades of his literary activity. That Saadia's attacks on the Karaites made a deep impression on his opponents may be seen from the violent abuse they heaped on him down to the nineteenth century. Poznanski has collected such attacks by forty-nine *Karaite Literary Opponents of Saadia Gaon*. His first work was a criticism of Anan, the founder of Karaism; but only a few quotations from this book, which he wrote in 905, in all likelihood in Egypt, have been preserved.

I shall limit myself to those books of which fragments have been recovered in recent years.

The most comprehensive was probably his *Book of Distinction*, which discussed in eight treatises nearly all the subjects of controversy between Karaites and Rabbanites. It is not written against any individual and, in contrast to the rest of his polemical works, is distinguished by its calm tone. It was composed in 926, after his appointment as a *Resh Kalla* of one of the academies.

While these works were written in Arabic, about a third of a Hebrew polemic by Saadia, in poetic form, *Esa Meshali*, has been recovered in the course of the last decade. In twenty-two chapters of twenty-six stanzas each, the author

gives praise to the talmudic authorities and deals with some
of the differences with the Karaites. This book with its
highly complicated technique of poetic composition was
perhaps directed against Ben Asher. Its language is very
difficult and not always clear. It is one of the works against
which a younger contemporary, Salmon ben Yeruhim,
wrote a sharp answer in poor Hebrew verses. His book of
the *Wars of the Lord* was published by Davidson in 1934,
almost exactly a thousand years after its composition. The
editor suggests, with good reason, that Salmon followed this
work with an Arabic treatment of the same subjects in two
books of prose, one about the talmudic literature, which he
called the *Book of Shameful Things,* the other concerning the
rest of the differences. Against these Saadia wrote two of
his treatises: *Refutation of Ibn Sakaweihi* and *Refutation of the
Unfair Aggressor* — of both of which fragments have been
published. Thus we know at last who this Ibn Sakaweihi
was. It was the Arabic name of Salmon ben Yeruhim.

The latter also attacks some statements in Saadia's
Open Book, which, as has been pointed out above, was
directed against the Exilarch David ben Zakkai. In writing
against the gaon, first in Hebrew verse and then in Arabic
prose, Salmon followed Saadia's example in that book.
Limitations of space do not permit me to discuss this most
interesting and most personal of Saadia's writings in greater
detail. Mention need only be made here of Saadia's
reference to his defense of Jewish tradition against the
Karaites and against Hiwi of Balk as especially meritorious
actions.

The polemic against Hiwi, about one-sixth of which was
discovered and published by Dr. Davidson, throws light on
a very curious movement among the Jews of the East in the
second half of the ninth century. Hiwi, in contradistinction
to the Karaites, not only denied the validity of the Talmud,
but also that of the Bible. He wrote his *Two Hundred*

Questions on the Bible with an absolutely destructive tendency, pointing to inconsistencies in the biblical narrative. Deeply influenced by an early Pehlevi work of polemics against the Bible, he even denied the unity of God, His omnipotence and omniscience. He claimed that the teachings of the Bible led to dualism, like that of the Persian religion, and to trinity. He believed in the eternity of the world. He denied free will and the possibility of miracles, and he objected to circumcision. These heretical ideas spread widely and were even taught in schools for children.

It was the great merit of Saadia that he put an end to this movement which disappeared in consequence of the refutation which he wrote in verse and with acrostics. Since he called himself *Alluf* and *Resh Kalla*, we see that the book was written in Babylonia before he became gaon. Many more polemical works are recorded, but we know them only by title.

As pointed out above, the heads of the Babylonian academies had centered their activities for three centuries on the study of Talmud and rabbinic law. New contributions of fundamental, even epoch-making importance in this field could only be the work of a genius. Without going into details, suffice it to state that Saadia was the first to write an "Introduction" on the methodology of the Talmud, of which five passages were translated into Hebrew by a famous Talmudist of the sixteenth century; commented on the Thirteen Rules of Interpreting the Bible; and composed a number of halakic compendia in which he, for the first time, discussed these laws systematically without regard to their sequence in the talmudic sources. Theretofore, all the geonic codes had followed the unsystematic order of the Talmud with only slight deviations. It is hard for us to realize what courage this new departure required. In some of his early works in this field he did not even give the sources for his statements, a procedure in which Maimonides followed his example and for which he was subjected to violent criticism. Whether such criticism was directed against Saadia also, and whether it was for this reason that he followed a different method in some of his codificatory work, we do not know.

He probably also wrote commentaries on Mishna and Talmud which, however, dealt mainly with lexicographical explanations. It goes without saying that, like all the geonim, he answered questions directed to him from various countries even as far as distant Spain. In the Jewish Theological Seminary Library I came across a torn leaf of an introduction to a series of such questions which have not reached us.

Saadia's *Siddur*—the *Collection of Prayers and Hymns*, as he calls it—also partly belongs to the field of law. It was preceded by a short treatise, the *Obligation of Prayers*, composed somewhat earlier, which he, or perhaps some copyist, placed in front of the *Siddur*. Here he discusses the necessity of prayer on the basis of Bible, reason and tradition, and enumerates the various categories of prayer occurring in the Bible.

The *Siddur* is not the first in this field. One of his Sura predecessors, Rab Amram, in the middle of the ninth century, had composed such a prayerbook, and the comparison between the two works is enlightening.

Saadia's *Siddur* is a work of quite different caliber and shows the pronounced individuality of the author. He does not merely codify the current customs, but uses his judgment in selecting the prayers, declares what is proper and valid, and criticizes and omits what he considers wrong.

He tells us that it was the lack of uniformity, the corruption of prayers, improper additions and omissions which he had observed in the course of his travels through the various countries, which induced him to undertake this work. He differentiates between the individual prayers and those recited with a quorum of men in the synagogue. His arrangement is very interesting. He does not hesitate to deviate from the old custom of the academies and, although one of his contemporaries raised objections against some of his changes, we are informed that he exerted a deep influence on the ritual even in Babylonia.

The text of the prayers is naturally Hebrew, but the rubrics are given in Arabic, briefly and without sources since he intended it as a handbook for the layman. The influence of Egypt, the land of his birth, is strongly evident in Saadia's *Siddur*, though it was composed in Babylonia. Only one manuscript has been preserved, and that one is not complete and does not bear his name. It was identified by Steinschneider in 1851 and published in 1941 in Jerusalem through the initiative of the late Israel Davidson, in collaboration with Professor S. Assaf and Dr. B. I. Joel. For this edition they consulted thirty-four *Geniza* fragments of the *Siddur*.

The *Siddur* includes a selection of later hymns, partly from his own pen. As an appendix, Davidson collected all the poetic compositions of a religious character by Saadia as far as preserved. In the spirit of the period, Saadia excelled in the artificial technique which was then considered the essential of poetic compositions. Rare expressions and difficult word-formations abound here as in the polemical treatises in verse form. They often make it hard to understand the meaning. While very objectionable to our taste, they were considered highly poetic in his time. But Saadia could also write in a prose which compels admiration. His two *Bakkashot* reveal him as a true master of Hebrew style and gained him the praise of so severe a critic as Abraham ibn Ezra, who, after a sharp condemnation of the early *payyetanim*, stated that the Gaon Rab Saadia avoided all these mistakes in his two *Bakkashot* the like of which no other author had composed.

Philosophy had occupied Saadia's attention since his youth, and philosophic discussions occur in his early commentary to the Bible and elsewhere in his works. His main philosophic books were composed towards the end of his life.

In 931, while he was engaged in the struggle with the exilarch, he wrote his commentary on the enigmatical *Sepher Yetsira*, the "Book of Creation." He did not consider it a mystical work but a philosophic attempt to express the process of the world's generation by the will of the Creator. The theory current at the time, that its author was the patriarch Abraham, he accepts with some reservation. The commentary contains important points of grammar, but is devoted mainly to philosophic problems.

Two years later he composed his chief work — the *Book of Philosophic Doctrines and Religious Beliefs*, which marks the beginning of the history of Jewish philosophy. With an exposition of his point of view he combines a continuous discussion of ideas opposing his own.

Saadia himself was a rationalist and belonged to the same school of thought as the Muhammedan school of the rationalistic Mutazilites. But he often discusses philosophic problems in an independent manner. His main problem is the relation between Reason and Revelation. To him, as to all religious thinkers, Scripture is of revealed divine origin. And this divine Revelation is identical with Reason. Philosophy and religion therefore do not contradict but supplement one another in making known the truth.

He discusses the problem of creation at great length, giving a survey and criticism of all the theories as to the origin of the world known in his time. He defends the theory of *creatio ex nihilo*. He further discusses the unity of God, at which point he touches on the doctrine of trinity. In his chapter on the revelation of law he also defends the eternity and immutability of the Mosaic law. The other problems which he discusses in special chapters are: freedom of the will, the value of obedience to the law, the immortality of the soul, resurrection, Messianic times, and reward and punishment in the world to come. He concludes the book with a lengthy section on ethics.

Saadia's book was the first comprehensive effort to take up the fundamental problems of Jewish philosophy and has had a deep influence on all later Jewish writers in this field. Some of his conceptions occur again even in Maimonides' *Guide to the Perplexed*.

It seems that the author first composed the various sections of the book as independent treatises and only later combined them into a volume. The two Arabic manuscripts of Saadia's philosophic work contain different versions of the seventh section, on resurrection. The ninth section, "Reward and Punishment in the World to Come," was revised by him after the book was published. In the Jewish Theological Seminary Library, I recently came across a leaf of this unknown treatise, in which the author states that he has dealt with the subject in the ninth section of his *Book of Doctrines*, but revises it now, omitting, however, the interpretation of the biblical passages he quotes.

The Arabic original of Saadia's philosophic work was not published until 1880. The Hebrew translation made in 1186 by Judah ibn Tibbon, under the title *Emunot veDeot*, was printed in Constantinople, in 1562, and several times later. It is this Hebrew translation of the book which made it accessible to wider circles. Of another, more paraphrastic Hebrew version, two sections appeared in the sixteenth century and were reprinted a few times.

It is with a feeling of deep admiration for the genius of the great scholar to whose memory this essay is devoted that I conclude this inadequate appreciation. It is no small tribute that, a thousand years after the death of a scholar, we can look back to so rich a harvest of literary work of permanent value which he left behind.

We pay homage to him for the tremendous contributions he made to Jewish learning and for the lasting influence he exerted on all branches of Jewish scholarship.

2

Rabbenu Gershom, Light of the Exile

IT IS a curious and hitherto unexplained phenomenon
that Jewish spiritual and intellectual life emerged
suddently, without any recognizable cause, in the tenth
century, appearing simultaneously in Spain, Italy and the
Franco-German empire.

During the first millennium of our era, Palestine originally held the center of the stage. In the third century, the
Babylonian center arose as a mighty rival to the old mother
country. The decline of the once great Palestinian schools
had already set in, and it continued as a result of deterio-
rating economic conditions, occasional persecutions and the
abolition, in the year 425, of the quasi-autonomous internal
political organization under the Patriarchate. The opposition of the ruling Church, culminating in forced conversion
under the Byzantine emperor Heraclius in the seventh
century, brought about the final disappearance of the
Palestinian academies. They were never able to regain
their ancient glory even after the Muhammedan conquest
of Palestine had resulted in a great amelioration of conditions. Not that the Palestinians did not try; but the galaxy
of heads of the Babylonian academies during the last
century of their flowering, men like Saadia and Samuel
ben Hofni, Sherira and Haya far outshone their Palestinian
colleagues. Until the discoveries of the last half century
even the names of the Palestinian leaders were forgotten.
The Babylonian academies, on the other hand, in spite of
occasional persecutions which caused brief interruptions of
their activity, carried on successfully till the middle of the
eleventh century. In the ninth or tenth century, their

ancient seats were transferred to Bagdad, the capital of the Caliphate, and from there they extended their influence over all the countries which had yielded to the sword of victorious Islam, i. e., North Africa and Spain, whose Jewries turned to the Babylonian academies with all their legal problems.

Only the Jewries of the Christian countries continued to recognize the Palestinian mother-country, with which they had been connected all through the period of the Roman Empire. This relationship was not disturbed by the Muhammedan conquest of Palestine. Jews from Christian Europe made their pilgrimages to Jerusalem for the Succot festival to participate in the procession to Mount Olivet on *Hosha'ana Rabba* and they turned to the Palestinian school for advice on religious questions. Only few traces of this relationship with Palestine on the part of Italian Jewry, and even fewer for that of the Jews of the Frankish empire, have come down to us; their correspondence was not carried on via Egypt where the Cairo treasure-trove — the *Geniza* — has preserved so many important documents of that period.

Jews of Spain carried on their correspondence with Babylonia for several centuries; we have ample evidence of that, but so far as we know there was no active spiritual life in Spain until the middle of the tenth century. In Italy such a revival had taken place a little earlier. We hear of a school and an academy in Venosa, for instance, through two tumular inscriptions of the ninth century. The *Chronicle of Ahimaats*, though replete with legends, and some old liturgical poems give evidence of somewhat earlier spiritual life in southern Italy. The oldest literary monuments, however, do not date before the middle of the tenth century.

We observe the same phenomenon in the Frankish empire. Here also, in the tenth century, we suddenly come across a scholar of the highest caliber, one of the great builders of Judaism in the Western world, Rabbenu Gershom, whose outstanding position has been recognized by posterity who referred to him with the epithet *Meor ha-Golah*, the "Light of the Exile." His unique personality and colossal achievements compel our admiration even today.

Our information about the history of the Jews in the neighborhood of the Rhine or, for that matter, of those of northern Europe during the tenth and eleventh centuries, is very scanty. Hardly any detailed facts are known to us. But if we read the contemporary liturgical compositions in which their poets expressed their feelings and their hopes, we get a dismal picture of prevailing conditions. The *selihot*, the prayers for forgiveness, especially are replete with cries about the intolerable fate, the continuous oppressions and persecutions; they complain of the efforts to force the Jews into conversion to Christianity. The ten *selihot* of Rabbenu Gershom which have been preserved — like those of his contemporary, R. Simon ben Issac, who lived in the same city, Mayence — give vivid expression to the troublesome times when "from day to day my suffering increases, the next day is harder than the one that passed." "I am tired to bear the yoke of the accursed who says: 'Measure and bring a large gift'." And he continues: "The oppressing enemy urges Thy possession to forsake its Hope (its God)."

In another poem he appeals to God to take up the case of the children of Jacob and to redeem them from the hand of the oppressor, "for strength is gone, and no money is left in our pocket." He prays that the Lord might look down from heaven and take pity and "say 'enough' to the sufferings of Thy chosen ones and restore in Thy grace Thy city and Thy people." This prayer for restoration naturally occurs in practically every one of these *selihot*, as it does in

Jewish liturgy all through the ages. The sufferings are always looked upon as punishment for sinfulness, and repentance is urged upon the community. "When we learned of their secret counsel we trembled, and we turned to the 'vocation' of our forefathers to return to Thee when we are in danger in our exile. Merciful one, hear our cry and do not let us perish."

It is not possible to determine which events called forth these cries of anguish from the soul of the unhappy poet. We frequently must leave the question open whether they refer to troubles in their immediate neighborhood or in some distant place — there are some records of persecutions at Limoges and elsewhere in France at that time. There is only one *seliha* which seems to refer to a definite event, the persecution and expulsion of the Jews from Mayence in 1012. A brief note in the *Annals of Quedlinburg* records this expulsion, ascribing it to the king, i. e., Emperor Henry II. We have no information whatever about the cause of this expulsion. It has been conjectured that it had some connection with the conversion of a clergyman, Wezelin, to Judaism mentioned in another chronicle among events of 1005 and 1006. Another hypothesis associates the expulsion with the effort of the archbishop of Mayence to found a national German Church under his aegis. But the dearth of sources does not permit any certainty on this question.

Whatever the cause, this event seems to be mirrored in one of Rabbenu Gershom's elegies. He complains bitterly of the enemy who rose against the Jews and ordered them no longer to direct their prayers to our Redeemer, the Lord of Hosts. When the community indignantly refused to yield, they turned against it and, after despoiling them of their property, expelled the unhappy Jews from their pleasant homes and dispersed them in every direction. Exhausted and sorrowful, they raised their eyes to their old

Refuge. The second half of the *seliha* is a fervent prayer for God's intercession in behalf of His unfortunate people.

It was undoubtedly in consequence of the upheaval connected with this expulsion that the marriage contract of Rabbenu Gershom with Bona, daughter of R. David, was lost and was replaced before the Mayence court, in January, 1013, by a new instrument the wording of which was preserved by chance in a manuscript formulary now in Oxford. This document proves that, either the expulsion of the preceding year was only a partial one, or that permission to return to their old homes was granted the Jews after a short time.

The saddest experience in the life of Rabbenu Gershom, the apostasy of his only son, was possibly also connected with the expulsion. In this case, our information is not derived from an account of the event, but from the record that, when this son died without having had the opportunity to return to the faith of his fathers, the unhappy parent observed the regular mourning rites for a period of two weeks in place of the customary seven days. This fact is mentioned in a discussion of the question whether one should observe the rites of mourning for a member of the family who had left the faith.

Rabbenu Gershom, according to a source dating back to the end of the thirteenth century, was born in Metz. Whatever the reliability of this statement, the city with which his name and activity were permanently linked was unquestionably Mayence. The Jewish community of that city is mentioned for the first time in historical records in connection with a church council held there in about 900, which decided that whoever killed a Jew or a pagan out of hatred or cupidity should be punished for murder. Half a century later we find the first Jewish scholars of eminence in Mayence: R. Judah ben Meir ha-Kohen, called R. Leon or Leontin, the teacher of Rabbenu Gershom; and R. Meshullam ben Kalonymos, known as a legal authority and as a famous author of religious poems. R. Meshullam was probably active in the middle of the tenth century. Rabbenu Gershom mentions him once in reply to the question whether it is permissible to interrupt the solemn 'Amida for the holidays by poetic insertions. Referring to scholarly poets of the past who had composed such additions, among them R. Kalonymos, he adds "and of his son, R. Meshullam, I know that he was a great scholar and is the author of such poems (*kerobot*) for the Day of Atonement." The statement does not sound as if he knew him personally; when R. Gershom wrote the responsum, R. Meshullam, it seems, was no longer among the living.

The tombstone of this R. Meshullam and, more recently, that of Rabbenu Gershom himself have been found in Mayence. Unfortunately they do not contain any dates, since the inscriptions on both stones are incomplete, lacking their last lines. Moreover, they seem to be of a later date and to have been made to replace the original monuments which in all probability had been destroyed during a persecution, perhaps that of the first crusade. We may have to be satisfied with the assumption that Rabbenu Gershom came to Mayence after the death of R. Meshullam or that he was still very young at the time of R. Meshullam's death. The lack of dates for both men makes a more definite conclusion impossible.

We are equally poorly informed about the dates of the life of Rabbenu Gershom. Some later sources record the year of his death, but here we have two differing traditions: the one places it in the year 1028, the other in 1040. We may assume that the latter — the Hebrew year 4800 — is a round, approximate figure and that the former, 1028, is the exact date. Accordingly he was born probably around 960.

These few facts exhaust all our information about the life of this great leader of his time. As is the case so frequently in the long annals of our history, contemporaries as well as subsequent generations were deeply concerned with the opinions, the interpretations and the literary output of great scholars, but paid no attention whatever to the personal life of their revered masters. Every student of Jewish history is constantly confronted with this dearth of information about facts which we nowadays deem essential but which our forefathers considered of no importance.

Even when one turns to the activity of Rabbenu Gershom, the lack of authentic material makes the biographer's task a difficult one. Until half a century ago it was generally assumed that his greatest literary work was a comprehensive commentary on the whole Talmud which is frequently quoted in the *Aruk*, the great talmudic dictionary which R. Nathan of Rome compiled during the last decades of the tenth century. Quotations indicate that this commentary extended to thirty-two treatises of the Talmud, ten of which have been preserved and were printed in the eighteen-eighties in the great Wilna Talmud edition. Half a century ago, however, Abraham Epstein submitted the whole body of material to a searching examination and reached the conclusion that the ascription to the famous scholar is without scientific basis. Only Italian authorities had referred to it as Rabbenu Gershom's work; none of the early German scholars who were acquainted with the commentaries ever connected them with his name. Two quotations by Germans on the treatise of Hullin probably refer to his copy of the Talmud text of which we shall speak presently. The commentary in question, in some instances, actually disagrees with readings known to have been found in Rabbenu Gershom's text.

The work is a product of the school founded by Rabbenu

Gershom at Mayence. It was composed by the pupils of one of his successors, R. Isaac ben Juda, a teacher of Rashi. The disciples of R. Isaac attended his lectures and wrote down his interpretations with various additions of their own. But many of the explanations probably go back, directly or indirectly, to the inspiration of the great master, Rabbenu Gershom himself.

If Rabbenu Gershom did not formulate his explanations of the Talmud in written form, except perhaps for a few passages on which he was questioned, he did do a great deal for the text of the Talmud. We know nothing of the condition in which this text had reached northern Europe during the early stages of talmudic study. That its condition was very unsatisfactory we may conclude from the innumerable instances in which, two generations later, Rashi found it necessary to point out the correct readings by stating in his commentary: "We should read thus." The current texts probably varied greatly from one another. A reliable text, however, was the first prerequisite for a proper understanding. Therefore Rabbenu Gershom did not shirk the tremendous labor of copying the whole of Mishna and Talmud with his own hand. We know from a single quotation that the above-mentioned R. Meshullam had shortly before undertaken the same task for the Mishna which, it seems, he even vocalized. Why Rabbenu Gershom should have considered it necessary to prepare a standard text anew we cannot tell, but his copy of the Mishna is quoted twice by Rashi's grandson, R. Samuel ben Meir, and references to it occur in other works of the French school.

There are many quotations from the copy of the Talmud written by Rabbenu Gershom's own hand. Rashi and his grandson, R. Tam, refer to it repeatedly, and a little later we hear of a copy belonging to R. Tam which had been made from Rabbenu Gershom's autograph. We may be permitted to conjecture that Rashi, during his student years in Mayence, when collecting material for his commentary on the Talmud, had a copy made of Rabbenu Gershom's codex, which later came into the possession of his grandson. If this hypothesis is correct, we may assume that many of the statements of Rashi as to the correct text of the passages which he interprets go back to this model. The tosafists, the school founded by Rashi's grandchildren, several times quote readings of Rabbenu Gershom and once refer to a copy of the master's autograph as their source. They evidently had before them the same copy that was once owned by R. Tam, probably the source of all the quotations in the works of the French school. References to the readings of Rabbenu Gershom's copy are to be found even among Italian scholars as late as the end of the fifteenth century, e. g., in a manuscript of that period, now at the Library of the Jewish Theological Seminary.

Most of these quotations refer simply to the Talmud which Rabbenu Gershom copied, but in several instances they indicate specifically the *Seder* of the Talmud to which they belong. Rashi himself quotes the *Seder Yeshuot* of Rabbenu Gershom; the *Seder Nashim* is quoted once, and the *Seder Kodoshim* especially is repeatedly mentioned. Evidently Rabbenu Gershom copied the Talmud in four volumes, each *Seder* by itself. It seems that the text was accompanied occasionally by short interpretations, which may have come from the pen of the copyist himself; but we have only one or two examples of these. Their number is not sufficient to form an opinion on the character of this text, especially since most of these quotations are very brief.

It is, of course, not impossible that Rabbenu Gershom merely transcribed the books in order to have a copy for his studies in view of the scarcity of manuscripts. But his pupils would probably have been glad to do that work for

him and spare his valuable time. Furthermore, he copied
not only Mishna and Talmud but also a Bible with *Masora*
and other books.

R. Jacob ibn Adoniyya, the editor of the famous first-
printed masoretic Bible (Venice, 1524), printed a marginal
note, derived from one of the manuscripts he consulted, on
a passage in Leviticus (4.35) about the accent found in the
Pentateuch copied and vocalized by Rabbenu Gershom.
Numerous notes of this kind occur on the margins of a
thirteenth-century Pentateuch in Leipzig. Some of these
indicate that the text was accompanied by the *Masora*.
The annotator indicates whether a reading is supported by
a masoretic note or not. He states that sometimes a letter
was erased or a correction made; we cannot tell, of course,
whether these corrections came from the hand of the master
himself or were added subsequently.

We learn from a curious note in a British Museum
manuscript that Rabbenu Gershom copied the rest of the
Bible as well. The scribe tells that he had copied the two
verses from Chronicles inserted in many texts of Joshua
(between chapter 21, verses 36 and 37), but repented of
his action when he found that the verses were lacking in
Rabbenu Gershom's copy and in another famous codex
(called *Sinai*). No further references to the rest of his Bible
have been discovered.

Rabbenu Gershom's interest in the text of the Bible
must have been very deep. Besides the text with the small
Masora, he also prepared a copy of the Great *Masora* which
was in the hands of the scribe of the aforementioned
Leipzig manuscript. The latter refers to it at least ten
times. It is quite possible that Rashi's references to the
Great *Masora* apply to this copy which he may have consulted in Mayence.

If it is unusual to see a scholar, famous mainly as a

Talmudist, devoting so much time and effort to textual studies of Bible and *Masora*, we are amazed to find that he even copied with his own hand a more secular work like the *Yosippon*. This is a Hebrew abstract and free retelling of Josephus which probably originated in Italy in the early Middle Ages. It was the only source for the history of the Second Commonwealth that the Jews of these centuries had. Again, the evidence is supplied by a single manuscript, now in the Library of the Jewish Theological Seminary. Rapoport pointed out more than a century ago that one of the *Selihot* of Rabbenu Gershom shows acquaintance with this book. In one place, where the Hebrew author of *Yosippon* states that he omitted most of the letters sent by Roman rulers to the Jews, he uses the expression "I was too lazy to incorporate them all." The copyist of our manuscript, believing this statement which he found "in the copy of the great rabbi, Rabbenu Gershom, in his own handwriting" to be not the author's but Rabbenu Gershom's, adds therefore at the end of the paragraph: "Thus did Rabbenu Gershom abridge the text." It is only due to this erroneous assumption that we hear of this copy of the Mayence scholar.

The exacting and laborious work of copying must have occupied him for years; and the fact that this man of action had the patience for it shows how much stress he laid on correct, reliable texts. As a matter of fact, R. Tam relates that Rabbenu Gershom denounced those who corrupt the text of the Talmud — i. e., take liberties with it by arbitrary emendations — and that he pronounced a curse against them.

It is noteworthy that Rabbenu Gershom himself did not compose any larger work. The only original work of his that we know of is a lost compilation of the laws of *trefot*, ritually forbidden meat, of which a number of quotations can be collected from rabbinic literature. This could hardly have been an extensive work. An extract from one part of the book, preserved in a manuscript of the British Museum, fills merely a couple of pages.

Of much greater significance are Rabbenu Gershom's responsa, his answers to questions on civil and ritual law which came to him from various localities, mostly, in all probability, from the adjacent communities. The custom had developed, after the conclusion of the Talmud, to direct questions on all kinds of problems to a central authority. Responsa, the answers to such questions, had played a most important part in the geonic period. Nothing but responsa have been preserved from most of the earlier geonim, whose literary activity was restricted to this branch. We find in these Babylonian responsa the germs of the various subsequent branches of Jewish literature, such as commentaries to the Talmud, lexicography, Bible exegesis and philosophy. Rabbenu Gershom's responsa, of which a considerable number have been preserved, do not cover many fields. They are concerned with ritual and, to a greater extent, with questions of civil law, particularly with problems of business.

His responsa follow the old pattern that had developed in the East in the course of centuries. But Rabbenu Gershom's responsa have an individual character; they differ, in some respects, from those of his predecessors and express his personality. They show, first of all, his mastery of the Talmud and the independence of his mind. Sometimes, to be sure, his decisions are based entirely on his interpretation of biblical passages; but generally his authority is the Talmud. It often must have been very difficult to find a basis for a decision in this vast treasury of Jewish law. Under the new conditions in Western Europe, new questions had arisen caused by the different economic circum-

stances under which the Jews were living; new customs
had come into being; and German Jewry, from the very
beginning, showed more respect for local customs than
did the Jews of any other country.

One of the customs which seem to have been characteristic of Germany was that which is called *Maarufia*, the
appointment of a Jew of the neighborhood as financial
agent for a knight or a merchant. Rabbenu Gershom speaks
repeatedly of a *Maarufia shel Komrim*, such an appointment
for a monastery. The position was recognized by some
Jewish communities as a monopoly with which no one had
a right to interfere. In others, this type of business venture
was considered open to competition. In our responsa
several such cases are discussed. In one instance, a man
had paid the community a certain sum of money for an
ordinance binding all members to assure him monopolistic
rights; in another instance, such an agency was in the hands
of a scholarly person who taught in public without remuneration. In the latter case, merchants who attended the
classes of this scholar were envious of the rich income
derived from this source and wanted to compete with
him. The community forbade the pupils to interfere with
the scholar's business and turned to Rabbenu Gershom
with the question whether it was proper to extend the
prohibition against competition to all members of the
community. The decision was that in this particular case
such a prohibition was justified in order to permit the
agent to devote his time to study and teaching, but that
generally the local custom was to be followed.

Contrary to the decision of a certain local scholar,
Rabbenu Gershom permitted the acceptance, as security for
a loan, of ecclesiastical robes used at services and the
dealing with Christians on their holidays. They are not
idolators, he states, and, since they have so many holidays,

such a prohibition would seriously interfere with commerce on which the livelihood of the Jews depended.

Naturally, the problem of interest came up for discussion, especially in cases where the taking of interest from a fellow Jew was veiled by the interposition of a non-Jewish middleman. Another important question dealt with wine left in the house of a non-Jew or carried by him from one place to another. The Jews in the Rhine district often made their living from their vineyards. In all such cases Rabbenu Gershom tried to alleviate conditions.

The following is another actual case. A Jew had an oven in which, for compensation, he permitted others to cook; Christians used it on Fridays and left their dishes there for Saturday or forced their way in to use it on the Sabbath. In this situation, the owner was held not responsible for the desecration of the Sabbath, but was forbidden to accept payment for the use of his oven on that day. On the other hand, a Jew who had bought a horse on a Sabbath was ordered punished by flaggelation; any profit he might later derive from the transaction would have to be given to charity. If the Sabbath observance was lax in the town, more severe punishment by the community might be advisable.

A custom, which was common at the time but which Rabbenu Gershom declared illegal, was for a merchant to pay a silver mark (*zakuk*) worth twelve ounces of small coin (*Peshittim*) at the Cologne fair and to receive back thirteen ounces on his return to Mayence or Worms. Only if the lender received the merchandise for which the money was borrowed, and if he or his representative brought this merchandise home at his own risk, was such a transaction declared permissible.

Several responsa deal with questions of an oath. We learn that taking an oath at a Torah scroll had been abolished, since a false oath of this kind would "cause punishment not only for the sinner but also for his family and the whole world." Instead, it was instituted that the person appearing before the Jewish court be threatened with excommunication (*niddui*) and with curses which would fall on him if he utter a lie. In some places, people were reluctant to take an oath and tried to shift it to the other party. Rabbenu Gershom decided that even an oath prescribed by the Bible could be shifted; the man who is sued must either swear that he does not owe anything to the other party or pay.

Just as the cases here cited throw interesting light on the commercial activities of the Jews, others illustrate the uncertainty of conditions in that period. A Jew borrows money from a neighbor to pay a debt to a Christian; on his return he finds that during his absence the houses of all the Jews of his village, including his own and that of his creditor, have been despoiled; he claims that the money borrowed would have been lost in any case and he therefore refuses to pay his debt to his fellow Jew. Rabbenu Gershom decides that the debt must be paid and, as in another case, adds that God favored the creditor by saving the amount he had lent his neighbor. In another instance, when a feudal lord had taken away from a Jew a piece of his land and sold it to another Jew, the latter had to return it to the original owner for the amount paid.

An interesting litigation came about when three Jews boarded a ship with all their property; the ship foundered but the people were saved. One of them then hired a man to rescue his property which was in a box at the bottom of the river. The box had become filled with water and was so heavy that it had to be broken open under the river. Part of his clothes and other merchandise were saved. During the night strangers saved and appropriated for themselves some silver, gold and other property. The next day

the Jews bribed the local authorities to order restitution of
their property and then collected whatever they could.
According to local custom, every Christian who was suspected of having retained some of this property had to pass
through the ordeal of placing his hand in fire; in one
instance a single combat between the contestants was
ordered. The neighboring communities enacted an ordinance that anyone buying any of the salvaged goods was
to return them to their original owner, "as is customary
among all Jewish communities." In spite of this, a Jew
bought some salvaged gold, claiming that property which
a river had carried away was free to anyone. The argumentation of Rabbenu Gershom's responsum in this instance is
very instructive. It is based equally on Talmudic law and
on the local ordinance of the non-Jewish authority declar-
ing anybody a thief who retained the recovered Jewish
property.

A curious, though not very edifying, picture of contemporary life is offered by the background of another responsum which deals with the question of the re-marriage of an
agunah (a woman the death of whose husband is not absolutely proved). Somewhere in France a man had many
customers within a radius of one or two days' journey from
his home town. He would sell them merchandise and give
them credit or lend money on securities. In payment he
sometimes received cattle which his customers had robbed
from their enemies and which they gave him at a low price.
He made many enemies by this practice; people claimed
that his readiness to buy the booty encouraged the knights
to rob them. Repeatedly he and other Jews were captured
and had to be ransomed; once this happened to his children.
In spite of such hazards, he carried on this trade for six
or seven years. Then the kings of France and Burgundy
laid a three-month siege to a city in his neighborhood. (It
has been suggested that the responsum here refers to the

siege of Valenciennes in 1006.) With other people of his
home town this man went daily to the besieging army to
buy booty. Towards the end of the unsuccessful siege he
disappeared and various rumors were current about his
capture and death at the hands of his enemies.

There are a few cases dealing with apostates. If a man
dies without leaving any children, his wife, if she wants to
contract a second marriage, has to undergo *Halitsa* — a
biblical ceremony — with her convert brother-in-law. A
convert, Rabbenu Gershom decided, does not share in the
inheritance of his father. Yet one who returns to his faith
is to be considered a Jew in every respect and, if he is a
priest (*Kohen*), is to have all the privileges which he enjoyed
before at the synagogue services.

Two responsa deal with teachers. A man engaged a
teacher to live in his home and instruct his three children
at an annual salary of three *litra*. The man stated that the
teacher might earn as much as ten *litra*, since he would try
to get more pupils for him and would throw business
opportunities his way. It seems that teaching paid so
poorly that the income had to be supplemented by other
activities. In this case, however, none of these prospects
materialized. On the contrary, for the second year the
miserly housewife reduced the salary to two *litra*. (Rabbenu
Gershom decided that a contract cannot be changed one-
sidedly.) For a period of several months when the children
were ill, the teacher was not paid. The agreement had been
that he was to teach the children the entire Bible. When he
left the house and continued teaching in his own premises he
still received no more than the stipulated pay.

The other responsum begins with the statement that
teachers and scribes must be righteous and trustworthy
and fulfill their tasks religiously; theirs was a godly work
which would find its reward in the world to come. The
compensation in this world evidently was very scanty at

the time. The teacher, who was a skilled scribe, had copied
books mornings and evenings, probably for sale. Now the
man who had engaged him to teach claimed these books
for himself. Rabbenu Gershom decided that, if it was
stated in the agreement that he was to teach mornings and
evenings during the winter, he would have to fulfill this
condition; if, however, that was not in the contract, it
depended on the local custom. If other teachers in that
locality devoted these hours to their own affairs, then this
teacher, too, was entitled to use his free time for his own
profit, otherwise he was not.

These are some of the cases which came up for decision
before the great master. They are mentioned here because
they illustrate the prevailing conditions. Reading his
decisions, we find that Rabbenu Gershom was thorough
and independent in his judgment and concise in his language. He gave a clear, logical analysis of each case and of
the sources on which he based his opinion. He rarely
quoted older authorities. Once he spoke of his teacher,
R. Leon, "who" he said, "taught me most of my knowledge
of the Talmud, an outstanding scholar in his generation
whose decision one must not change." In another instance
he stated, "This is my opinion according to what my
masters taught me," or "On these arguments I rely and
on what I have learned, and this is my opinion." Like
his geonic and other predecessors, he often stated, "Thus
they showed me from heaven and this is my opinion."
These and similar phrases, which occur about ten times in
some sixty of his responsa which have been preserved, imply
that the writer possessed a measure of self-confidence and
considered his reasoning quasi-inspired. Sometimes he
added at the end, "and thus is the law." He did not,
however, force his decision on his questioner, but placed
all the proofs and arguments for his opinion before him
and thus enabled him to examine them and reach his own

conclusions. He never hesitated to pronounce a clear decision even where he could not quote a precedent. Often he took occasion to refute possible counter-arguments which an opponent might bring forward. His approach to the involved litigations has rightly been characterized as classical. In the sixteenth century, an oriental scholar, R. Bezalel Ashkenazi, was still in possession of a collection of Rabbenu Gershom's responsa from which he quotes No. 64. But this manuscript has since disappeared.

Rabbenu Gershom repeatedly emphasized in his responsa the right of the communities to make new enactments according to the needs of time and place; such enactments were to be absolutely binding on every member, and whoever transgressed them was to undergo severe punishment. These ordinances were necessary to adapt rabbinic law to European conditions, and it was in this field that Rabbenu Gershom acquired the greatest fame. Some of his enactments were fundamental for Jewish life and were accepted far and wide as normative. When and how they were enacted we do not know, nor do we have the texts of some of his most far-reaching ordinances — *takkanot*, as they are called. It is not likely that these were his own individual decisions. In all probability they were accepted by a synod over which he presided and in which his towering personality exerted great influence. Such synods, we know, gathered often in the next two centuries. Later generations forgot the participation of others and were satisfied to ascribe the inauguration of the *takkanot* to Rabbenu Gershom alone.

Contrary to biblical and talmudic law, he forbade polygamy and took away the right of a man to divorce his wife against her will. He ordained that, thenceforth, a divorce should be valid only with the consent of the wife. In spite of their departure from traditional law, these ordinances found general acceptance because they were in consonance with the prevailing ideas. Plural marriages had become rare in the course of time and undoubtedly the influence of the surrounding world made itself felt in Jewish circles. Polygamy was no longer in keeping with the respect Judaism always granted to women and it needed only a prominent and farseeing leader to do away entirely with customs which had become obsolete. We do not hear of any opposition to Rabbenu Gershom's fundamental changes of law; they were readily accepted in all of Western Europe except Spain, at that time still under Muhammedan rule. It stands to reason that under the Moslems the Jews did not object to the Islamic custom of polygamy. Rabbenu Gershom's ordinances have thus become an integral part of Jewish law. Only later on were exceptions allowed in cases of undue hardship, and then only by permission of a hundred rabbis.

An important ordinance along a quite different line was the prohibition against reading somebody else's letters without permission. Since generally letters had to be forwarded by a traveller going to the place of their destination, it was in many instances a matter of vital importance to the writer to have the secrecy of his correspondence protected, e. g., against competitors in business or enemies and rivals. In this instance, what could not be accomplished by ordinary legal method was accomplished by the ordinance forbidding such unauthorized reading under threat of excommunication. A century ago it still was not unusual to read on an address: "to N. N. and forbidden under R. G.'s *herem* to anybody else."

As mentioned above, conversion during persecutions and subsequent return to Judaism was not uncommon during that period. Those who had remained steadfast under the duress would frequently taunt those who for a time had yielded. Rabbenu Gershom, whose own son had been a victim of such circumstances, had a deep sympathy for the mental suffering of such unfortunate people and, therefore, in one of his enactments called for the excommunication of anyone who would remind a penitent of his former apostasy.

Besides these most famous and far-reaching enactments, there is another group of ordinances which have been preserved in several texts as *takkanot* of Rabbenu Gershom. Dr. Finkelstein has rightly described them as a kind of crude constitution for the German communities. Unfortunately, we have no authentic texts of these and there are considerable differences among the various manuscripts, all of which were written centuries after the death of Rabbenu Gershom. We, therefore, cannot be sure whether they all go back to Rabbenu Gershom or whether they have been amplified at a later period. We can only mention a few of them. The jurisdiction of the local courts was extended to include transients. The poor were assured their day in court by a custom that had developed permitting any member of the community to stop services in the synagogue until a day was set for the trial. The methods of procedure in interrupting the services were now defined by ordinance. A person who had lost an object, and suspected that someone in the community might have information which would enable him to recover it, could compel anyone knowing the finder of the object to inform against him under a *herem* (excommunication). If someone had offered his house to the community as a synagogue, he could not exclude even an enemy from attending services. An ordinance enacted by agreement of the majority in the interest of the poor, or for some other purpose, was binding on all, and the minority could not bring the matter to court for a legal decision. A tax-assessment for the community had to be paid or security had to be given before its validity could be tested in court. If there was a quorum of ten in the synagogue and the reader had started the prayers, no one was permitted to leave and break the quorum.

These and some minor matters make up this group of ordinances of Rabbenu Gershom. Most of them were generally accepted immediately, though some were not known in the following generations. They were re-enacted and enlarged in the subsequent centuries at various synods and left a lasting impression on Jewish communal life in Germany.

Rabbenu Gershom towers over the preceding and following generations. Only Rashi may be considered his real successor. His contributions to the intellectual life of the north European communities by the great school he founded, and to the communal life by his responsa and even more by his enactments, cannot be overestimated. The most competent judge, Rashi, expressed his opinion of the great master of Mayence in these words: "May the memory of the righteous and saintly Rabbenu Gershom be for a blessing; he enlightened the eyes of the exile; we all live from his instruction and all the members of Jewry in the Frankish lands and in Italy are the pupils of his pupils."

3

Rashi

THE last century and a half have made us, as Jews, more conscious of our history than ever before. In recent decades this awareness has expressed itself in many ways, among them memorial celebrations for some of the oustanding personalities of our past. In 1904, the seven hundredth anniversary of the death of Maimonides and, in 1905, the eight hundredth of that of Rashi were widely utilized for commemorating the achievements of these two great men. Again, in 1935, the eight hundredth anniversary of Maimonides' birth was celebrated far and wide and received considerable publicity, especially in this country. In 1940 we commemorated the nine hundredth anniversary of the birth of Rashi, the greatest and most popular commentator of the Bible and the Talmud.

It strikes the observer that in former centuries only very few were aware of such occasions; as a matter of fact, the dates of the lives of these and other personalities were of little interest and hardly known even to scholars, let alone the mass of people. Perhaps we today talk more of Rashi and Maimonides themselves, whereas the Jews of earlier centuries found infinitely more meaning in their works. Every Talmudist studied the commentaries of Rashi and the Code of Maimonides as a matter of routine and their names were household words in wide circles. Nowadays, outside of small groups of specialists, very few people are familiar with their works, and it is in order to make wider circles acquainted with the enormous contributions of these two giants to the development of Judaism that we endeavor to illustrate their literary activity and influence by exhibitions and public meetings. For Rashi's commentaries still retain their importance for a proper understanding of the basic texts of our rich literature, and one cannot suppress the wish that these celebrations of his anniversary would lead to a wider study of his works.

Rashi undoubtedly had greater influence than Maimonides on the Jewish people at large. Maimonides had an aristocratic disdain for the multitude and was more concerned with instructing the elect few. Rashi, on the other hand, wrote for the people and by his genius succeeded in opening the closed pages of the intricate rabbinic discussions to anyone who cared to learn how to navigate the stormy "ocean of the Talmud." His incomparable commentary on the Pentateuch became the means of initiating countless generations into rabbinic lore and gave a taste for a general understanding of that literature to thousands of people who otherwise would never have known anything about it. It was the most popular and perhaps the most valuable textbook in Jewish education. The reading of "Rashi" in the primary schools was a stepping-stone to the understanding of the basic elements of rabbinic literature; and those who, in the struggle for their daily bread, had neither time nor opportunity for further study were saved from the opprobrium of being *'amme aratsot*.

Before turning to a discussion of Rashi's great literary achievements, we shall consider the little we know of the great man's life.

His full name was R. Solomon ben Isaac, and so he signed some of his responsa. A German authority of the thirteenth century maintained that Rashi generally signed his name *Shin Yod*, i. e. Shelomo Yitshaki, and this abbreviation sometimes occurs in our sources. From a letter of R. Nathan, author of the *'Aruk*, and his brothers, who were the heads of the Academy of Rome, we learn that Rashi signed a letter he sent to them "Shelomo ha-Yitzhaki." His pupils generally referred to him as *ha-Moreh*, the teacher, or *Rabbenu*, our master.

In the thirteenth century, Raimund Martini, the author of the famous *Pugio Fidei* ("Dagger of Faith"), the most learned work by a Christian against the Jews, erroneously resolved the abbreviation "Rashi" into R. Solomon Yarhi, i. e., of Lunel. This interpretation of the abbreviation was accepted by the great Christian Hebraist, Johannes Buxtorf, in his *Bibliotheca Hebraea* (1613), and through his authority it became common among Christians and was accepted by some Jewish scholars. It is on this basis that we sometimes read that Rashi was born in Lunel.

The great critic, R. Abraham ben David, who lived in Provence during the thirteenth century, called him *ha-Rab ha-Tsarfati*, the Rabbi of Northern France, and treated him with more respect than he did most other scholars. A thirteenth-century scholar of Provence, R. Asher ben Saul, as well as an Egyptian contemporary of Maimonides and the latter's son Abraham, and a Yemenite author of the fourteenth century, Abraham ben Solomon, quoted him as R. Solomon *Tsarfati*, the Frenchman, a name which otherwise occurs only rarely. Occasionally, he was referred to as R. Shelomo of Troyes, but the abbreviated form of his name — RASHI — is the one most commonly used; it has replaced his full name for the last six or seven hundred years, and all his works have been published under it.

We do not know the exact date of Rashi's birth. Tradition has it that, even as "the sun also ariseth and the sun goeth down" (Eccl. 1.5), so Rashi was born in the year of the death of the great pioneer of Jewish learning and culture in the Frankish empire — Rabbenu Gershom ben Solomon, the "Light of the Exile." The latter's death occurred, according to the same tradition, in the year 1040. Some sources, however, date R. Gershom's death in the year 1028.

And as if to tease us, his tombstone, which was discovered towards the end of the last century and correctly deciphered two decades ago, no longer shows the date of the death of the great leader in whose memory it was erected.

Further doubts about the year of Rashi's birth have been expressed quite recently. Among other reasons it has been argued that in the short span of sixty-five years he could not have produced the enormous amount of work that has been preserved. But since several of the sources which record the year of his death add expressly that he died at the age of sixty-five, we may as well stick to the traditional date of Rashi's birth as 1040.

We are better informed about the date of his death; several sources record that the great man passed away on Thursday, the 29th of Tammuz, 4865 (July 13, 1105). And the fact that literary tradition has preserved this date is striking evidence that his contemporaries realized the outstanding merit of the scholar; for it is altogether exceptional, exact dates transmitted by medieval Jewish literary sources for the lives of scholars being very rare.

These dates and the fact that Rashi was born at Troyes, the capital of the duchy of Champagne, are about all the direct information we have about him. There are half a dozen compilations by Rashi's pupils, but they were interested in transmitting to us the opinions and interpretations of their great teacher; the "facts" (ma 'asim) which they record are his legal decisions, but never incidents of his life. Only by the way, here and there, do some points of personal interest occur in these works and in the master's own writings. With their help a few bare facts of his biography can be pieced together.

Nothing is known about his parents. We cannot even tell whether his father was a scholar. He never refers to him in his writings; he may have died while his son was still very young. Twice he mentions a brother of his motner — R. Simon the Elder, a pupil of Rabbenu Gershom — but we do not know where he lived and whether he exercised any influence on his nephew's education.

It was the merit of my revered teacher, Professor Abraham Berliner, whose publications on Rashi have thrown much light on his personality and work, to have pointed out for the first time that the city of his birth gave the young man an opportunity to become familiar with many aspects of practical life and that he made good use of this opportunity. Rashi's commentaries indicate that he was not a man of books alone, removed from problems of everyday life; they show an unusual familiarity with practical matters which he could not easily have acquired anywhere but in Troyes. For the capital of the Champagne was a mercantile and industrial center of importance, an importance which it maintained until the expulsion of the Jews in 1306. The great fairs arranged twice a year at Troyes were attended by merchants from France and Germany, Flanders, England and Italy. From visitors to these fairs Rashi learned about the city of Venice and its wonders, where one had to travel by boat from house to house, or about a great wall in Hungary. Conversations with seafarers and perhaps inspection of their ships were helpful for an understanding of Ezekiel's prophecy on Tyre (ch. 27), and it was from them that he learned about tides. In connection with Tyre he states that the foreign visitors were not permitted to deal directly with one another, but had to call in the services of the inhabitants as brokers; evidently Rashi transferred the experience of his own day to biblical times. He became familiar with the Cologne standard of coinage, which was used in Western Germany, saw tokens without engravings and learned about the procedure of coining, which, he tells us, followed certain practices of the blacksmiths. He knew of soldering and of engraving, of weaving figures into the material and of embroidering silk with gold. He evidently had observed these processes at the workshops of Troyes. He also speaks of the import from Lucca, Italy, of expensive taffeta interwoven with silver, of gold buckles and other jewelry, of belts worn by noble ladies when on horseback, and of many other items. He mentions buffoons who appeared during the fairs to entertain the people. What is of particular interest to us is that he knew of the preparation of parchment, manufactured in the tanneries of Troyes, which thus made available the indispensable material for a scholar of his type. Berliner informs us that owing to the high price of that material the scribes of the eleventh and twelfth centuries utilized every strip and corner of the skin. There are two manuscripts in the Jewish Theological Seminary Library which illustrate that old custom — one is a thirteenth-century copy of Rashi's commentary on the Prophets.

From his own experience — for Rashi earned his livelihood as a vinegrower — he describes to a son-in-law the difference between the wine-presses then in use and those formerly employed. In one of his responsa he apologizes for the briefness of his letter on the ground that he and his family were all busy that day with the vintage.

Thus Rashi went through life with his eyes wide open and was able to utilize the observations he made in his own day for the interpretation of practical matters in Bible and Talmud. He frequently gave the equivalent of these things in the French vernacular in his glosses, about which we shall have more to say later on.

In Troyes, Rashi could not find any teachers to give him a deeper understanding of Bible and Talmud; he therefore decided, after his marriage, to turn to the great academies which, in the preceding generation, had been established on the Rhine by the scholars of Lotharingia, as they are called in Jewish literature.

In Mayence, R. Judah ha-Kohen, also called R. Leontin, had opened the first academy in northern Europe (10th century). Under the leadership of his pupil, the afore-mentioned Rabbenu Gershom, the school quickly grew and developed; it trained a large circle of prominent scholars who continued the work of the Mayence academy and established similar schools in Worms and other cities.

In these academies the study of the Talmud was culti-vated with great zest and devotion. There the interpre-tations of the great master, Rabbenu Gershom, and of other scholars were eagerly collected by groups of younger scholars who preserved them in writing. The "Mayence Commentary" (*Kuntres Magenza*) — a product of this activity — enjoyed considerable fame and was excerpted by Rashi's contemporary, R. Nathan of Rome, in his *'Aruk*. In Italy it was ascribed to R. Gershom himself; it is under his name that the commentary on several treatises has been preserved and was so printed half a century ago in the great Wilna Talmud. A similar compilation origi-nated in the Worms academy.

The Jews of the Frankish empire, like their Italian brethren, had been dependent on the Palestinian acade-mies, and in the tenth and eleventh centuries they still turned to Palestine for decisions in difficult cases. The Spanish Jews, on the other hand, looked up to Babylonia for centuries and received their inspiration from the Baby-lonian center. As Dr. Louis Ginzberg has shown, the Babylonian Talmud had replaced the Yerushalmi even in Palestine as the main subject of study; in Europe, so far as we know, it had been the textbook of the academies from the very beginning. Somehow Babylonian traditions also reached northern Europe and were incorporated into the German commentaries on the Talmud.

These great schools of Mayence and Worms now at-tracted Rashi, and here, he felt, his thirst for knowledge could be quenched. It was generally assumed that he first attended the Worms school; but recently Dr. V. Aptowitzer has brought forward good reasons for the assumption that Rashi first directed his steps to the academy of Mayence, where R. Gershom himself had taught and where prominent pupils of his carried on the work of that great master. R. Jacob ben Yakar, who died in 1064, and R. Isaac ben Judah were the heads of the academy while Rashi attended it, and he refers to the former as his "old teacher" and his "teacher in Bible and Talmud." Incidentally, among Mayence tombstones recovered in recent years has been found that of R. Yakar, the father of R. Jacob, but, like that of Rabbenu Gershom already mentioned, it lacks the date. The other teacher, R. Isaac ben Judah, was related to Rashi, as was R. Isaac ha-Levi, the head of the Worms academy to which he went from Mayence.

We do not know when and at what age Rashi went to these academies, nor how many years he studied at each. From a note in one of his letters we learn that from Worms he went home — we do not know whether just for a visit or for a longer period — and later returned to the academy. He tells us that he had received instruction from his teacher on a certain point, but that when he came back to Troyes and studied the subject thoroughly he became convinced that his master had been wrong; on his return he had an opportunity to point out his error to him. Even after Rashi's final return to Troyes he probably intended to go back to his school in Worms; for on another occasion he expressed the hope that, although he had failed to prove his point by correspondence, when he saw his master again he would show him that he was correct. It is from such casual notes that we gather the few facts about Rashi's biography.

About his family the sources are very scanty, too. He had no son, but two or three daughters who were married to prominent scholars. One of them, Jochebed, was married to R. Meir ben Samuel who attended the Mayence academy together with Rashi. Four sons were born to them and they all became famous scholars: Isaac, Samuel, Solomon, and the youngest and the greatest of them, Jacob, called Rabbenu Tam. All but Solomon, who was forgotten until recent times, belonged to the outstanding French scholars of the following generation; they were the founders of the great school of Tosafists, who contributed so much to the interpretation of the Talmud and its practical application to the changed conditions of European life. Rabbenu Tam, indeed, outshone his grandfather Rashi himself as an authority on practical decisions.

Another daughter, Miriam, was married to R. Judah bar Nathan, a famous commentator on the Talmud, whose commentary on the last pages of the treatise Makkot is included in all editions. Large parts of his commentary on Ketubot, which were heretofore considered as belonging to a first version of Rashi's own commentary, were shown a few years ago by Professor J. N. Epstein of the Hebrew University to be the work of Rashi's son-in-law, R. Judah bar Nathan; they were collected together with some remnants of his commentary on Nedarim. This couple also had a learned son, Yom-Tob, and a daughter.

Whether Rashi had a third daughter, Rachel, is rather doubtful. R. Tam, in a responsum to his cousin, the Yom-Tob just mentioned, speaks of the divorce of their aunt Rachel, called Belle-Assez, from Eliezer, called Joselin. But it is possible, as several scholars assert, that *dodah* here does not mean aunt, but cousin, relative. Accordingly, the information given by Italian authorities of the sixteenth century that Rashi had three daughters cannot be verified, and the matter will have to be left in doubt unless new sources of information come to light. Incidentally, we learn from this case that among the French scholars it was quiet

common for a person to have a French name besides the
Hebrew one.

When Rashi returned to Troyes he opened a talmudic
academy of his own, and many students flocked to the
teacher who evidently very quickly succeeded in gaining
recognition and fame. Although he was the rabbi of
Troyes, he did not receive a salary but earned his living
from his vineyard which, as mentioned before, he cultivated
with the help of his family.

Turning now to the literary activity of Rashi, we come to
his commentaries on the Bible and, in the first place, to
that on the Pentateuch. No other Bible commentary ever
had greater success and influence. It is noteworthy that
it is the first edition of Rashi on the Pentateuch which bears
the earliest date for a Hebrew book printed in Italy, namely
February 1475, though the printing of a larger work had
probably started a little earlier. A year later, in 1476,
printing in Spain, too, began with an edition of this commentary. And still a third edition preceded the text of the
Hebrew Pentateuch itself, which appeared in print for the
first time in 1482 — accompanied by Rashi.

Without entering upon a bibliographical study of the
various editions that have appeared, it may be of interest to
state that the Library of the Jewish Theological Seminary
has about fifteen editions of Rashi on the Pentateuch without the text and over a hundred and eighty of the Pentateuch accompanied by Rashi, besides twenty-three editions
of the entire Bible with Rashi. The total number of such
editions is vastly greater; but these figures will give an
idea of the great popularity of the work.

Its popularity was richly deserved. It is a masterpiece
in every respect. Rashi's aim was to offer a literal interpretation of the text. Up to his time homiletical interpretation based on the Midrashim — works that originated

from the first or second to about the tenth century, mostly in Palestine — had predominated among the Jews. These books, containing the comments of the great authorities of Mishna and Talmud, include many a simple explanation, but these are almost lost in the mass of homiletical interpretations. A desire for a proper understanding of the Bible made itself felt in France at that time, and Rashi had at least one predecessor there. But it is his great merit to have succeeded in combining the two methods in masterly fashion and, with unerring instinct, to have selected such explanations from the rich storehouse of midrashic literature as fitted the biblical text best, without forcing its sense. He was aware of the homiletical character of these works, and at times expressly stated that there are many haggadic interpretations which the rabbis collected in various Midrashim; but it was his purpose to give *peshat*, the literal explanation of the Bible, and to combine it with "the haggadah which explains the words of the Bible." He emphasized that many of the midrashic interpretations actually offer an exact understanding of the biblical word. But he fully realized the fundamental difference between literal and homiletical exegesis, and not infrequently rejected interpretations which did violence to the text.

This happy blending of the two methods was responsible for the unique success of Rashi's efforts. His pupils and successors in the schools of northern France carried the desire for literalness much farther than the great master and even criticized his method. Perhaps the best of them, Rashi's grandson, R. Samuel ben Meir, called Rashbam, related in his commentary to the Pentateuch that Rashi had intended to revise his own work and adapt it to the new literal interpretations which were turning up every day. Rashbam's own commentary was a high achievement in this field and has found generous appreciation in modern times. It certainly was considered an advance over Rashi in his time, but it is dry and lacks the warmth so characteristic of Rashi's work. It is sufficient to record that his commentary had to wait for publication till 1705, when innumerable editions of Rashi had appeared and a whole literature had been written about it.

The Library of the Jewish Theological Seminary has about ninety different printed supercommentaries on Rashi's Bible commentary, and nearly twenty in manuscript. Among the authors of such supercommentaries we find some of the most prominent scholars — a fact which again permits us to gauge the influence of this popular work.

Rashi's commentary is thorough and deals with the narrative portions in the same way as with the legal ones, including even minute descriptions of the Tabernacle and its vessels. Here his practical sense and his observations of daily life, to which I have referred above, proved most helpful. He sometimes even added drawings to his explanations of Bible and Talmud; which, however, have been omitted by copyists and printers, and only the indication "like this," followed by a blank space, has remained in our texts.

Grammatical studies had made great progress, by the time Rashi began his literary activity, through the efforts of the great Spanish scholars; but their works, written in Arabic, were inaccessible to Western Jewry. Rashi only knew the first groping steps in this field, the Hebrew dictionary of Menahem and its criticism by Dunash. He quoted these frequently, but his fine sense and intuition led him in many instances to avoid their mistakes so that, compared with these early Spaniards, Rashi's linguistic explanations, to which he gave considerable space, represented real progress. A grammarian like Abraham de Balmes (1523), rated these grammatical notes in Rashi's commentaries very highly and stated that Rashi revealed the true nature of the Hebrew language. His occasional remarks on the shades of meaning of various synonyms are still of real value. Many a Jewish scholar in former centuries owed his grammatical training to his study of Rashi.

A characteristic of Rashi in all his commentaries is his use of the vernacular for the interpretation of difficult words. It has been noted that about 3,000 French words occur in his works. These words are of the highest value for the study of old French, for they belong to the very oldest remnants of that language. There is, so far as I know, only one French epic dating from Rashi's time. Rashi's French glosses have therefore been much studied during the last hundred years; and it is an American scholar, the late Professor David S. Blondheim, to whom we owe the most important contribution in this field. Unfortunately Blondheim died in the midst of his work, which would have thrown much further light on both French and Hebrew literature. These glosses, moreover, give evidence of Rashi's many-sided interests. He mentions the titles of French dignitaries, such as count, senechal, treasurer, provost, master of cuisine, etc. In one place he tells us that it was customary in France to hand a glove to a man as a sign of appointment to a position of dignity.

Rashi generally followed the *Masorah* in the interpretation of the Bible, and only rarely did he deviate from the accents of the text. He treated the *Targum*, the official Aramaic translation of the Pentateuch and the Prophets, with the greatest respect, constantly referring to them, for he considered them of the highest importance for exegesis. He was not so much concerned with the anthropomorphisms which the *Targumim* are at great pains to avoid; apparently such locutions offered no serious problem to the people of his time. He occasionally referred to them, however, and once he stated that it was the method of the Bible to speak of Divinity in human terms in order to facilitate

understanding. He paid as much attention to the interpretation of the single word as to the context, subject
matter and order of the verses.

Rashi's commentary on the Pentateuch is a truly popular
work. It offers instruction to the scholar and to the layman;
even children can easily follow its simple language. It
earned him the honorary title *Parshandata*, "the interpreter
of the Torah." His language is quite remarkable; clear
and simple, it avoids all unnecessary phrases, always uses
the right word and displays great felicity in explaining one
Hebrew word by another.

The Rashi commentary on the other parts of the Bible
is not as popular as that on the Pentateuch; the midrashic
interpretations do not occupy quite so prominent a place
and more emphasis is laid on pure literalness. Otherwise
it has the same characteristics. We find here occasional
polemics against Christian interpretations, with which
Rashi evidently was familiar.

There was a flourishing Christian school in Troyes in
Rashi's days. As his relations to his Christian neighbors
seem to have been friendly — to judge from various expressions in his works which suggest great tolerance towards
Christians — he may have heard such interpretations from
the clergymen of Troyes, who probably cultivated the alle-
gorical interpretation of the Bible so prevalent at that
time.

We find in the later books a few references to suffering
and persecution of the Jews; and we may be justified in
assuming that these passages, like some of the *Selihot* he
composed, were written after the first crusade which cast a
gloom over the last decade of Rashi's life. But of that we
shall have to say more later on.

Theological ideas rarely occupied Rashi, but a well-
known saying in his commentary on Psalms (49.11) may
be mentioned: The term *mitah*, death, is there employed

in reference to scholars, for only their bodies die in this world; for the foolish and ignorant, however, the Psalmist uses the term *abedah*, perishing, indicating that both their bodies and their souls perish.

Rashi always began with the interpretation of the text, without any preliminary remarks; in two instances only did he write short prefaces — to the Song of Songs and to the Book of Zechariah. In the former he points out that a biblical text has more than one meaning, but ultimately always retains its plain sense; and although the prophets speak in allegories, we have to explain them properly according to context and order of verses. This he proposes to do for the Song of Songs, though with constant references to the midrashim. He then goes on to speak of the reason why King Solomon composed the book in the prophetic spirit. In the case of Zechariah, the difficulty of the prophecy causes him to remark: "The prophecy of Zechariah is very mysterious, for it contains visions which, like dreams, require interpretation; but we cannot understand their real meaning until the teacher of truth (the Messiah) comes. I shall try to expound every verse in accordance with fitting interpretations and the explanation of the *Targum*." In the course of the commentary he says (11.13): "I have seen many interpretations of this prophecy which I cannot understand." In all his commentaries, Rashi, with his customary modesty and love of truth, never hesitates to admit that he does not know the solution to a problem or does not understand a certain passage.

He is also ready to admit an error without any effort to defend his original interpretation. Thus he states on one occasion that he has reconsidered his explanation of a passage in Ezekiel and now, having gone over the book once more with one of his pupils, Shemayah, and found that he had contradicted himself, offers a more acceptable interpretation. This pupil, Shemayah, who, like one of

his grandsons and several other persons in his entourage,
occasionally served Rashi as secretary, inserted quite a
number of explanations into his master's works, even during
Rashi's lifetime. Of another pupil — the excellent exegete
Joseph Kara — Berliner collected over eighty such additions to the commentary on the Pentateuch; in some
instances Kara states expressly that they met with the
approval of the master.

One of the Seminary manuscripts which I have examined
contains a few further brief additions by Kara and one by
Rashi's grandson, R. Samuel ben Meir. Some of these
additions have found their way, without any indication of
their secondary character, into the printed texts of Rashi,
which are marred by many other corruptions.

The necessity for critical editions based on the extant
old manuscripts has therefore long been felt. The first
serious effort in this direction was Dr. Berliner's famous
edition of the commentary on the Pentateuch, in 1866.
Based on a number of manuscripts and early editions, it
represented an enormous improvement over the existing
text. For a second edition, 1905, Berliner consulted many
more manuscripts, though without recording their readings.
During the last decade, Dr. I. Maarsen, Chief Rabbi of the
Hague, started work on a critical edition of the commentaries on the Prophets and Hagiographa, of which those
on the Minor Prophets, Isaiah and Psalms have already
appeared and that on Job was in press when World War
II broke out. The manuscript of the Jewish Theological
Seminary had been consulted for this edition, as well as the
Seminary copy of the extremely rare first edition of the
commentary on Psalms and Job. But our hope that in
the course of time we may be able to study Rashi's masterly
biblical commentaries in adequate editions was shattered
when the scholarly rabbi fell victim to the Nazi terror.

Rashi occasionally quotes his sources by name; more

often he refers to them in general terms: "I have found," "some say," "some explain," or similar expressions. Frequently we read that he "heard" or, more definitely, that he "heard [or received a tradition] from his teachers." As against such explanations by others, he expressly states in some instances: "I have not heard or found," or, more definitely: "I say," "I explain," "it seems to me," etc., thus emphasizing his originality on the points at issue.

In one instance (Ez. 42.3) we read in our editions: "I had neither teacher nor helper in [the interpretation of] this building [of the Temple of Ezekiel], but [explained it] as they showed me from heaven." (This remark, however, is not found in any of the eleven manuscripts consulted by A. J. Levy for his edition, Philadelphia, 1931.) Sometimes again we find an indefinite "one could say," "one could explain," "the explanation of this passage is," occasionally with the addition "according to its context," or "one also could explain the passage." The latter expression shows that, at this point, Rashi offers more than one interpretation of a passage. It is not an unusual phenomenon for him to give several explanations for a verse, though he generally introduces such additional interpretations with a simple formula: "another way." The above-mentioned modern editions, especially that of Berliner, have made very successful efforts to trace most of Rashi's sources and thus enable us to get a clearer notion of Rashi's original contributions.

But it is not only his new suggestions which make Rashi's work on the Bible of outstanding importance; his judicious selection from the works of his predecessors and his restatement of their opinions in his own classical diction are deserving of just as much recognition.

Such recognition Rashi's biblical commentary found from the very beginning, not only among his co-religionists, but also among Christian scholars. One of the most famous Christian exegetes, Nicolas de Lyra, a French Franciscan of

the first half of the fourteenth century, quoted Rashi
constantly, and this commentary was one of the main
sources used by Luther in his translation. The collaborators
in the King James version of the Bible also made ample
use of Rashi.

If the commentary on the Pentateuch is the book that
made Rashi famous among wide circles, that on the Talmud
is of no lesser importance. So far as we know, only two or
three parts of the Talmud were ever printed without this
indispensable work.

The widespread influence of the Talmud commentary
may likewise be illustrated by the fact that the Seminary
Library has forty-four editions of the complete Talmud
and some two hundred and fifty individual treatises, and
all but one of them are accompanied by Rashi. Even when
an enterprising publisher decided, half a century ago, to
print a one-volume edition of the Talmud, in small type,
he did not dare omit Rashi. The few Spanish and Portu-
guese incunabula, with one exception, also added the
commentary of the French scholar, though they did not
print the *Tosafot* by Rashi's pupils which appear in all the
Italian, German and Polish editions.

We do not know whether Rashi had already conceived
the plan of the commentary on the Talmud when he went
to the Rhenish academies; but undoubtedly the commentaries of the Mayence scholars and the direct instruction
received from his teachers there were of a very material
help to him. It has been shown that he generally follows
the interpretation of the teacher under whom he had
studied the part of the Talmud in question, adding diver-
gent explanations he had received from one or another
teacher, or found in earlier works, with the introduction:
"some explain," or "another interpretation." Often he states
that either the first or the last interpretation is preferable.

He collected, during his years of study, all the material available in the academies, that is, the Mayence and Worms *Kuntresim* which may be compared to notebooks of Talmud students recording the instruction of their masters. Only thus can we understand why some serious errors have been discovered in these early works. Whatever geonic interpretations were accessible in the Rhenish schools were carefully copied. At the same time, Rashi looked for all available material for the text of the Talmud, which in the course of transmission had suffered corruption and unauthorized additions before it had reached the academies of Western Europe. Scholars had made free with the text and had corrected and interpolated it. R. Gershom, therefore, had with his own hand prepared a careful copy of this fundamental work and had issued a prohibition against any change or correction. Rashi naturally used this autograph, which probably was considered normative in the schools. He, however, was not satisfied with this work, but collated all the other manuscripts he could procure. His numberless notes on the text in his commentary, which he introduces with the words "we should read thus," are undoubtedly based on the authority of some manuscript or perhaps on a parallel in one of the *Baraita* collections. It is unlikely that he often resorted to mere conjecture to emend this book for which he had such great respect, as in his modesty he hardly would have trusted his own judgment without some such authority.

His pupils, on the other hand, permitted themselves great freedom in the matter of emendation. Rashi's grandson, R. Tam, complained bitterly about the rashness of his elder brother, R. Samuel, whom he otherwise greatly respected, in changing the readings of the Talmud. He says that, unlike his grandfather, R. Samuel changed the texts themselves, whereas Rashi had merely noted his corrections in his commentary without touching the text.

In our editions, Rashi's readings have for the most part been introduced into the text; often it is only by consulting manuscripts or the readings collected in Rabbinowicz's invaluable work that we can determine the readings which Rashi rejected. Rashi's authority was so great that his statement on the correctness of a reading was considered sufficient to change the text of the Talmud, although such action was contrary to his warnings and objections.

We cannot tell whether Rashi merely collected material for his work at Mayence and Worms or actually started there on his great task. Nor do we know in what order he commented on the various treatises. In two of them his commentary stops in the middle in our editions and manuscripts — Baba Batra 29b and Makkot 19b. In that on Makkot, *tahor*, "pure," is one of the last words, and we read: "Our master with his pure body, whose soul expired in purity, did not comment any further; here begins the commentary of his pupil and son-in-law R. Judah bar Nathan." But Berliner found in one manuscript merely "Up to this point is the commentary of the master, from here on we read the words of the pupil;" and explanations of his on later passages of these treatises are quoted in comments of the French school. The commentary on five treatises printed under Rashi's name has been the subject of much discussion, and their authenticity has been doubted with good reason. It is not impossible, as Lipschütz, the latest comprehensive biographer of Rashi, suggests, that we have here an early, unrevised version of Rashi's commentaries, which therefore do not show all the characteristics and the excellence of the rest of the work. This question deserves further study.

Rashi worked constantly on the revision of his commentaries. We have a curious description of his autograph by a German scholar, written a century after his death. He relates how Rashi crossed out words, wrote and corrected between the lines and made additions on the margin. There are a few such references to Rashi's holographs with author's corrections, but unfortunately not a line from his own hand has been preserved.

Much has been written in modern times about the various recensions of Rashi's commentary on the Talmud. It is claimed that we have for the greater part the third and final revision. I doubt that he actually rewrote his books entirely and did not, rather, simply keep on correcting and, when the accumulation of such changes made parts of the book difficult to use, copy these and eventually add new corrections and revisions. In spite of this, there are a number of contradictions in different parts of the commentary due to the fact that he generally followed the interpretation of the teacher under whom he studied the particular treatise. Since we do not know the chronology of his works, it is impossible to state which was his earlier and which his later opinion.

On the other hand, differences in the interpretation of biblical passages between the commentary on the Bible and that on the Talmud can easily be explained. On the Bible he gives the explanation which he considers correct in the context. In the commentary on the Talmud, however, he offers the interpretation of the text in the sense of the talmudic authority who invokes it.

Rashi's commentary on the Talmud is extremely brief and to the point. Often he answers a question that might occur to a student by the insertion of a single word. The Tosafists, who carried on his work, at times did not realize this and added discussions which more careful attention to the wording of his comments would have made unnecessary. One of the greatest German Talmudists of the last century, R. Jacob Ettlinger, occasionally calls attention to such cases. Rashi is interested in establishing the general methodological rules which the Talmud follows; he is careful about the chronological succession of the generations of tannaim and amoraim and tries to interpret points of archaeology. His attention is generally directed towards the details. He always finds the points which require elucidation and expounds them briefly; what is easily understood he passes over. He never tries to show either his vast knowledge or his acumen; he keeps his personality entirely in the background and considers nothing but the text and the need of the student.

There is a great and basic difference between Rashi and all his predecessors. They all tried to facilitate the understanding of the Talmud by giving a brief outline of the talmudic discussions while adding relatively few explanations of details. Rashi, on the other hand, refrained from doing so. He left it to the student to find the context and the logical development of the discussion, of which, however, he never lost sight and to which he occasionally pointed with a brief remark. His main aim was to give the necessary help without ever distracting the reader from the text for any length of time. He thus created an indispensable and incomparable tool for the study of the Talmud, which became the basis for practically all work in this field. The simplicity and lucidity of his interpretations — a rare gift which he possessed to an unusual degree — made his work as valuable to the scholar as to the beginner. It has been justly asserted that his commentary restored the Talmud to us, that without his masterly interpretation it would have remained a closed book to the majority of students, that it was his commentary alone which made possible the great development of talmudic knowledge by the northern French scholars. It is the work of a genius and a master craftsman who, penetrating into the very structure of the Talmud, enables us to see its growth and evolution. It is only thanks to Rashi's commentary that the proper study of the Talmud did not gradually cease, as Maimonides had feared. Maimonides tried to save the subject matter from oblivion by a marvelous digest, since he saw no real hope for the revival of its study. Rashi, however, forged a key to the treasure-house of the Talmud which enabled an easy entrance into it and thus made it again the cornerstone of Jewish learning and culture.

The commentary on the Talmud is gigantic in size, and there is still a possibility that parts of it may have perished. Who can tell what wealth of ancient and medieval literature was lost to us when twenty-four carloads of Jewish books were consigned to the flames in the market place of Paris around the year 1240?

Rashi's commentary is a phenomenal piece of work, which hardly has its equal in any other literature. It has become almost an institution. We cannot imagine the study of the Talmud without this indispensable guide. All of us, like countless generations before us, have been introduced to it by his help; and, although modern scholarship may occasionally interpret the Talmud more scientifically, it recognizes its indebtedness to the genius of Rashi and still stands on his shoulders.

A little over a century after Rashi's death, a member of the later Babylonian schools, Daniel ha-Babli of Damascus, referred to Rashi as the "greatest commentator who enlightened the eyes of the people in exile." The members of the Babylonian schools considered themselves the true successors of the geonim and looked with disdain on the results of Western scholarship; they refused to recognize the great Code of Maimonides and bitterly attacked it. The praise of a critic from this circle is therefore a rare recognition of Rashi's outstanding merit.

It is a curious phenomenon that in the eleventh century, after the close of the geonic period and the decline of the Babylonian schools, there arose three contemporaries who summed up the work of the five centuries after the conclusion of the Talmud: Rashi, by his commentary; R. Nathan of Rome, by his talmudic dictionary; and R. Isaac Alfasi, of Lucena, Spain, by his great code. Of the three, all of whom died within a space of four years at the beginning of the twelfth century, Rashi was the greatest genius.

There is only one side of talmudic study to which Rashi, again in contradistinction to his predecessors, paid little attention in his commentary — the practical application of the talmudic discussions to legal decisions. In his capacity of rabbi, however, he was naturally deeply concerned with questions of Jewish law. Some brief legal summaries of his are incorporated in the legal compilations composed by his pupils which go under his name and which have mostly been published only during the last century. These books also give us information about Rashi's opinions and decisions on numerous legal questions. They include a large number of his responsa, some of which have been found separately in manuscripts and were also published during the last century. An edition of the about two hundred and sixty responsa of Rashi has been published by Dr. Israel Elfenbein. Through these letters, which contain more personal references than all the other, greater writings of our sage, we get a clearer perspective of the beauty of his character and personality. He corresponded with his teachers, his colleagues and his pupils. To all of them he wrote with the same modesty and loving interest. It would be tempting to discuss these utterances of Rashi in greater detail, but space permits the mention of only a very few characteristic points. They show Rashi's independence of judgment; he does not follow his teachers when his own study of the sources leads him to different decisions. They give evidence of his love of peace and of his great tolerance, which finds expression especially in his dealings with the victims of the first crusade. Though French communities had suffered very little, the crusade had caused the destruction of the ancient Jewish communities of the Rhine, so dear to Rashi since his student days. Many Jews had embraced Christianity to save their lives, and most of these returned to their ancestral religion as soon as circumstances permitted. Rashi insisted that these unfortunate persons should be treated with the utmost consideration, since they had not given up Judaism of their free will but only to save their lives and in many instances had been baptized by force and under direct compulsion. He permitted men of priestly descent to function in their communities as before, declared a marriage entered into during the period of conversion valid and strictly forbade reminding these unfortunate victims of their lapses. He was guided in this by Rabbenu Gershom, whose attitude we know through a responsum of Rashi.

Time and again we are struck by the ideal relationship between master and pupils. His teachers address Rashi with love and admiration as an "honored and great scholar;" they show their deep concern over his well-being and inquire after him from every foreign visitor. "The generation to which such a man belongs is not orphaned," one of them writes to him; another asks him to pray for him. Rashi shows the same loving concern for his own pupils, whom he addresses as: "my brother," "my beloved."

I may quote one of his most characteristic utterances: "It is not my custom," he writes, "to consider myself chief judge and to pass final decisions; far be it from me to consider myself a prominent court of law (to decide for other communities). If I were in your midst, I would vote with you to permit this matter; but who am I to take for myself authority elsewhere, a little man like myself whose importance is slight, an orphan of orphans."

Let us in conclusion compare his modest self-appraisal

with the remark of a competent judge, one of the great German scholars of the following generation, R. Eliezer ben Nathan of Mayence. Speaking of a responsum of Rashi, he says: "His water we drink, and from his mouth we live . . . We must try to understand the perfect teaching of R. Solomon, who searched and explored the Torah and, so to speak, provided it with handles . . . The words of that Gaon are straightforward for the learned, correct for those who know the law; his lips guarded understanding and the interpretation of the law was asked and requested and renewed from his mouth; true learning was in his mouth, in peace and in righteousness he walked, established for the world one of its three pillars (the truth) and enlarged and glorified the Torah."

Few facts, as we have seen, are known about Rashi's life, but as he somewhere remarks: "The true biography of a man is the record of his deeds."

4

Moses Maimonides

THE year 1935 marked the eight hundredth anniversary of the birth of Moses Maimonides of whom it has been said: "From the time of [the law-giver] Moses to that of Moses [Maimonides], there arose none like Moses." He was the greatest genius Judaism has brought forward in the course of the Middle Ages, and one of the greatest sons of our people in all times.

In many-sidedness and fertility only that great pathfinder in all fields of Jewish learning, the Gaon Saadia, can be placed beside him; but, while the latter stands at the beginning of the fruitful development he inaugurated, the work of Maimonides was its culmination.

There are richer sources for Maimonides' biography than for that of most mediaeval heroes of Judaism, but there are many points on which our information is very inadequate. As I fortunately have access to an unusually large collection of Maimonides-manuscripts in the Library of the Jewish Theological Seminary, I shall occasionally take the opportunity to refer to these.

Scion of an illustrious family of scholars, he was born, the son of the eminent judge of Cordova, R. Maimon, on the 14th of Nissan — March 30, 1135. The boy showed unusual gifts at an early age and profited greatly from the instruction of his learned father. But the happy days of Spain's golden era were waning for the Jews, and Moses had hardly reached his thirteenth year when the invasion of the fanatical Almohades put an end to the flourishing Cordova community and compelled its members, unless they consented to do lip-service to the Mohammedan

87

confession, to go into exile. A period of restless wanderings for Maimon and his family followed. Of this time we have little information. Ultimately the fame of a great scholar of Fez, R. Judah ibn Sosan, attracted Maimon and his sons to settle there. But after some time, conditions in North Africa became unbearable for the Jews and many outwardly embraced Islam. At this juncture a fanatical scholar, living elsewhere in undisturbed safety, issued a sharp condemnation of those yielding under compulsion, though observing Jewish ritual at home; he declared their private observance to be without any value and even a desecration. The young Maimonides replied to this man in his *Treatise on Religious Persecution.* He refuted the statements of the fanatic in his own systematic way, but pointed out that faithful Jews were in duty bound to leave the country whenever possible. The treatise was printed twice, from two different manuscripts; three more manuscripts in the Jewish Theological Seminary Library throw new light on this important letter. Maimonides must already have enjoyed considerable authority at the time he wrote it.

When the persecutions became unbearable and his teacher, Ibn Sosan, died a martyr's death, Maimonides decided to leave by ship for Palestine. The trip from Fez to Acco lasted a month; during a terrific storm the little ship nearly foundered — an experience which made a very deep impression on him. We have a copy of an autograph note stating that he would observe the day of this storm all his life as a fast-day to be spent in solitary contemplation. Thirty-four years later, when Ibn Tibbon planned to visit Maimonides, the latter, evidently still remembering his own sufferings, was concerned about Ibn Tibbon's exposing himself to the dangers of the voyage over seas.

In the early part of the year 1165 Moses arrived in Palestine, and his brother David joined him there ten days later. After a five-months' stay in Acco, they visited the holy places, Jerusalem and Hebron. Shortly afterwards they went to Egypt and, possibly after a sojourn in Alexandria, Maimonides settled in Fostat. Whilst his brother supported the family by trading in jewels, Maimonides devoted himself exclusively to his manifold studies. He was gifted with a remarkable memory which, according to his own statement as reported by a younger contemporary, enabled him after a single reading to remember the contents of any book and to teach it to others: "Unlike many people, I never suffered in my youth from forgetfulness."

But this happy time was not to last. A few months after leaving Palestine, he lost his revered father. Then he fell ill. Later, he seems to have been accused of apostasy and subsequent return to Judaism. This accusation is recorded by Arabic writers with many contradictory details. Some modern scholars have accepted his apostasy as a fact, but the weight of evidence is strongly against them, and it has been suggested that the charge was due to the jealousy of some less successful physicians. Maimonides refers in a letter to the attacks of informers who threatened his life; he probably had these accusations in mind.

The hardest blow for Maimonides was the death of his beloved younger brother in a shipwreck in the Indian Ocean on one of his business trips. Through this catastrophe he lost a devoted brother and an apt pupil, together with the fortune of the family. Eight years after the event he expressed his sorrow in a touching letter to the Palestinian judge, Jefet ben Elijah, and mentioned that in consequence of his loss he had been ill for a full year.

We may assume that soon after his arrival in Egypt, Maimonides started to lecture on talmudic lore and on the sciences of astronomy and medicine. He also devoted himself to the practice of medicine, especially after the heavy financial reverses to which he refers in the above-mentioned letter to R. Jefet. In all these fields he soon acquired considerable fame, and he became a very influential member of the Jewish community. We do not know when he first became a member of the Jewish court and the spiritual guide of the Jewish community of Fostat, but we hear at an early period of important enactments made with his cooperation and at his instigation. He counteracted the influence of the powerful Karaite community and took an active interest in the administration of the civil and marital law as well as in the synagogue services. Numerous decisions of his, sometimes with the added endorsements of prominent members of the rabbinical court, have come down to us, testifying to his successful efforts to improve conditions.

When an unworthy person had, through political favoritism, procured the position of *Nagid* (the official lay head of Egyptian Jewry) and oppressed the people, Maimonides was instrumental in depriving him of his power. At a later period Maimonides himself became the actual head of Egyptian Jewry, though we nowhere find that he bore the title *Nagid*. This office was filled, however, by his only son, Abraham, and by his descendants for two centuries.

In accordance with his conviction that a rabbi had no right to draw a salary for his rabbinical work, he did not accept any remuneration for the public service to which he devoted a great part of his time. Owing to his great fame as the outstanding scholar of his generation, he was consulted on questions arising not only in Fostat and other parts of Egypt, but also in foreign countries. He answered all these inquiries with characteristic, concise clearness and thoroughness. A large number of his responsa to legal questions have come down to us. Some are written in Arabic and others in Hebrew, for he always answered in the language of the questioner. Recently an excellent edition of nearly four hundred responsa has been published in Hebrew, in part original, in part translations; but we are still waiting for an edition of those transmitted in Arabic which Dr. B. Halper had practically ready for the press at the time of his lamented death.

Even stronger evidence of Maimonides' outstanding position is shown by the question directed to him from Yemen. There, through a change of rule, the position of the Jews had become very unfavorable and they were sorely oppressed. A messianic pretender had risen in their midst and they asked the great leader in Egypt whether they should trust his promises. Maimonides' famous *Letter to Yemen* comforted them in their perplexity and made such an impression that thenceforth Yemen Jewry included Maimonides' name in their prayers and added a blessing for him in the *Kaddish*. It is to the devotion of the Yemenite Jews that we owe the preservation of the Arabic originals of many of his works, as they continued copying them until recent times. The Seminary Library has about one hundred manuscripts of parts of his works or commentaries on them written by Yemenite scribes. Of the unpublished Arabic original of the *Letter to Yemen* a copy is found in the Jewish Theological Seminary Library. It is the more important since it contains a long historical passage about false messiahs which was omitted in all Hebrew translations. The late Professor Friedlaender prepared an edition of this important text and there is hope that it will be published soon.

In this epistle Maimonides expresses himself very sharply about Mohammedanism. Its religious teachings compared to our Torah, he says, are like a statue as compared with a living man. While he asks to have copies of his letter spread throughout the country, he implores the addressee to be very careful that it should remain only among his coreligionists. If it became known to Mohammedans, it might involve the author in dire consequences. Though realizing this danger, Maimonides felt it his duty not to shirk responsibility and to do his share to relieve the mind of the people who had appealed to him. The *Letter to Yemen* was written about 1172.

In the following year he started a movement to redeem a number of Jewish captives, possibly Yemenites, who had left the unfriendly shores of their old home. He raised money in his home and sent a representative to communities of another country, hitherto unidentified, with a letter bearing his autograph signature, asking his coreligionists there to follow the generous example of Egyptian Jewry. The original letter which this representative had taken with him on his trip was discovered by Doctor Schechter in the *Genizah* and is now the property of the Seminary Library. The wording of the letter shows that its author held a position of considerable authority.

We know through some thirteenth-century Arabic historians of medicine that Maimonides was considered one of the most eminent practitioners of his time. A prominent physician of Bagdad, Abdu'l-Latif, tells us that he went to Cairo to make the acquaintance of three great men, one of them being Maimonides, whom he characterizes as a man of great merits, but tainted by ambition and by excessive readiness to cater to the great. This must have been a hasty visitor's fleeting impression, contradicted by the testimony of other contemporaries and by many utterances of the sage himself.

Another Arabic author, Ibn Abi Usaibia, who was born a few years before Maimonides' death and was a colleague of the latter's son at the great Cairo hospital, relates that in theoretical as well as in practical medicine the Jewish scholar held the highest rank among the physicians of his time and that he was very well versed in the sciences and possessed a deep knowledge of philosophy. He was appointed by Sultan Saladin and afterwards by Saladin's son, Al-Afdhal, as court physician. Ibn Abi Usaibia quotes the verses of a Mohammedan judge in honor of Abu Imran (Maimonides' Arabic name). These verses, though written with true oriental exuberance, still convey an idea of the unique position held by Maimonides even among non-Jews:

> Galen's medicine is only for the body; that of Abu Imran is suited for body and soul.
> If with his knowledge he had made himself the physician of the century, he would have cured it by his knowledge from the sickness of ignorance.
> If the moon had resorted to his art, it certainly would have obtained the perfection it lacks.
> On the day of full moon he would cure it of its spots, and from its disease on the day of conjunction.

A third writer, Ibn Al-Kifti, who was an intimate friend of Maimonides' favorite pupil, Joseph ben Juda, has a long article about the master in his *Dictionary of Scientists*. Although the information is partly confused, Ibn Al-Kifti adds some valuable points. Thus we learn from him that Maimonides was invited to become the court physician of a Frankish king at Ascalon — either Richard the Lionhearted or King Amalric of Jerusalem — but declined the honor. Saladin's vizier, Al-Fadl al-Baisami, overwhelmed him with kindness and granted him an annual stipend.

In the year 1190, Maimonides wrote to his pupil, Joseph ben Juda:

> I inform you that I have acquired a very great reputation among the great, such as the chief kadi, the emirs, the house of Al-Fadl and others among the great in the city who do not pay much. As for the ordinary people, I am placed too high for them to reach me. This obliges me continually to waste my day in Cairo visiting the sick; when I return to Fostat I am too tired for the rest of the day and night to pursue the study of medical books which I need. For you know how long and difficult this art is for a conscientious and exact man who does not want to state

anything which he cannot support by argument and without knowing where it has been said and how it can be demonstrated.

This utterance is very characteristic of the man and the scientist.

At that time he evidently was not yet the court physician of Saladin, who died in 1193. For the time of the reign of Saladin's son, who ascended the throne in 1198, Maimonides gives us a striking description of his daily routine in a letter to Samuel ibn Tibbon, who wanted to visit him in order to discuss with him some difficult passages of the *Guide of the Perplexed* before completing its translation. Although anxious to make his acquaintance, Maimonides advised Ibn Tibbon first to finish the translation. To explain why the visit would not give them sufficient opportunity for scholarly discussion, he gives the following account of his regular duties:

> I dwell in Fostat and the Sultan resides at Cairo and the distance between the two places is a double Sabbath-day's journey (circa 1½ miles). My duties to the Sultan are heavy. I must visit him early every morning; if he feels weak or any of his children or the inmates of his harem are ill, I do not leave Cairo but spend the greater part of the day in the palace. Also if one or two of the officials fall ill, I have to attend to them and thus spend the whole day there.
>
> In brief, I repair to Cairo every day in the early morning, and even if nothing unusual happens, I do not return to Fostat till after the noon hour. Then I am fatigued and hungry and I find the courts of my house full of people, prominent and common, gentiles, theologians and judges, waiting for the time of my return.
>
> I dismount from my animal, wash my hands, and go forth to them and entreat them to wait for me while I take a slight refreshment, my only meal in twenty-four hours. After that I attend to the patients and

prescribe for them. Patients go in and out until night-
fall or sometimes, I assure you, until two hours in the
night. I talk to them lying on my back because of
weakness. When the night falls I feel so weak, I cannot
speak any more.

Thus no Israelite can have a private discussion with
me except on the Sabbath. Then they all come to me
after the services and I advise them what to do during
the week; afterwards they study a little till noon and
depart. Some of them come back and study again
until the evening prayers.

This is my regular daily routine.· I have here related
to you only part of what you will see, please God.

This precious letter, which also contains some illuminating remarks on correct methods of translating, together
with Maimonides' careful judgment on the works of the
Greek and Arabic philosophers, was partly written in
Arabic. Two translations of the most important passages
have been preserved, one frequently printed, the other
known from one manuscript in Breslau. Recently a second
manuscript of this translation was discovered in the Seminary Library and both were published together.

How the court physician could find time and strength
for literary activity after such a daily routine is hard to
understand; but we have two important and interesting
medical works which he composed at the request of the
young ruler who complained of various disturbances of
his health and of his nervous system.

The *Treatise on Dietetics*, one of the most famous of his
medical works, was written shortly after Al-Afdhal had ascended the throne, and in the thirteenth century it was
translated into Hebrew and twice into Latin. One of the
Latin translations, probably by the eminent physician
Armengaud of Blaise, was printed circa 1477 and reprinted
at least five times during the sixteenth century — an evidence of its popularity. A manuscript of the Arabic text

and the first four Latin editions are found in the Seminary
Library. This treatise is of great interest, as it contains
general rules for a healthy life and shows the author's
understanding of human psychology.

The strain of the arduous practise which Maimonides
described in the letter of 1199 — five years before his
death — proved too much for him, and the last work he
composed — likewise for Al-Afdhal — informs us that at
that time (probably in 1200, the year when Al-Afdhal was
deposed), he was no longer able to attend his royal patient
personally. The sultan informed him of the various opinions of the physicians in attendance and requested him to
express his judgment about them and to give his own advice
as to the mode of life to be followed. Although not satisfied
with some of the methods of the other physicians, Maimonides, who, we are informed, was always on good terms with
his colleagues, treated them with respect. He gives the
ruler a detailed regimen for every hour of the day and
prescribes a strict diet. In a curious passage he excuses
himself for recommending the use of wine and song which
the Mohammedan religion forbids. As a physician he has
to state what his calling requires. He points to that which
is useful for the body and warns of the harmful, but he
does not compel obedience; that is left to the free will of
the patient. The non-Mohammedan physician had to be
very careful and pay attention to the court intrigues!

It may be stated in this connection that we know of ten
medical works by Maimonides, all written in Arabic, five
of which have been published in the original by a German
rabbi, Dr. H. Kroner, in the course of the last thirty years.
A hitherto lost treatise, giving the names and use of the
principal drugs in Arabic, Greek, Spanish, Berber, Persian
and sometimes Syriac, has recently been discovered in a
Constantinople manuscript and has been published by Dr.
Meyerhof of Cairo. Of the others, one was translated into

French and German, and one was published in Latin and also, very incorrectly, in a Hebrew translation. The latter, his medical aphorisms or the *Chapters of Moses*, as he called them, are the most important and the most interesting of his works in this field. The Latin translation was printed in 1489; twice again in the fifteenth and once in the sixteenth century. Through the mediaeval Latin translations Maimonides' work became known to certain great Christian physicians who considered him an authority in several fields of medicine and not infrequently quoted his views. While his works are based on those of the famous Galen, Maimonides shows a certain originality and critical ability in his treatment of medicine. (Dr. S. Muntner, a Jerusalem physician, began in 1940 the publication of *Maimonides' Medical Works* in their mediaeval Hebrew translation; two volumes have appeared.)

Maimonides' literary activity ceased with his last medical work which he wrote in the year 1200. A few of his letters and responsa come perhaps from his last years. But although his mind retained its power and clarity to the last moment, his physical weakness did not permit him to carry out some of his literary plans. He died on the 20th of Tebet — December 13, 1204, three months before his seventieth birthday, mourned far and wide by the Jewish people in whose service he had been active during all his life and to whom he left an incomparably rich inheritance. He was buried, according to his last wishes, in Tiberias, Palestine.

While some of his minor works have already been mentioned in this short sketch of his life, I shall now turn to the great books which have made the name of *Rambam* a household word among his coreligionists. In spite of repeated attacks by certain opponents of his rationalistic views, his fame has not been dimmed in these eight centuries.

So far as we know, he started his literary career in Spain as a young man, not yet 16. His first work was the *Treatise on Logic*, composed at the request of an unnamed scholar of prominent position. The Arabic original is preserved only in part; in Moses ibn Tibbon's translation it has been commented on repeatedly since the fourteenth century, by Mendelssohn and Heidenheim, amongst others. This minor treatise was translated twice more: by the Sicilian physician Ahitub of Palermo and by the Spaniard Joseph ibn Vives. Thus the three translators represent the Jewish communities of three countries. All three translations, together with the fragment of the original, were published in 1938 by Israel Efros for the American Academy for Jewish Research.

Another early writing of Maimonides shows his mastery of astronomy; it is a short *Treatise on the Calendar*, composed in 1158, again by request. It was probably written in Arabic but is extant only in Hebrew. It is an elementary treatment of the subject with which he deals more comprehensively in his great Code.

Maimonides was at that time engaged in several larger works which he never revised and published: a book on the laws in the Palestinian Talmud, which supplement those of the Babylonian, and a commentary on the greater part of the latter. He occasionally refers to these works, and his son who possessed his manuscripts quotes some of the talmudic interpretations. It is still doubtful whether the *Commentary on Rosh Hashana*, published under his name, is actually his work.

In his twenty-third year he started on his first great work, the *Commentary to the Mishna*, which occupied him for the next decade. The Mishna, the groundwork of post-biblical Judaism, in which R. Juda the Patriarch, about 200 C. E., had summed up the activity of the preceding centuries, had become the basis of the Talmud which expounded and occasionally modified its dicta. Only some parts of the Mishna had been explained independently by the Babylonian geonim and their successors. We know of only one commentary to the Mishna as a whole, prior to his time, and that was unknown to Maimonides. His predecessors in general had limited themselves to an interpretation of the difficult words of the text, but only rarely had entered into a discussion of the subject matter. The work of the youthful Spanish scholar was a much more ambitious undertaking. He gave an exhaustive explanation of the whole Mishna in all its aspects.

His explanations of words, based on the tradition of the schools as well as on personal observation and studies in the various fields of science, are of lasting value. He pays special attention to the realia — names of animals, plants, utensils, etc. for which he gives the Arabic equivalents. His statements about plants, with which the physician naturally was well acquainted, are of such interest that historians of botany have not passed them over; his descriptions and identifications are correct and valuable; it is characteristic that he noticed the differences in the flora of the countries in which he dwelt. Recent works in the field of talmudic archaeology always refer to his explanations and rarely find them incorrect.

But all this was only of secondary interest to the author; his main concern was the interpretation of the subject matter. While he generally follows the interpretation of the Babylonian Talmud which was considered normative in the whole of Jewry, there are a number of cases in which his philological conscience could not reconcile him to forced talmudic comments and where he went his own way, although such instances never concern the legal decision. To this he also paid special attention and, where the Mishna records various opinions, he always indicated which of these are to be accepted in practice. He rarely passes over a

difficulty and he explains the intricacies of the different
laws of purity or the treatises about the sacrifices with the
same thoroughness and mastery as those dealing with the
laws in daily life.

The whole work is preceded by a comprehensive introduction to the Mishna, the first of its kind, which shows a
point of view far ahead of his time. Since the laws of
sacrifices and purity were very much neglected by scholars,
he found it advisable to precede the interpretation of the
sections dealing with these subjects with illuminating introductions which for the first time reveal the underlying
principles of the mishnaic legislation, and which in themselves have been declared sufficient to establish their author
as one of the greatest Talmudists of all time.

His theological and philosophic interests found expression
in excursuses; in the one added to the tenth chapter of
Sanhedrin, the Creed of Judaism is formulated for the first
time in thirteen articles, which found entrance into the
liturgy and have been treated in poetic form in about a
hundred poems. His interpretation of the ethical *Chapters
of the Fathers* is of particular interest. Here, for example, we
find his vigorous objections to a salaried rabbi. The interpretation of this section of the Mishna is preceded by the
famous *Eight Chapters* — a popular exposition of his system
of psychology and ethics. Both his commentary to Abot and
its introduction, as well as his treatise on the Creed, were
translated very early, the last of these several times, and
they became so famous that they were incorporated into
numerous manuscripts and editions of the prayer books.
An inadequate Hebrew translation of the whole work
accompanied the first edition of the Mishna in 1492.

The introductions and excursuses were made accessible
in their Arabic original in 1655 by the great English orientalist Pococke who had brought manuscripts of the *Commentary to the Mishna* from the East. During the last fifty

years many parts have appeared, mostly as doctoral dissertations, but only the sixth volume is available in a reliable
scholarly edition. The complete publication of the other
five volumes in proper editions is a crying need. The
Seminary Library has good manuscripts of all the parts,
altogether about twenty-five. Maimonides' autographs of
two parts are found in the library of the late Mr. David S.
Sassoon, that of another part in the Bodleian.

In a postscript, Maimonides points to the difficulties of
his task which will be evident to any sensible and fair-
thinking reader.

> In addition, [he continues,] I was troubled by the
> suffering and exile which God had decreed on me, since
> I was driven from one end of the world to the other;
> yet perhaps I have received reward for that, since
> exile atones for sin. God knows that I have explained
> some chapters whilst on my wanderings, and others on
> board ship. Besides I have also devoted time to the
> study of sciences.

He only mentions these personal matters as an excuse to
the critics and as an explanation for the long time consumed
in the work. The commentary was finished in 1168 at
Fostat, but was continually corrected, and he probably
reissued it in a revised edition; an interesting instance of
his revision I have found in one of our manuscripts.

This *Commentary to the Mishna* has not been surpassed or
even equalled by any of its successors. It is printed with
most editions of the Talmud; but the very poor translations
have interfered with its popularity.

Immediately upon the completion of this work, Maimonides turned to a larger task, the codification of Jewish law.
As a preliminary study, he prepared a summary list of all
precepts occurring in the Bible. The talmudic statement that there are six hundred and thirteen biblical

precepts had given rise to various enumerations which did not seem acceptable to his critical mind. He began, therefore, with a characteristic attempt to establish the principles according to which we are to determine which precepts may be considered biblical. After this discussion of principles, the *Book of Commandments* continues with an enumeration of the two hundred and forty-eight positive and three hundred and sixty-five negative precepts and their derivation from the Bible. This book was published in our time in the Arabic original from Yemen manuscripts of which several are found in the Seminary Library. Translated three times into Hebrew at an early period, it was made the subject of various commentaries, as well as of an acute criticism by Moses Nahmanides in the thirteenth century. Nahmanides pointed out that Maimonides' enumeration was no less arbitrary than that of his predecessors. An important manuscript of this criticism in the Seminary Library contains several passages omitted in the printed editions.

Having cleared the ground and made sure of including all biblical precepts, Maimonides undertook the arduous task of composing his great Code, inserting in the introduction the enumeration of the commandments as he had established them. The Code, which he called *Mishne Torah*, consists of an introduction and fourteen books; it is also called *Yad ha-Hazaka*, "The Strong Hand," *Yad* (hand) having in Hebrew the numerical value fourteen. In order to find a decision quickly without a long search in the "Sea of the Talmud," he originally started to write down notes for his private use. He realized the importance of supplying an authoritative code, which should give final decisions, omit all differences of opinion and be as free from mistakes as possible. He determined to supply the desideratum and for ten consecutive years devoted day and night to the completion of this gigantic task, which he brought to an end on November 28, 1180. He wished to facilitate the study of the Talmud and to provide a reliable guide which would enable a judge to give a correct decision quickly, without wasting much time in the study of long discussions. He omitted all names of the authorities and simply enumerated them in the chain of tradition stated in his introduction. His systematic mind rebelled against books, such as those of his predecessors, who combined discussions of talmudic arguments with the codification of laws; "you write either a commentary or a code; each one is a distinct task in itself." He wanted to provide a work in which the student who knew his Bible would have the whole of the Oral Law conveniently arranged.

> In times of persecution like the present [he states], people lack the mental equanimity to devote themselves to intricate studies, and nearly every one finds serious difficulties in deriving a clear-cut decision from the works of the earlier codifiers where the arrangement is as unsystematic as in the Talmud itself. Still fewer persons are able to deduce the laws directly from the talmudic sources.

Maimonides' Code, the greatest of his works, is superior to those of his predecessors and successors in various respects. It is the only complete code which comprises the whole of biblical and post-biblical law, whether applicable at the present day or obsolete after the destruction of the Temple and the exile from Palestine. It is arranged in a more systematic order and in a language which is by far clearer and better. His prototype is the Mishna and he follows it in its neo-Hebrew language, avoiding the admixture of the talmudic idiom of Aramaic which was found in all the others. He tries to be as concise as possible and, as he says in one of his smaller treatises, if he had been able to put the whole of the Oral Law into one chapter, he would not have put it into two. His aim to have his work accepted as *the* Code, which everybody would follow, he accomplished only partially and for a limited time; we may perhaps say fortunately, for an absolute, final code would have tended to stop further development and would have led to petrification of law and life. Against the author's intention his *Mishne Torah* gave a great impetus to talmudic studies, in a direction which was far removed from his aims.

In 1893, Jellinek published a bibliography of Hebrew works commenting on the Code from its publication down to his own time. This bibliography enumerated no less than two hundred and twenty titles, yet is not quite complete, and a goodly number of further works have appeared from that time to the present year. Some of these books explain the words of Maimonides and supply his sources, but a great part of them are specimens of their authors' acumen and try to reconcile the irreconcilable.

Naturally Maimonides' novel procedure of stating conclusions without the sources, which would have enabled the Talmudist to check them, gave rise to considerable differences of opinion. The first book in particular was not acceptable to those unacquainted with philosophy, because it contained much that was irrelevant in the formulation of talmudic law. Included were a brief outline of the physical universe, as it reflects its Creator, and rules of diet, the latter finding a place since the knowledge of God demands healthy senses. In the course of his treatment of the calendar, Maimonides discussed astronomy in much greater detail than was needed for his immediate purpose. He wished his work to be encyclopedic, so that his people might not be compelled to resort to non-Jewish books.

Maimonides became the subject of numerous attacks; the critical remarks of his contemporary, R. Abraham ben David of Posquières in Provence, accompany the Code beginning with the third edition (1509). The Seminary

Library has one of the rare manuscripts of these criticisms
of the great Talmudist.

The lack of sources once disturbed the author himself,
when a visitor asked him about his authority for a certain
statement and he looked in vain in the treatise of the Talmud where the subject is discussed. Only after the man
had left did he remember that it was taken up incidentally
in another treatise. He planned to add a supplement giving
such remote sources, but he did not find leisure to carry
out this plan. Perhaps that was the aim of his son's *Commentary on the Code* which is mentioned in a letter to a
friend as not yet finished and revised. Eight leaves from
Abraham Maimuni's autograph in the Seminary Library
seem to be part of the introduction. He quotes there from
several of his father's letters and relates the answer given
to a visiting Talmudist who maintained that the Code could
only be used if explained with the help of the Talmud.
"If it had been my intention to explain the Code through
the Talmud, I would not have composed the Code," the
author stated on that occasion. Later commentators supplied the missing sources as far as they could; but they did
not have access to all the books consulted by the author,
nor did they realize that with his critical mind he paid far
more attention to the works of the tannaitic literature than
did any of his contemporaries. He frequently accepted the
statements of these authorities, occasionally even against
the Talmud. He followed the authors of the Talmud in
his respect for these early sources.

A Spanish contemporary tells us that in many cases
judges opposed the new work, for it enabled the laymen to
check judicial decisions, since anybody could consult this
well-organized book, written in a clear and easy language.

Especially the heads of the Babylonian school, who felt
themselves the direct successors of the Babylonian geonim,
objected to the work of the Egyptian scholar and raised

questions against some of his decisions. Parts of Maimonides' correspondence with Samuel ben Ali of Bagdad have come down to us and they are of great interest. The most important discussion between them dealt not with a legal matter but with the utterances of Maimonides about resurrection. The Babylonian scholar, as well as a Spanish contemporary, protested against these utterances of Maimonides on this subject, and he answered them with a special treatise, the Arabic original of which was considered lost until a few years ago when the Seminary Library received an incomplete copy. Later we were fortunate in obtaining an additional copy, this time complete. On the basis of these copies and one other, the treatise was published, with Samuel ibn Tibbon's Hebrew translation, by Joshua Finkel for the American Academy for Jewish Research.

The Code was composed between 1170–80, but Maimonides continued revising it, partly on account of certain criticisms which he considered valid, for he kept an open mind and was never dogmatic in his personal views. He always welcomed honest criticism which was not provoked by ulterior motives. In a letter to a group of scholars from Southern France who had sent him twenty-four questions on various points of his Code, he expressed his happiness at having found such able critics. This was a group of great admirers of Maimonides who turned to him repeatedly. Their first letter asking about the value of astrology has been preserved in the manuscript which also includes the *Letter to Yemen*. His answer, which shows his advance beyond his time and his freedom from superstition and pseudo-science, is one of the gems among his minor treatises. Incidentally he tells us here that he had read every book or treatise dealing with astrology, just as he informs us elsewhere that there was nothing written on the subject of idolatry which he, with his thirst for knowledge, had left unread.

About five years after the completion of the Code, Maimonides had the good fortune to be visited by a younger scholar who had emigrated from the western part of Morocco on account of the persecutions which still continued in that country. R. Joseph ben Juda, who had already acquired a certain fame by his literary achievement, became the favorite pupil of the great master with whom he studied mathematics and astronomy as well as philosophic subjects. Later, he went to Aleppo, but he kept up his relations with his beloved teacher and it was at his urging that Maimonides took up an old plan to write about prophecy.

About the year 1185, he began the composition of his great philosophic work, the three books of *The Guide of the Perplexed*, which he dedicated to his pupil. He sent it to him in instalments; in a letter of 1189 or 1190 he included the end of the first part. The whole book in all likelihood was finished soon after that, but one of our manuscripts states that the autograph gave October-November of the year 1200 as the date of completion. This may be due to a scribal error — a *yod* having been added by mistake — or the author made a final revision in that year as a result of the questions directed to him by the translator, Samuel ibn Tibbon.

In his Code, Maimonides had presented the religious content of Judaism in its practical aspects; he now supplemented it in the *Guide* by a systematic presentation of the theoretical side, which offered perhaps even greater difficulties. The author is first concerned with the pure idea of God and discusses the biblical passages which speak of God in anthropomorphic terms. These expressions which already troubled the old Aramaic translators are to be understood in an abstract, metaphorical sense. He objects to all positive attributes to God, because they cannot express His real essence. It is only possible to conceive His attributes in a negative sense or as describing divine action. He then turns to the philosophic proofs for the existence of God and discusses the heavenly spheres and the question of creation. The problem of prophecy, which was the starting point of his philosophic speculation, is dealt with at the end of the second part of the *Guide*. After an interpretation of Ezekiel's vision, a problem which the Talmud only permits for oral instruction between the master and a single pupil, he turns to the problem of evil and to God's providence and omniscience, and concludes with a most interesting discussion of the aims and purposes of the Mosaic legislation and the rational reasons for the biblical commandments. The positive and negative commandments are to educate us in the fear of God and the perception of God; and these doctrinal truths will lead us to love Him.

With masterly clearness the author presented the various theories of the philosophical and theological schools, and for a long time his book was the main source for our knowledge of the Islamic philosophy of the Kalam.

The *Guide of the Perplexed* is the greatest philosophic book produced in Judaism. It is an effort to reconcile the Jewish faith with the ideas of the Aristotelian philosophy. It quickly became a classic. Two Hebrew translations were made during the author's lifetime, one by Samuel ibn Tibbon at the request of the Southern French scholars whom I mentioned before; the other, much inferior and more superficial, was composed by the famous poet and wanderer, Judah al-Harizi. The latter rendering was soon translated into Latin and was used extensively by the great Christian schoolmen who, like the great medical writers, often referred to "the Egyptian Moses." Ibn Tibbon took his task very seriously and corresponded with the author about the meaning of some difficult passages. I have quoted above from this correspondence, part of which is still unpublished. In this translation by Ibn Tibbon the book was even more influential than in the Arabic original which appeared together with a French translation by S. Munk in 1856–66.

Steinschneider compiled a list of over sixty commentaries on the book, and at least one other, now in the Seminary Library, remained unknown to him. The book was translated into many languages and exerted a tremendous influence on Jewish and even on Christian and Mohammedan thought. In the thirteenth century a Mohammedan wrote a commentary on some parts of the *Guide*, while in the following century Jews taught the book to Mohammedan students at Fez. (A Mohammedan scholar, it may incidentally be mentioned, also wrote a commentary on the first, philosophical, chapters of the Code). All the later Jewish philosophers depend on the *Guide* even where they contradict it. Together with the philosophic part of the Code it gave rise to vigorous controversies all through the thirteenth century and even later. Down to the eighteenth and even nineteenth century it gave the first inkling of philosophic thought to many a gifted youth. Its influence is still felt.

I have tried to give an outline, although a very inadequate one, of the life and the great works of Maimonides. As to his personality, we have no statement about his appearance, such as a contemporary gives of his son. The picture which Ugolini reproduced in the first volume of his work in 1744, from an old plaque without indicating its source, has naturally no authority and seems to be a pure invention. It has been repeated time and again, with variations, since the last century, and Maimonides' appearance has accordingly changed.

But we do get a picture of his character and personality from some of the utterances in his letters. His character was worthy of the intellectual gifts with which nature had blessed him. He was charitable, peace-loving and devoted to truth to a degree rarely found.

He writes to his pupil Joseph ben Juda about his Babylonian opponents: he understands that the more his fame spreads, the more they feel the necessity to speak slightingly of his works in order to maintain their superiority among the people; even if they feel compelled to declare that he is irreligious and not a man of good deeds, he is neither injured nor annoyed. To quote his own words: "Even when men insult me I do not mind, but answer kindly with friendly words or remain silent. I shall never fight on my own behalf, for my dignity and the honor of my character are too dear to me to engage in a war of words with the ignorant." He enjoins his pupil to follow in his footsteps and rather to be cursed than to curse.

In another letter he states:

> I never pride myself on not making mistakes; on the contrary, when I discover one, or if I am convinced of an error by others, I am ready to change anything in my writings, in my ways and even in my nature.
> I never listen to slander, for I know how statements are altered and grow when they go from mouth to mouth. Thank God, even if I hear with my own ears and know definitely that someone seeks aggrandizement by slandering me and by treating my statements with contempt, I take no heed, but forgive him.

When a Bagdad opponent, seeking for honor at his expense, attacked him virulently, Maimonides requested Joseph ibn Jabir, one of his local admirers, to ignore the incident. "All the better if he thinks to gain credit by his conduct; he may win and I shall certainly not lose."

These utterances show a remarkable moderation and love of peace, although Maimonides, who possessed a rare combination of inner modesty and pride, was evidently fully conscious of his own importance. Maimonides was an aristocrat who cared for the few chosen ones and at times ignored the multitude. In the introduction to the *Guide* he says: "If I can see no other way except by pleasing one intelligent man and displeasing ten thousand fools, I prefer to address myself to the one man and to take no notice whatever of the condemnation of the multitude."

Maimonides was a man of deep piety who observed the laws to the smallest detail. He even took a part of his precious time to write a scroll of the Torah with his own hand.

His tolerance can be observed in his communal enactments and in his utterances about other religions. Three times he states in his Code that the pious of all nations have a share in the world to come.

He took no pleasure in poetry; music and song did not appeal to him. He objected to the addition of *piyyutim* to the prayers and even considered it a waste of time to read historical works.

He possessed a unique combination of deep philosophic thought and incomparable mastery of rabbinic literature. An unusual depth and width of knowledge were combined with a rare clarity and a systematic sense of organization. Using his rare gifts to best advantage, Maimonides enriched our literature by the best commentary to the Mishna, the best and fullest Code, and an epoch-making philosophic presentation of Judaism.

I cannot better sum up the importance of Maimonides than by quoting the words spoken a generation ago by my lamented friend and colleague, Professor Israel Friedlaender, at the seven hundredth anniversary of the death of Maimonides: "The uniqueness of Maimonides, which made posterity compare him with Moses, the man of God, lies in the fact that Maimonides, like Moses, took up the gigantic problem of Judaism in its totality and tried to solve it in its totality."

5

Moritz Steinschneider

AMONG the small group of eminent scholars who, in the first half of the nineteenth century, laid the foundation for modern Jewish learning, the triad, Leopold Zunz, Solomon Juda Rapoport and Moritz Steinschneider, hold first place. The great master, Zunz, who in his first publication drew up a comprehensive program for the new science of Judaism, summed up his own researches on the development of the Midrash, the liturgy and religious poetry in his epoch-making works. He also clarified the share of the Franco-German school in the development of Judaism and Jewish literature. Rapoport, through his famous biographies notable for their critical depth, rare acumen and brilliant scholarship, was first to throw light on the end of the geonic period and the spread of learning in the West and to make invaluable contributions to a scientific study of the Talmud. Steinschneider, like no one else, mastered the entire field of Jewish literature, especially that of the Middle Ages, and by his pioneering works placed research in its various branches on a firm foundation. Though we still lack adequate biographies of these three great scholars, much has been written on the former two, while there has not been even an attempt at a biography of the third and most erudite of them. The present essay makes such an attempt, however inadequately, to present a sketch of the life and work of this unforgettable teacher.

Moritz Steinschneider was born in Prossnitz, Moravia, on March 30, 1816. Prossnitz was a progressive community and there was a strong desire among its members for modern culture. His father, Jacob Steinschneider (1782–1856), combined talmudic knowledge with general education, both of which he had acquired in Prague. His house was the center for a group of scholars, among them his brother-in-law, Dr. Gideon Brecher — the commentator on Judah Halevi's *Kusari* — with whom the nephew subsequently kept up close relations, addressing him as uncle and friend in one of his publications.

The father's broadmindedness showed itself in the education he gave to his son. He shocked the community by sending the boy, at the age of six, to the Christian school and by having him instructed also in music and dancing. To counterbalance the prevailing inclination among the Jews towards onesided intellectualism, he tried to interest his son in practical matters by taking him to the workshops of various artisans. It seems that he instilled in the boy a prejudice against the common run of *bahurim* (Talmud students) which kept him apart from his fellow students when, after the age of thirteen, he entered the *yeshiva* of R. Nehemiah Trebitsch. Subsequently (1830), his teacher was elected rabbi of Nikolsburg, and Steinschneider followed him there to continue his studies. Two Hebrew testimonials by Trebitsch, who in 1832 had been appointed Moravian *Landesrabbiner*, give evidence of the unusual industry and application and the extensive talmudic knowledge of the pupil as well as of his fine intellectual equipment. He calls him his favorite pupil and friend and expresses the hope that he would retain his attitude towards his studies and not, as is customary nowadays, turn to matters of secondary importance and devote himself to valueless speculation. Was the rabbi aware of the pupil's interest in secular subjects, or was he expressing the fear that he might be influenced by current Reformist tendencies? Trebitsch was a representative of the old school of Talmudists, bitterly opposed to any trend towards mod-

ernism and secular education. In Prossnitz, Steinschneider
had received a thorough training in French and Italian,
the latter through Adolf Bacher (a great-granduncle of the
famous Jewish scholar, Professor W. Bacher), who at the
time was tutor in a family at Prossnitz. This knowledge
enabled Steinschneider to earn a living, not only during
his stay in Nickolsburg, but also later as a teacher of French
and Italian and as an educator — an unusual situation for
a student of a *yeshiva.*

Trebitsch's fear that his pupil might be diverted to
secular subjects was only too well founded. In 1833,
Steinschneider went to Prague to devote himself to the
study of philosophy, esthetics, pedagogy and modern languages. Philosophy in particular captivated him for the
next two years. He did not, however, neglect his Hebrew
studies; he attended the Talmud lectures of Rabbi J.
Schlesinger and the classes of the *Hebraeische Lehranstalt* in
Bible and Hebrew language. In 1835, he passed an examination in the latter two subjects with signal success. A
testimonial by the well-known teacher, Wolf Mayer, given
in August 1836, states that he was fully prepared to teach
Bible and Hebrew and praises his biblical knowledge, his
sound method, as well as his ability to express himself in
Hebrew. The famous — or notorious — Herz Homberg,
imperial *Schulrat,* testified that he attended his lectures in
"religious morals," exegesis, theoretical and practical
pedagogics and that he passed his examinations "first
class with distinction."

With these certificates, Steinschneider went to Vienna
in 1836 in the hope of entering the Oriental Academy of the
Austrian capital and there obtain a thorough grounding
in the Semitic languages. The reaction prevailing at that
period, however, precluded the admission of a Jewish student to the academy. In order to receive permission to
stay in Vienna, he had to become a pupil at the Poly-

technical Institute. He succeeded in realizing his desire
to study Semitic languages by attending the lectures of
Professor Joseph Kärle in Hebrew, Syriac and Arabic at
the Catholic Theological Faculty of the university, where
evidently fewer obstacles were placed in the way of the
young and eager student. As in Prague, he devoted much
time to his Jewish studies and faithfully attended the
classes of Rabbi Lazar Horowitz in Talmud and Codes.
His knowledge of Bible, Mishna and Talmud, his skill in
writing and speaking Hebrew and his mastery of other
languages, as well as his diligence and assiduity, deeply
impressed the rabbi, who invited the promising student to
his home. Like Trebitsch, he observed the deep piety of
young Steinschneider, for whom he predicted a great
future as rabbi and preacher. The breadth and comprehensiveness of Steinschneider's studies showed that his
conception of his future calling was a very high one.

In Vienna, Steinschneider made an acquaintanceship
which was to have a great influence on his whole life.
Leopold Dukes, the literary historian, a man of wide,
though unorganized, knowledge of Jewish literature and of
broad general education, introduced his young friend into
the field of medieval Jewish literature and bibliography to
which he was to devote the greatest part of his life and to
which he was to make such tremendous contributions.

To gain his livelihood during the two and a half years
of his stay in Vienna, he again gave instruction in Italian
and other subjects. He became the tutor of two brothers,
the Counts Lichnowsky, and their sister, the wife of Prince
Richard Khevenhüller-Metsch. His relations with these
young students were very friendly and they received much
stimulation from their Jewish mentor.

His first publication appeared in Vienna in 1838. It
was a German translation of a versified collection of moral
sentences by Abraham Belais, a curious personality who

was for some years rabbi of Tunis and treasurer of the Bey of Tunis and who later travelled through Palestine and many parts of Europe. Steinschneider received the munificent sum of 12.30 florins for his translation. Probably the work had been given to him by the publisher. In the following year he entered into his account book the receipt of 23 florins for reading proof of *Marpe*, probably the Aramaic grammar by E. I. Blücher which appeared that year in Vienna.

It was perhaps the influence of Dukes that made him eager to become acquainted with the Hebrew treasures of the Imperial Library. But access to a library was not an easy matter during those years. He was not even permitted to make extracts from the catalogue, and the future bibliographer was not given the opportunity to enrich his knowledge by delving into the rarities accumulated during the centuries, but kept under lock and key against the scholarly curiosity of a mere Jewish student who, in addition, happened to be a foreigner.

Since a Moravian Jew was considered a foreigner in the capital of the empire of which Moravia formed part, he was not granted permission by the police to extend his stay after he finished his studies; and thus, in 1839, he applied for a passport to Berlin. Without awaiting the answer to his application, he started on his way and, despite some difficulties, went to Teplitz and Dresden, reaching Leipzig in the middle of April to learn that he had been refused the passport. He could neither return nor proceed. He stayed in Leipzig and used the opportunity to continue his Arabic studies under the greatest master of the subject, Professor Heinrich Leberecht Fleischer, with whom he kept up very friendly relations afterwards. Though Steinschneider did not remain there long, this teacher, too, was very greatly impressed by his character, intellect, industry and erudition. A close friendship was formed in Leipzig with the famous theologian, Professor Franz Delitzsch, with whom Steinschneider undertook Hebrew and oriental studies and together with whom he published the Hebrew text of a Karaite theological work, the *Ets Hayyim* by Aaron ben Elija. This edition appeared in 1841 without the name of Steinschneider as co-editor on the title page, owing, as he said, to the conditions imposed by Austrian censorship. Delitzsch admired the integrity of his friend's character, his cheerfulness even under privations, his indefatigable industry and the scrupulous exactness he exercised in every detail of his researches. Their intimate relationship was continued at intervals when Delitzsch came to Berlin and Prague. Nearly half a century later he wrote to Steinschneider of the unforgettable days he had spent with him in his modest bachelor quarters in Berlin.

How extensive and successful Steinschneider's studies in Arabic literature were is evident from the invitation, extended to him while in Leipzig, to collaborate on the second edition of Pierer's *Universallexikon* (1839–43) for which he wrote a large number of shorter or longer articles, mostly on Arabic literature and religion — very few dealt with Jewish subjects. Most of them occur in the first half of the alphabet. Though in his years of struggle he depended on any available source of income, he terminated his collaboration because his articles were treated by the editors in a way which went against his scholarly conscience. A Hebrew rendition of the Koran, which he began in Leipzig, was discontinued when the appearance of Reckendorf's translation made its publication impractical.

This was the period when Samson Raphael Hirsch, for the first time, tried to formulate Jewish creed and rabbinic law from a strictly Orthodox point of view in a way that would appeal to a modern, well-educated Jew. Steinschneider, it seems, was deeply stirred by Hirsch's books and regretted the fact that no scholarly review of them had appeared. He sent the polemical *Erste Mittheilungen aus Naphtali's Briefwechsel* (Altona, 1838) and the *Horeb* to the rabbi of his home town, Hirsch B. Fassel, and asked him for a frank statement about the new spokesman of Orthodox Judaism whose point of view had become a vital issue to him as a rabbinical student. He was anxious to know whether Hirsch's formulation of rabbinic law could stand the test of an unbiased critical examination.

In a series of seven letters, Fassel discussed especially Hirsch's *Horeb* and pointed out a number of inexactitudes and errors in the legal statements of the book. He treated the author with great respect and showed appreciation of his aims and purposes; nevertheless, he found Hirsch too one-sided and extreme in his acceptance of post-talmudic additions to Jewish laws. He added, at Steinschneider's request, an appendix "on the possibility of abolishing existing Jewish customs from the Orthodox point of view." Steinschneider published these letters during his stay in Leipzig under the *nom de plume* M. S. Charbonah, a Hebrew translation of his name.

The slender volume is preceded by an introduction which claims to reproduce a discussion between several friends, among whom the editor seems to be represented by the letter *I[ch]*. We find here some highly characteristic utterances: Even under the most oppressive circumstances, teachers and educators — and all Jewish scholars belong to that category — should never speak against their inner convictions. We need not always pay for the truth with our life; but we must never bargain for our life with an untruth. He complains of the lack of unity among Jewish scholars and the consequent impossibility of winning their collaboration in some of the great tasks which exceed the powers of any one individual, such as a dictionary of

literary history or of the Semitic languages. He regrets
that there does not exist a dictionary of the Hebrew Bible
by a Jewish author which can be used by young people.
Empty phrases and a barbaric striving for originality
replace serious scholarly work; collecting and indexing
material are looked down upon as mere mechanical labor.
Before writing on Talmud and Midrash, we must create
a complete index of the subject matter contained in these
books. Popularization will lead to superficiality if it does
not aim to propagate ideas attained by thorough research.

The discussion which started with Hirsch's *Horeb* returns
to it again and Steinschneider gives expression to his
objection to discussing casuistic law in the German language. This could be done well only in Hebrew. One must
not try to occidentalize everything. The holy tongue must
remain the international language of Jewish scholarship:
it has been shown in modern times that it is quite possible
to write adequately in Hebrew even on matters of natural
science.

Though Steinschneider was opposed, on the one hand,
to certain liturgical compositions which consisted of a
mosaic of mysticism, legend and casuistry, characterized
by tautology, letter-juggling, silly jingles and linguistic
distortions; he condemned, on the other hand, the removal
of Hebrew from the synagogue service. He had no use
either for manuals of religion dispensing with Hebrew
quotations from the Bible, or for religious instruction without teaching the Hebrew language, or for a "periodical for
Jewish theology" which has not even a Hebrew division.
The last was an attack on the periodical of Geiger.

I have dealt with this little publication at some length
because it shows Steinschneider's deep concern in questions
with which he never dealt again except in casual remarks.
On some of these questions he changed his point of view
later, in the course of the following period, but it is worth-

while to learn his attitude on these vital problems during his formative years. His high appraisal of scholarship, his emphasis on objective truth and his objection to superficial popularization are characteristic of his whole life's work.

Steinschneider stayed in Leipzig only six months and attended two courses: one by Professor M. Becker on the domestic life of the Greeks, the other on the Koran by Fleischer.

A university passport from Leipzig now enabled Steinschneider to reach Berlin, the goal of his yearnings. He attended the university there during four terms, enjoying the instruction of such famous masters as Bopp in comparative philology (German, Sanscrit and the classical languages); Boeckh in the history of Greek literature; Petermann in the history of Oriental literature and Ethiopic; and Ritter in the geography of Palestine. He also attended a term in homiletics and one in Church history under the convert Neander; the last was the only subject in which his unusual industry was not praised. Some of the carefully prepared elaborate notebooks which he preserved give evidence of his deep interest in his studies. During these two years he became Leopold Zunz's admiring friend and also came into intimate contact with Abraham Geiger. That he had devoted himself during his stay in Berlin with great industry to Hebrew studies and rabbinic literature was testified by Zunz. Incidentally, it may be mentioned that at this time (1841) the first catalogue from his pen appeared, though anonymously. It was an auction-catalogue of Hebraica to be sold by the famous antiquarian bookseller A. Asher.

This first Berlin period brought one fundamental change in Steinschneider's outlook on Judaism. Among his fellow-students in Prague one, Abraham Benisch, had conceived a plan to promote the emigration of the Jews from their "step-fatherland" to Palestine in order to bring about the liberation of the Austrian Jews from the yoke of intolerance and oppression. His ideas made a deep impression on Steinschneider and for the next five or six years occupied the center of his thoughts. When the two young men had gone to Vienna they had founded a secret student society which they had called "Unity." In the residences of Steinschneider and Albert Löwy or during excursions to the outskirts of Vienna, Benisch used to propound his scheme and to discuss it with his fellow members. Steinschneider evidently was one of the leaders of this movement. When he came to Leipzig, he interested Julius Fürst, the editor of the *Orient*, in the Palestinian scheme; and in Berlin he founded a branch of the Vienna society of which he was the guiding spirit. He encouraged the others in their interest and urged them to literary activity. The group was in constant touch with the Vienna branch. Their correspondence roused the suspicion of the Austrian police, in whose archives some data about this group of students have been preserved. The police had confiscated the correspondence of Benisch which included an interesting letter from the famous French-Jewish statesman Crémieux; but they came to the conclusion that the movement was an innocent and immature expression of youthful idealism which would in all likelihood be given up when the young men came in contact with practical life.

Upon Steinschneider, however, whose letters they must have found among those confiscated from Benisch, the Vienna police looked as a suspicious individual who had to be watched, and they therefore turned to the Berlin police and informed it of the society which Steinschneider had founded. A letter of a member of the society, written to Steinschneider when he was visiting his parents, had been intercepted by the Austrian police who concluded from it the existence of a secret society with destructive and reformist tendencies. No less a person than the Austrian chancellor, Metternich, charged the Austrian ambassador in Berlin to inquire whether the society did not propagate rebellious ideas which were dangerous to the state. The chief of the Berlin police reported the existence of a students society working against the decay of Judaism, which he considered entirely harmless. Though Steinschneider had left Berlin at the time, he still was considered the head of the society, which consisted of nineteen members whose names have been preserved by the police. Several of them became well-known scholars and were always active in Jewish life and some of them remained intimate friends of Steinschneider with whom he maintained personal relations for many years.

The society, the Berlin police report says, aimed at instructing the Jewish people by articles and periodicals to insure its continuance and to counteract the increasing movement towards conversion. In weekly meetings the members discussed present-day questions; they read papers and reported on these meetings to those who lived elsewhere. They had no statutes. Most of the members came from various parts of Germany, a few from the province of Posen, one from Warsaw and one from Brody, besides the two Austrians, Steinschneider and Benisch. The latter had at that time already gone to London in the interest of his plan about which he constantly corresponded with Steinschneider. Steinschneider, during his sojourn in the more liberal and enlightened atmosphere of Berlin, reached the conclusion that the plan was unworkable and useless and in 1842 withdrew from further participation. But it was only after a severe inner struggle that he changed his attitude toward the idea of a restoration of a Jewish Palestine, as we learn from the fragments of his diary. He later asserted that only the conditions prevailing in Austria had produced these ideas, and his attitude towards newer Zionistic schemes became absolutely antagonistic. He bitterly condemned Pinsker's *Autoemancipation* and considered such trends more dangerous than antisemitism. As he wrote to his old friend, Löwy, in 1898, Zionism seemed to him, after those early years, an object of folk-psychiatry which could be cured only gradually by systematic education. "For the Messiah humanity perhaps needs the entire period of our earth's existence." When he added that no documents existed of the early movement with which both had been associated, he was not aware of the curiosity of the Austrian police.

Steinschneider's years of wandering were not yet at an end. Towards the close of the year 1841, he again went to Prague, where he earned a scant living by private tutoring. From 1842 to 1845 he was the principal teacher at an educational institution for Jewish girls (*Lehr- und Erziehungsanstalt für israelitische Mädchen*) established by a local lady, Charlotte Löw. He taught the upper class in all but the technical subjects and delivered Sabbath discourses which left an excellent impression on the pupils. He also introduced the confirmation of the girls on their leaving the institution. Miss Löw stated that his great ability and success as a teacher was accorded repeated public recognition, that he exerted a marked influence on the moral and religious attitudes of the girls and that his conduct and character secured him the love and respect of the pupils, the gratitude of their parents and the friendship of his colleagues.

His beloved Jewish studies were given strong stimulation through his association with the great chief rabbi of Prague, S. L. Rapoport, and with Zunz, one of the founders of modern Jewish learning. Rapoport praised his erudition in the whole field of Jewish literature, his great pedagogic ability and his exemplary moral and religious conduct; he recommended him warmly as an excellent teacher in Bible, Hebrew language, Talmud and codes, as well as in cognate fields.

In the same year, 1843, in which he received this testimonial from Rapoport, he received a German rabbinical diploma from Hirsch B. Fassel, the rabbi of his home town, Prossnitz. During a visit there he had preached twice in the synagogue and had earned the general approval of his audience. Fassel had examined him in Talmud and codes and testified to his thorough knowledge of the parts of the *Shulhan Aruk* required of a rabbi and his great familiarity with Talmud and Midrash. He recommended him as an excellent, learned, strictly religious person, gifted with great oratorical talent, who was able to act as rabbi in any community. A few months later, Fassel gave him a formal Hebrew *Hatarat Horaah*. In his library — which is located now in the Jewish Theological Seminary of America — Steinschneider preserved a large folio volume by Fassel, containing a recast of the second division of the *Shulhan Aruk*, which he probably used to prepare for the examination by Fassel.

David Cassel, one of Steinschneider's close friends among his fellow students in Berlin who, like him, aimed for the rabbinate but was to devote his life to Jewish learning, was approached (1843) by a publisher, Monasch of Krotoshin, to become the editor of a Jewish encyclopedia. Cassel, who at that time had a position as tutor in Wollstein, Posen, immediately turned to his friend in Prague and invited him to take charge of the field of post-biblical Jewish literature. Such an ambitious work required careful planning in general and in detail, and a very lively correspondence between the two developed in consequence. A lengthy letter of Steinschneider's with supplementary notes by

Cassel was published in the *Literaturblatt des Orients* for July and August, and by the end of the year an elaborate *Plan der Real-Encyclopädie des Judenthums* appeared under the name of Cassel who states that Steinschneider had at least as great a share in the contents of this pamphlet of over fifty pages as he. The purpose of their undertaking was to further Jewish learning and to propagate general information about Judaism which, they hoped, would lead to spiritual and social progress among their coreligionists.

A few months later Cassel returned to Berlin. The correspondence between the two continued for over two years. Cassel's letters show the devotion with which the two threw themselves into their great scheme which involved an enormous correspondence with all those who might possibly contribute to the work. Incidentally, the letters contain interesting judgments on some of the rabbis and scholars of the period. In his last letter on the subject, written a few weeks before Steinschneider's arrival in Berlin, Cassel informs him that he has sent the specimen articles to the printer and that as soon as he came to Berlin they would undertake the final redaction of the first issue. The specimen of four pages without a title or other indications, except for the statement that the "work" would be printed in a new and better type, contains, besides two very short articles, a lengthy one on abbreviations signed by both friends. Cassel's original article on the subject had evidently been very thoroughly revised and enlarged by his co-worker, who reprinted it over thirty years later in the *Archiv für Stenographie*. Why the whole plan was given up after all these prolonged efforts we do not learn. Perhaps the publisher, in the last minute, fought shy of the expense involved. Thus only the ambitious plan and the little specimen remained of this first scheme for a Jewish encyclopedia which was not to be realized until some six decades later, in the new world.

During the same period two plans were proposed to Steinschneider for bringing his years of study to an end and accepting a more adequate position. Samuel Goldenberg, editor of the periodical *Kerem Hemed* which was printed in Prague, had there made the acquaintance of the young scholar and experienced teacher and thought that he would be the right man to fill the vacant position of principal teacher at the modern school founded by Joseph Perl in Tarnopol, Galicia. He prevailed on Steinschneider to write an application and filed it in spite of Steinschneider's specific instructions not to hand it in until he would authorize him after having received information on various points. The school authorities immediately applied to the government for ratification of Steinschneider's appointment. This was received; but Steinschneider came to the conclusion that the position did not offer a desirable sphere of activity for him and would at best be no more than the first step to a possible appointment as rabbi after a couple of years. He declined the position.

Somewhat later Steinschneider met Auguste Auerbach, the young woman who was to share his life, and now became anxious to establish himself. For this reason he applied for the position of censor of Jewish books, after the death of Carolus Fischer (1844) who had held this position for 59 years. Fortunately his application was unsuccessful. The opinion about the various candidates rendered by Abbot Zeidler, director of philosophic studies and censor in Prague, considered Steinschneider unfit because he had not passed through a gymnasium and lacked the proper philosophic training. He pointed to his refusal of the position in Tarnopol after the government had confirmed his election as evidence of fickleness and unsteadiness of character.

A call to become the director of the Talmud Torah in his birthplace, Prossnitz, at least for a period of two years —

which shows how highly he was esteemed there — did not attract him.

After the failure of his attempts to find a congenial position in the Austrian empire, he came to the conclusion that he would never feel happy in that reactionary state.

Dr. Michael Sachs, one of the few men of wider interests in the narrow circle of Prague with whom Steinschneider evidently was intimate during these years, left his position as preacher, which he had occupied there since 1836, and went as rabbi to Berlin in 1844. Some of his friends expected Steinschneider's election as Sachs' successor, but he was not considered for the place and we do not know whether he himself aspired to the position. He decided to follow Sachs to Berlin, where the revered master, Leopold Zunz, and his charming wife, Adelheid, were a powerful attraction. The hopes he may have placed in Sachs' friendship were to be disappointed. Away from Prague, the famous preacher found a larger group of cultured men which surrounded and admired him and he showed less interest in the young, sensitive scholar who therefore felt himself neglected and gradually withdrew. At the same time, his attitude towards Orthodox Judaism, which he had accepted thus far, underwent a great change in the more liberal atmosphere of the Prussian capital. He himself stated that he now felt repelled by Sachs' Orthodox point of view, though he was vigorously opposed to the Reformers as well. In consequence, in his thirtieth year, he gave up the plan of becoming a rabbi which had been the goal of his studies all these years.

"Now I enjoy my studies," he writes to his fiancée (February, 1846), "owing to the fact that I have thrown off my neck the drudgery of the irksome, large literature of practical and ceremonial law, *Shulhan Aruk* and *Poskim*, and in consequence can breathe more freely. I see now that a conscientious and pious rabbi cannot be an *educated* man. He must become absorbed in a literature which consumes his entire energy. Still I do not regret that I have been clinging to the chain so long. I have the right to an opinion, for I have labored honestly." It would, however, be wrong to conclude that he had severed all inner relations with religion. A man who in his last years could write: *"Religious development* is the true ultimate object of Jewish history" must have retained a certain attachment to religion.

Though he gave up, during the following years, the strict observance to which his teacher and friends had often referred theretofore, the literature of his people remained central in all his thinking. He decided to devote his life to learning and research for its own sake. It was to be a life dedicated to the study of the Jewish past and to the clarification of the many fundamental literary problems which had been neglected up to then.

During his early years in Berlin, Steinschneider was mainly concerned with the effort to establish himself and to secure a fixed income which would enable him to marry his fiancée who felt very unhappy in her position as governess in Prague. But for that he had to wait several long years. It was an exasperating experience through which both young people had to pass before they were united in marriage on June 21, 1849.

Private lessons were his main source of income to provide for his modest needs. Though he was fond of teaching, some of his pupils, who were badly prepared and lacked all idealism and religion, could give him little satisfaction. The fees for his contributions to various periodicals and other scholarly work supplemented his revenues. In his first year in Berlin (1845), he, together with Jellinek, preached in Leipzig for the High Holidays with great success. His hope to be invited again for the following Passover did not materialize. In these early years he must have been a good speaker. Around this time he wrote a Jewish oratorio, *Saul*, based on the Bible with some use of the Aggada, for the composer J. Stern, the director of the choir of the Reform synagogue. Eventually it brought him five Louis d'ors (ca. $25).

It is characteristic for the position of the Jews in Berlin during that period that Steinschneider had to make formal application to the ministry of education for permission to visit the general reading room of the Royal Library (1846). It took six weeks before the permission was granted.

An academic career appeared the natural choice for a scholar of Steinschneider's wide learning and broad interests. He was encouraged in this direction by the professor and director of the Prussian Statistical Bureau, Karl Friedrich Wilhelm Dieterici, the father of the well-known orientalist, who befriended the Jewish scholar. He realized, however, that as a Jew he had no chance at a university and no prospect of establishing himself speedily. Instead, he therefore applied for a teacher's license. After a comprehensive examination in German, Latin, French, history and geography, arithmetics and geometry, natural sciences and pedagogics, after trial-lessons in mathematics and mathematical geography and after handing in a paper on Pestalozzi, he received a certificate (March, 1847) permitting him to act as teacher or director of a Jewish school. His examiners were deeply impressed both by his knowledge and his ability as a teacher and expressed to him their satisfaction.

A certificate was not sufficient, however; he had to be naturalized in order to be permitted to obtain a position even in a Jewish school. This proved to be a difficult problem. Steinschneider had taken the first steps long before, but the matter dragged on and on for several years, in spite of the warmest recommendations of the Leipzig professors, Fleischer and Delitzsch, and other prominent persons. His petition at last reached the king with a recommendation by the ministry, and the decree of his naturalization was signed by Frederick William IV on the very eve of the outbreak of the revolution, on March 18, 1848, perhaps the last document ever signed by the king.

His friend, A. Horwitz, head of the Jewish community school for Jewish boys, where Steinschneider had given his trial lessons for his *Rector-Examen*, had declared in his recommendation for the naturalization that he would be glad to give him a permanent position in his school if he were a citizen, since there was a great dearth of such scholarly and pedagogically experienced teachers; but we hear no more of such a position, although Steinschneider previously had taught a few hours a week at this school. Together the two men had published a *Spruchbuch für Jüdische Schulen* (1847) which was well received.

Even such publications for purely practical purposes, mainly undertaken as a source of income, were approached by Steinschneider with scientific seriousness. What was to be offered to schoolchildren and beginners, he insisted, should be prepared with the greatest care and exactness in text and conception. When he was asked (1860) to compile a primer for the educational institution established in Bombay by David Sassoon, he gave the subject most careful consideration, and his *Reshith Hallimud*, a systematic Hebrew primer, represented a great advance over all similar books published up to that time and shows a quite modern approach. A primer, in his opinion, should not merely enable the child to learn reading in an easy and speedy fashion, but was to be a preparation for a study of the language itself. It should keep out any examples which have no meaning; but be selected as far as possible from the storehouse of the Bible. Stress should be laid on correct reading with the right accent and the pupil should be gradually led to the study of the Bible itself. He also emphasized the necessity of getting the children used to reading without vowels at an early period. It is interesting that he tells us twelve years later that the reprints of the early part of the book which he had ordered had mostly been used by himself in teaching his private pupils. Thus we learn that this great scholar had spent considerable time in teaching little children the Hebrew alphabet.

The events of the revolution of March 8, 1848, aroused Steinschneider's interest in politics and he was among those who helped in the building of barricades in the streets of Berlin during the first days. But he abstained from further active participation. He became the reporter of the *Nationalzeitung* and correspondent of the *Prager Zeitung* for the sessions of the "National Assembly." He did not belong "to the wild democrats who are Jesuits in their own way," but favored a liberal government.

In his efforts to obtain an adequate position, he applied, in 1847, for the directorship of the Jacobson-School at Seesen, but refused to accept the call for a trial year. He corresponded with the *Landrabbiner* of Hanover, Dr. Samuel Meyer, concerning the position of *Oberlehrer* at the Jewish school of that city (in 1848) for which Zunz, without his knowledge, had warmly recommended him. Here again the conditions were not satisfactory and he finally declined the appointment.

There were times of bitter disillusionment in these years. He gave expression to it in his correspondence with his fiancée. "It is all over with *Wissenschaft* because the hopeful enthusiasm has sunk into the abyss. Jewish scholarship has no basis in reality, no institution, no encouragement." "I must not entirely neglect my scholarly work; it might perhaps, some day, ease life when I attain pedagogic activity." "I cannot any more be so absorbed in my work as not to stop suddenly in the midst of my research and ask myself 'what for?' The world will become neither better nor more sensible through such writings; and I have overcome the vanity of authorship since I have seen the judges on the Parnassus — I should like to say the *parnassim* (presidents of the synagogue) — face to face." "Teaching now is a pleasant change for me, sometimes four successive hours." "Formerly I considered an hour lost in which I neither studied nor taught. You will have to answer some day for the fact that it is not so any longer."

The only relaxation he permitted himself during these years was his music. Every two or three weeks he played his flute in a trio with a pianist and a cellist, and about once a month he played in a duet.

He began to retire from social evenings with his friends, but when he did visit them his lively talk gave no inkling of his depression and impatience with the slow progress of his affairs. He always refrained from giving expression to his emotional life in his conversation. During his student days, Adelheid Zunz told one of his intimate friends, Steinschneider often disavowed his heart and forced on himself a certain asperity of sentiment in contradiction to his real self. His friend was mistaken when he added that at last his intellect had permitted him a freer expression of his feelings. He remained consistent to the end of his life in his objection to any trace of sentimentality.

This retirement from purely social intercourse he continued ever after. In his last decade he once remarked that his untiring industry had demanded sacrifices on his part. He doubted whether he had gone out three evenings throughout his later years.

During his early years in Berlin, Steinschneider's friendly relations with the bookdealer, A. Asher, for whom he had prepared a catalogue during his student days, proved to be of great benefit to him. In 1847, upon the death of the great book collector Heimann J. Michael, Asher acquired the valuable Hebrew library brought together by that well-to-do scholarly Hamburg merchant. After the greater part of the catalogue of the famous collection had been printed, Asher asked Steinschneider to go to Hamburg in order to compare the Michael manuscripts with the printed list. In ten or eleven days he went through the more than eight hundred manuscripts, checked them with the catalogue and collected the material for his index of authors which was added to it. In this supplement he incorporated innumerable corrections and amplifications. In order to gain some valuable material for his scholarly plans, he worked through several nights, after an exhausting day's work, making the best of this opportunity in every way. He had to devote the last few days of his stay in Hamburg to a quick checking of the printed books.

It was perhaps this experience that showed Asher the energy and unusual capacity for work of the young scholar and caused him to recommend Steinschneider to Dr. Bandinel, the chief librarian of the great Bodleian Library at Oxford, for the preparation of a new catalogue of the printed Hebrew books of this, then the greatest existing, collection of Hebraica. Asher, through his business, was in contact with the heads of the great English libraries and his recommendation carried considerable weight. Steinschneider was engaged to prepare the catalogue. It was originally thought that it would be possible to accomplish the task from a distance, in Berlin, on the basis of the printed catalogues of the library and those of the Oppenheim collection, acquired by Oxford in 1829. The manuscripts of H. J. Michael, which the Bodleian had purchased, included a manuscript catalogue of the Oppenheim collection which was far superior to the printed ones and was placed at Steinschneider's disposal. He immediately

started on his work; but after two years he came to the
conclusion that, in spite of the information on many
dubious points readily provided by the staff of the Bodleian
and by his friend, Joseph Zedner, of the British Museum
(which had acquired the printed books of H. J. Michael), it
would be impossible to prepare a satisfactory catalogue
without inspecting the books themselves. Accordingly
Steinschneider was invited by Bandinel to come to Oxford.

For five years (1850, 1851, 1853, 1855 and 1858) he
spent the summer months in Oxford, working steadily
during the seven hours that the library was open, in order
as far as possible to settle the doubtful points. Between
these visits, sheets filled with new questions continued to
come to the ever-ready hand of the librarian, who followed the work with the deepest interest. He saw to it
that Steinschneider was charged with the task of following
up the catalogue of the printed books with that of the
Hebrew manuscripts. Steinschneider therefore at once
began to examine the manuscripts together with the printed
books. Many of the results of this examination were incorporated in the catalogue of the printed books and helped to
make it an unrivalled storehouse of information on the authors dealt with. The access to these manuscripts at the
same time convinced Steinschneider that the publication of
his planned *Bibliotheca Judaeo-Arabica* would be entirely premature, since it was based on the incomplete and unreliable
information of the printed catalogues without consultation
of the manuscripts themselves. In consequence his plan
was postponed for many decades.

The very extensive correspondence, carried on with
Dr. Bandinel during the thirteen years consumed by the
work on the catalogue, gives evidence of the warm friendship that developed between the aged librarian and the
younger scholar. The former retired as a man of eighty,
a few months before his death, just before the final com-

pletion of the catalogue in which he had taken so warm and active an interest. He had full understanding for the gigantic nature of the task and resented Max Müller's "very silly" question (in 1857) when the book would be finished. "He fancies that, because it is only a Catalogue of our *printed* Hebrew books, it is like all other Library Catalogues. He may as well compare Fabricius' *Bibliotheca Graeca* with our Catalogues!"

Bandinel took great interest in the printed specimen pages, discussing every detail. The original arrangement of the pages, proposed in 1850, was displaced by a new one two years later and when this was approved the printing started in Berlin. In that year Bandinel wrote to Steinschneider: "I assure you, I fully appreciate your labours and the difficulties you have to contend with at the distance from the Oppenheim Library and with such an inferior aid as myself." Occasionally Bandinel employed visiting Jewish scholars, like Edelmann and B. Goldberg, to answer some of the difficult questions. He asked Steinschneider to help him in the meantime to fill as far as possible the gaps in incunabula and other books printed before 1732, up to which date the catalogue was to include all Hebrew printed books. He authorized him to purchase for the Bodleian a selected number of manuscripts from J. H. Schorr and J. S. Reggio and permitted him to retain them for a long time in his house for a thorough examination. When Edelmann brought the Palestinian bookdealer, N. Coronel — a fine, turbaned man — to Oxford with a lot of Hebrew manuscripts, he immediately sent the list to Steinschneider with the request that he mark those worthwhile and suggest fair prices for them. He accepted his selection, but had to raise the prices a little. In reference to purchases from J. M. Goldberg and Asher, he wrote him: "You have always acted straightforwardly and fairly and have my best thanks."

Bandinel's relations to the younger man became more and more intimate and fatherly. He took a deep interest in Steinschneider's personal affairs and in his family and on occasion even offered him financial aid out of his own purse. We do not have Steinschneider's answers, but the proud scholar seems not to have taken advantage of the proffered help. The money paid by the Bodleian, altogether some £1,300 in the course of his employment, must have been a very great help during these years of struggle.

In spite of the enthusiasm with which Steinschneider had approached the arduous task of catalogue-making, he felt himself very much handicapped by the rules imposed on him for the work which, to complicate matters, had to be written in Latin. His friend Geiger, to whom he sent the sheets as they were printed, wrote to him (in March, 1855): "The book will become indispensable to the bibliographer; it shows a high degree of workmanship and suffers only from an *embarras de richesse*." The author's answer reveals his struggle with the unwieldy material: "The *embarras de richesse* in my Catalogue is due to the unfortunate arrangement which does not permit the addition of footnotes outside the text, so that my footnotes have become the real text. The Catalogue is not meant to be a book, but a work of reference. I have made every effort to make its arrangement convenient. *Ultra posse nemo obligatur.* Add to it the miserable, awkward, to-me-unfamiliar Latin!"

The accumulation of all possible references to every author and book from earlier and later writers, frequently accompanied by the critical remarks of the cataloguer to which Geiger refers, seems to have been objectionable also to the authorities of the Bodleian. After the printing had dragged on from year to year, they became very impatient. They were displeased with the size of the volume and the great cost involved and claimed that the amount of extraneous data made it hard for the user to find quickly the desired information. They likewise objected to the excessive use of uncommon abbreviations and the clumsy Latin style which, in accordance with German custom, departed too much from the classical models followed in England. Its lack of "brevity and perspicuity" made it less useful than had been anticipated.

It was the first draft of the introduction submitted by Steinschneider which brought this feeling of the curators to a head. Even the old librarian was disappointed and wrote him a letter of severe criticism, advising him "not to introduce anything personal — finding fault with others" — into the introduction. Most of the criticism was conveyed to the author by the famous Syriac scholar, Prof. Payne Smith, author of the *Thesaurus Syriacus*, who was designated by the curators to supervise Steinschneider's catalogue of the Hebrew manuscripts which was to follow that of the printed books immediately upon its completion. It seems that the purpose of the criticism was largely meant to prevent a repetition of the objectionable features in the new book. At the same time Smith suggested corrections for the introduction, which apparently underwent a thorough revision before it was approved.

Smith's letters were written in the first half of 1860, while the introduction went to press. In the following year (February 18, 1861), when the catalogue of the printed books was about to be published, Bandinel's successor, H. O. Coxe, requested Steinschneider "that you undertake the sole charge of the Catalogue (of the Hebrew manuscripts) and proceed with it with all the expedition you can," and he expressed the hope to have him spend the coming summer in Oxford.

It is a great pity that we do not have the answers to all these letters and therefore do not know Steinschneider's reaction to the criticism and to the repeated invitations to take up the cataloguing of the manuscripts. Steinschneider fell sick in 1861 and was therefore unable to proceed immediately. Whether he waited for a new invitation, which did not come, we cannot tell. Ten years later, in a letter to Coxe of which he kept a draft, he took the opportunity to complain that he had heard indirectly that the task had been turned over to other hands (Adolph Neubauer). For many years he resented this arrangement whereby he was prevented from carrying out the plan for which he had collected so rich a body of material and to which he had been looking forward for a long time. When Neubauer's catalogue was in press, he sent him numerous additions and corrections which the latter incorporated in his "Additions." But Steinschneider's material was still not exhausted.

For the first fourteen years of the Berlin period Steinschneider did not find a suitable position. He gave occasional public lectures on general topics for various organizations and he preached on the High Holidays (1848–1853) in the Baruch Auerbach Orphan Asylum with great success. He participated as an expert in the preparation of a changed liturgy for the New Synagogue of the Berlin community (1862–1866) and, in recognition of his services, received for life a seat in the Old Synagogue. For some time after the death of Sachs (in 1864), and during the absence of Rabbi Joseph Aub (in 1869), he occasionally officiated at weddings in the community. He was invited to deliver the official address in the synagogue at a general thanksgiving celebration after the conclusion of the peace of Vienna (December 18, 1864) and, together with the famous Lewandowski, to arrange an appropriate program of selections for the choir. He evidently continued to cultivate the interest in music implanted in him in his early years. This had brought him close to Adelheid Zunz during his student years in Berlin. It enabled him, in his eightieth year, to discuss the old synagogue melodies with an expert like Eduard Birnbaum whom, according to the testimony of his young admirer, G. A. Kohut (who was present at this meeting), he impressed by his knowledge and understanding of such matters.

For a year and a half (1858–1860) he taught geography and German at the Jewish girl's school — eight hours a week for the munificent remuneration of about eight dollars a month. For ten years (1860–1869) he functioned as Jewish scholar in the administration of the oath *more judaico*; he had to read a prescribed admonition to the witnesses, occasionally with special additions at the request of the judge. He used every opportunity to point out the inexpedient and unjust character of this special oath, which at last was abolished by law in 1869. In the meantime, however, this time-consuming activity served him as his main source of income.

The first regular position he attained (in 1859) was that of lecturer at the *Veitel-Heine-Ephraimsche Lehranstalt*, with an annual salary of three-hundred thaler ($225), a position which he filled for forty-eight years until the end of his life. This institution had been founded, in the second half of the 18th century, as an old-fashioned *Bet ha-Midrash* by the court-jeweler of Frederick the Great and bore his name. It had been modernized in 1856 and was open to all Jewish and non-Jewish students who, in the opinion of the teachers, were prepared to follow the lectures to advantage. Steinschneider, after the death of Lebrecht (1876), became the principal teacher and lectured there — and in later years in his home — twice a week. His main subject was to be rabbinic literature (i. c., works composed after the conclusion of the Bible in the language developed by the Jewish scholars out of the Hebrew and Aramaic) and the subsidiary branches of knowledge. On these he was to lecture according to a purely philological and archaeological method. He opened the series with an introduction to the Jewish literature of the Middle Ages which he published during the last decade of his life, just as he did with his lectures on Hebrew manuscripts, on Arabic literature and on historical literature. Other subjects with which he dealt were the philosophic, dogmatic and polemical literature of the Jews, with special attention to the Arabs; the history of the Hebrew language, philology and exegesis; Halakic literature from the conclusion of the Talmud to Joseph Caro; biographies of famous Jewish scholars of the tenth and eleventh centuries; and other topics of similar nature. In his late years he devoted one weekly lecture to one of these literary subjects, the other to a philological interpretation of outstanding philosophical and polemical works.

He gathered around himself for these lectures a group of students, mostly pupils of the liberal *Hochschule für die Wissenschaft des Judentums* and the orthodox *Rabbinerseminar*, who attended his classes very conscientiously and found them, as well as his interpretations of texts, very stimulating.

Once only, in 1875, did an exciting episode disturb the quiet circle. When the first report of the *Hochschule* appeared, Steinschneider, in his *Hebräische Bibliographie*, recorded its publication with some caustic remarks about "the new ghetto for Jewish learning" and drew attention to the fact that while the report speaks of the regular students and those "from countries of a lower state of culture" who were permitted to attend, it omits figures for either group. Thereupon the student body of the institution directed (1875) a letter to the scholar stating that, in view of his unjustified sharp attacks and the disdainful terms applied to their *Alma Mater*, they felt compelled to say that to their great regret they could no longer attend his lectures.

Steinschneider was evidently annoyed and on the margin of the letter he remarked that of the six *Hochschüler* attending his lectures during the term, three were not worth mentioning; of the others, one, Dr. Klein, had left for Copenhagen before the letter was written, M. Löwy, the writer of the letter, had come back to him after two years, and Immanuel Loew, who had drafted the letter, returned afterwards to consult him on his researches. From the expression of thanks to the revered teacher by the latter two in their publications, we see that the master's resentment did not prevent him from extending to the rebels his invaluable scholarly advice and assistance. He also noted that an article in a German-Jewish weekly making fun of the rebellion was published without his knowledge.

The lectures at the Veitel-Heine-Ephraim Institute were strictly scholarly and were attended by students of Orthodox and Liberal points of view alike. Dr. Siegmund Auerbach, later the renowned Orthodox rabbi of Halberstadt, was his pupil as well as such men as Ignatz Goldziher, Joseph Jacobs and Solomon Schechter. I did not come across any record of the students who took his courses. During the years I had the privilege to be his pupil, his classes were attended by Drs. Moses Auerbach, Arthur Biram, now head of a school in Haifa, Hayyim Brody, David Herzog, George A. Kohut, Judah L. Magnes of the Hebrew University, Henry Malter, Isaac Markon, Julian Morgenstern, Samuel Poznanski, Max Schloessinger, Gotthold Weil, now at the Hebrew University, and many others. Steinschneider liked to state on occasion that several non-Jewish scholars also had attended the courses of the *Bet ha-Midrash*, such as the famous professors of Semitic languages Georg Hoffmann, H. L. Strack, and Paul de Lagarde, the well-known antisemite.

From 1869 to the end of his life Steinschneider held the position of *Hilfsarbeiter* at the Royal Library in Berlin, where, in his late years, he came every Wednesday to work on the catalogue of the oriental and especially the Hebrew books. The services he rendered in ever-ready kindness and selfless devotion, as helper, counsellor and bibliographer, to the members of the staff and to visiting scholars, were warmly appreciated by his colleagues at the Library. They found expression in a congratulatory letter on his ninetieth birthday which was written by the director of the Library, the world-famous scholar Adolf Harnack, and signed by forty-five members of the staff.

His work in the Library brought him in contact with many outstanding non-Jewish scholars in different fields. Men like H. Diels, Ludwig Stern, Valentin Rose and many others turned to his incredible erudition for help in the most complicated problems of medieval and oriental literature and bibliography.

In the same year (1869) in which he received this appointment at the Library, Steinschneider — then a man of fifty-three — at last was given a position which, though utterly inadequate for a scholar of his rank, provided him at least with security for the future. He was appointed for life head of the girls' school of the Jewish community. For this he received a salary of a thousand thalers ($750) with the obligation to teach up to twelve hours a week. He was not to accept any other position, whether remunerative or not, without the permission of the board.

Steinschneider had, since his youth, shown great pedagogical talent and by this time had gathered rich experience in the teaching field. He threw himself with his full energy into the new task to which he devoted the best that was in him. In his simple way, he treated everybody with equal friendliness and took the deepest interest in the welfare of teachers and pupils. He never asked from others what he was not ready to give himself. In many respects he was ahead of his time in his educational theories. Opposed to all sham and pretense, he refused to draw the attention of the public to his school by theatricals or other unessential activities. He laid stress only on the real educational work — to prepare the girls for practical life; to aim for thoroughness in limited fields rather than for superficial many-sidedness. To achieve a proper balance between intellectual and practical education, he took an interest in the introduction of gymnastic training, wanted the girls to be able to handle tools and to have understanding for handicraft and trade. Occasionally he took them to a printing shop or discussed with them the practical problems of the home. He tried to develop self-reliance among his pupils and interest in continuing their own education. Having laid the greatest possible stress on the study of German, which he personally taught in the higher classes, he had the satisfaction of hearing the inspector of schools, himself director of one of the Berlin high schools, assert that the best German was spoken in this Jewish school in spite of the fact that a large proportion of the girls were foreign born. He especially liked to teach little children, for he enjoyed watching the young mind awaken.

Thus he, with the depth of his understanding and the clarity of his intellect, guided the school for twenty-one years. In 1890, a man of seventy-four, he decided to retire, partly because of an ear ailment; and the community pensioned him. He was offered, besides the modest pension of 3,200 mark ($800), an additional honorary compensation of 2,000 mark in recognition of his great merits for Jewish learning. In a highly characteristic letter, he absolutely refused the additional money. His pension together with some other income and savings, he said, would be sufficient to provide him and his wife with their modest requirements. It had always been his principle, he continued, to take money only for services rendered and to keep his scholarly activities and his convictions free from any external consideration; nor did he want to bequeath to his children money he had not earned. The recognition of his work, he felt, would have the higher meaning the less it was of a material nature.

Twice Steinschneider refused positions which would have enabled him to develop a more extensive teaching activity in the field so dear to him, that of Jewish learning. In 1871, Professor Moritz Lazarus offered him a place on the faculty of the newly established *Hochschule für die Wissenschaft des Judentums*. He had previously objected to the aims and purposes of this institution, and his curt refusal stated that he could not teach there without placing himself in opposition to the statutes of the institution or renouncing his convictions.

An invitation to a professorship at the Budapest Seminary, in 1876, conveyed to him by his old friend, Dr. M. Kayserling, he answered at greater length, pointing out that even if he were a younger man — he was then sixty years old — objective considerations would prevent his acceptance. The subjects which he could teach and his conception of Jewish scholarship would not fit an institution which held itself aloof from the university. He objected to special institutions for the training of rabbis and claimed that they nowadays promoted systematic hypocrisy and scholarly immaturity. What is scientific in Jewish history and literature does not have to fight shy of the universities and should be made available to Christians. He rather favored endowing chairs at philosophic faculties for unsalaried instructors (*Privatdocenten*) in order to induce the government to establish professorships in this field. This very one-sided and prejudiced attitude towards the Seminaries prevented him from accepting these positions. His optimism regarding the possibility of creating a place for Jewish learning at German universities, as has happened in England and America, was entirely unfounded. But we see the proud independence of the great scholar who did not even for a moment consider the acceptance of a more adequate and undoubtedly higher-salaried position if it did not fully coincide with his principles. Money and titled positions never played a part in influencing his decisions.

At the age of seventy-four, on his retirement from the directorate of his school, Steinschneider at last was granted leisure for his scholarly labors. At an age when most people retire from all work, he threw himself with undiminished ardor into the completion of some of the great tasks which had occupied him all his life. He now sat at his desk from the early morning to seven o'clock in the evening and presented Jewish learning with a continuous flow of invaluable contributions to its various fields. In the late afternoon he took a walk with one of his pupils or his devoted secretary. Once a week he spent a day in the Library, keeping up the catalogue of new acquisitions. He always had time, however, for his old friends and his pupils when they came to consult him on their work or their private concerns. He suffered much from noise in his ears and complained that he continuously heard the musical band of a whole regiment. Otherwise his health was unimpaired and his vitality unusual, though the natural discomforts of his advanced age made themselves more and more felt. When he once was run over by a carriage and broke his knee, the physicians were astonished by his quick recovery; he soon was able to go out again. He jokingly remarked that he had been passed over so often, why should he not be run over for once? When the all-inclusive Association of German Rabbis (*Rabbinerverband*) was being founded, in 1896, he was undergoing an operation for rupture (from which he quickly recovered). Again he could not suppress one of his customary puns and remarked: "In my case the rupture preceded the bandage (*Verband*); with them the *Verband* precedes the rupture."

On June 11, 1898, his wife, Auguste, passed away after a few months' illness, shortly before their forty-ninth wedding anniversary. The loss of his brilliant and vivacious companion, the mother of his children, must have left a deep scar on the personal and emotional life of the aged scholar. There were no other noteworthy events in the grand old man's last years. He carried on his scholarly work, his lecures at the Veitel-Heine-Ephraim Institute and his cataloguing at the Royal Library, till December, 1906, six weeks before he passed away. He died during the night of the twenty-third to the twenty-fourth of January, 1907, ten months after his ninetieth birthday. His mind was clear to the end, and he was still making literary plans. As Schechter fittingly remarked: "His vision never became dimmed and his freshness never disappeared until his dying day."

An interviewer once asked Steinschneider in his later years about the course of his life. "My life — it is my scholarly work" was his only answer; any further information was refused.

The above outline of the external events of his biography hardly touches upon the gigantic scholarly work which made Steinschneider one of the small group of founders of modern Jewish learning and established his fame as the most erudite in the entire circle of Jewish luminaries of the last century. We have to turn now to this real life of the scholar. An exhaustive appreciation of his innumerable books and articles, however, cannot be attempted within the frame of an essay. It would require a bulky volume and wider knowledge than any single Jewish scholar possesses. Only his outstanding and more extensive contributions can be briefly considered here.

The central theme of Steinschneider's researches — the theme he selected at the outset of his scientific career — was the relation of Jewish literature to the other literatures of the Middle Ages, especially in the fields of science. In Leipzig, Fleischer's lectures and the collaboration with Delitzsch stimulated him to investigate the relations between Arabs and Jews. Upon coming to Berlin, he submitted a plan for a work — on the general subject: Jewish Contributions to the Literary History of the Middle Ages — which was to occupy him for nearly six decades. The vast theme was divided into three parts. The first part, entitled *Bibliotheca Judaeo-Arabica*, was practically ready for publication and he approached the Culturverein, of which Zunz was the president at the time, for a subvention. He received a grant of a hundred thalers, but the work was to appear only after fifty-seven years, grown in the meantime from a slender book to a large volume. He proudly stated in its introduction that this was the only subvention he ever received for his scholarly labors.

Before he could realize his plan, the editors of the great *General Encyclopedia of the Sciences and Arts*, edited by Ersch and Gruber — a tremendous undertaking of which 167 large quarto volumes appeared in the course of eighty years without completing the alphabet — invited Steinschneider to contribute the article "Jewish Literature" which Zunz and Lebrecht had refused to undertake. It required the bold daring of youth to approach so enormous a task. It involved bringing order and method into the chaos into which the subject had been plunged. Material had to be gathered from the amorphous volumes of Wolf's *Bibliotheca Hebraea*, the books of J. B. de Rossi and other, less reliable works. The opportunity to show the whole magnificent phenomenon of Jewish literary development as an organic entity attracted Steinschneider very strongly. He felt it would clarify the problem in his own mind, would give him a lucid conception of the subject and, incidentally, would establish his position in the circle of the learned. The essay was to cover two printed sheets; it soon turned out, however, that it could not be confined to so narrow a compass. It grew to seven times the planned size and occupied the author for three years (1845–1847). It was a great satisfaction to Steinschneider that the editor of the encyclopedia decided to accept the lengthy article without any cutting. It was printed three years later, in 1850. Subsequently, in 1857, *Jewish Literature from the Eighth to the Eighteenth Century: with an Introduction on Talmud and Midrash* appeared as a book, in English translation by William Spottiswoode, carefully revised by the author. The translator had become interested in the essay when searching for information on the history of mathematics among the Jews.

For the first time, the literature of eighteen centuries was thus properly organized according to subjects and periods. The first period, that of post-biblical literature preceding the contacts with the Arabs — the traditional literature of Talmud, Midrash and Liturgy — was dealt with briefly in an introductory chapter which was indispensable for the understanding of the later developments. Here Zunz's *Gottesdienstliche Vorträge* served as an invaluable guide. The second period, from the eighth to the fifteenth centuries, offers a brief outline of all branches of Jewish literature, arranged chronologically and according to countries, with short, often piquant and epigrammatic remarks and characterizations of the essential contributions and the intellectual currents in every field. What was known at the time about the authors and works is briefly recorded. The third period, from the sixteenth to the eighteenth centuries down to Mendelssohn's time, is dealt with similarly and is shown to be generally a period of decay. Secular and religious works are treated with equal thoroughness.

One does not know what to admire more, whether the erudition of the author, then thirty years old, or his powers of organizing the enormous material which had to be collected from, for the most part, very unsatisfactory sources. These, as a rule, showed no appreciation whatever of the value of the individual contributions and of their interrelationships. As an article of an encyclopedia, Steinschneider's book could only offer a bare outline and could not do full justice to the requirements of a proper history of Jewish literature. The hand of the master, however, is evident at every step and the completeness of the work for its time is truly amazing.

This publication put its author immediately into the front rank among the pioneers of Jewish scholarly research. It was probably in recognition of this achievement that the University of Leipzig conferred on him, in 1851, the degree of Doctor of Philosophy. The English translation, which has been out of print for more than seventy years, has, curiously enough, never been reprinted. George A. Kohut's plan for a new edition, authorized by Steinschneider a few months before his death, unfortunately was not carried out. The Hebrew translation by another pupil of the author, Henry Malter (1897–1899), contains only part of the indispensable notes with their important contributions to research in all fields.

The article "Jewish Typography and Book-Trade," which appeared in the following volume of the same encyclopedia a year later, served as a kind of supplement to the "Jewish Literature." It was written in cooperation with David Cassel and is still indispensable, though Steinschneider's later works made corrections on many points.

His study of Jewish literature in its entirety enlarged the

scope of Steinschneider's original plan which had been limited to dealing with the contributions of the Jews to the sciences in the countries under Arabic dominion. He now realized that European Jewry also had devoted attention to these fields, although their coreligionists under Muhammedan influence had excelled in it. After finishing his gigantic task, he intended to return to this, his favorite subject. Again external circumstances interfered, as it happened, to the great advantage of the work.

As stated earlier in this essay, he was invited at this time to prepare the *Catalogue of the Printed Hebrew Books of the Bodleian Library.* Again the task turned out to be much greater than had been anticipated and, instead of being completed within a few years, it took thirteen years to finish the great work which was to establish Steinschneider's fame for all time. It became *the* reference book on all questions of Jewish literature, "the Urim and Thummim of every Jewish student," to quote Dr. Schechter. Many years later, Kayserling remembered the celebration of the *bar mitsva* of the catalogue by a small circle of friends of whom, next to the author, Zunz and his wife were the center. Steinschneider himself tells us that he had put into this catalogue one fourth of his life and the greater part of his strength. Twice, sickness had compelled him to break off his stay in Oxford prematurely. The printing of the catalogue lasted from 1852 till 1860. For the first anniversary of his father's death (1857), he published, as a *Specimen,* five of the longest and most instructive articles of the catalogue, and they fill no less than a hundred and five quarto pages; that on Maimonides covering eighty-two and that on Saadia seventy columns. A wealth of new information on these great scholars had been gleaned for this work from manuscripts as well as from out-of-the-way printed sources, so that even today, despite all the publications on these scholars which have appeared in connection with the anniversaries of their birth and death, these monographs of the master bibliographer and historian of literature are still indispensable.

The Bodleian catalogue — *Cat. Bodl.*, or *C. B.*, as it is generally quoted in literature — is a tremendous volume filling seventeen-hundred and fifty pages of double columns. It records all Hebrew printed books up to 1732, the year when Wolf had concluded his bulky repertory of Jewish literature and when Oppenheim had practically ceased to collect books. Up to the time indicated, even the *desiderata* of the Oxford Library are carefully recorded.

The book begins with a section on anonymous books, headed by Bible, Talmud and Liturgy, and then lists the authors in alphabetical order. After each name we find the most important information on the author and his unpublished works, and these notes become fuller and fuller as the work proceeds. Errors of Steinschneider's predecessors are corrected; new information gathered from hitherto inaccessible sources greatly enrich our knowledge. The wealth of learning, of originality, the combination of breadth and minuteness of research, evident in these notes on the biographies of the authors is truly astounding. The printed works of every author are enumerated with all the titles and editions that appeared before 1732, and later ones as far as they were found in the Library. Wherever necessary, bibliographical notes and references are added to every item, again frequently correcting earlier mistakes.

The full index of printers includes the names of typesetters, correctors, maecenases and is an invaluable source for the history of Hebrew typography, correcting his and Cassel's previous article on this subject in many points. A geographical index records over seven hundred Hebrew names of cities and their modern equivalents. The Bodleian catalogue is an unrivalled tool for every serious scholar and has become the sound foundation of scholarly Hebrew bibliography. It served the author for all his later works.

Though Steinschneider, to his great disappointment, was not to describe the unrivalled manuscript collection of the Bodleian, we are indebted to him for catalogues of several important, though smaller, continental European collections of manuscripts. While he was working for Oxford, the authorities of the Leiden University entrusted him, in 1854, with a description of their important little collection of a hundred and fourteen codices, among which those of the Karaite sectarians were especially well represented. It is characteristic of the industry and quick perception of Steinschneider that he examined all but four of the manuscripts during a single month's stay in Leiden; the four which required more detailed study were sent to him to Berlin. The exhaustive catalogue which appeared in 1858 furnished an accurate, full and lucid account of every manuscript, the more detailed if the works were little known.

Like the Bodleian catalogue, this one had to be written in Latin. More concerned with accuracy than with elegance of style, he tried, as always, to be as brief as possible. He therefore used a great many, frequently uncommon, abbreviations, which still contribute to the difficulty of reading his catalogues and books by those not thoroughly familiar with the subject.

The cataloguing of the greatest and most important collection of Hebrew manuscripts in Germany, that of Munich, was entrusted to him in 1862. In the course of eighty ears he examined the three hundred and sixty manuscripts, in Berlin, and prepared the catalogue. It exceeded the space allotted to the volume and had to be shortened repeatedly before it was printed in 1875. This catalogue had the rare good fortune that after twenty years a new edition became necessary. This time the author was not so strictly limited and thus was able to incorporate much of the material excluded from the first edition insofar as it had not been published in the meantime. It consequently became to some extent a new work.

Shortly after the publication of the Munich catalogue, Steinschneider was asked to describe the three hundred and fifty manuscripts of the Hamburg Municipal Library. He examined them there in the course of a month (July, 1876), again setting a few volumes aside for detailed examination in Berlin. The Munich collection was characterized by its varied content, showing the interest of the Jews of the East and of southern Europe in secular subjects as well as in Cabala; that of Hamburg, on the other hand, was mainly limited to the segment of Jewish literature cultivated in Germany. Apart from some late material of slight worth, it was rich in old vellum manuscripts of high value.

In the same year as the Hamburg catalogue (1878), there appeared the first volume of the Berlin catalogue. It comprised a hundred and twenty-four numbers, of which eighty-eight had been catalogued by Steinschneider ten years earlier. This collection was largely acquired during the nineteenth century and selected on the basis of expert advice. The volumes were therefore throughout of considerable scientific value, in contradistinction to most other collections which had been gathered in the course of centuries. A second volume (1897) brought the number of entries to two hundred and fifty-nine. The two volumes of the Berlin catalogue are the acme of his work in this field and can serve as models for all time.

Besides the catalogues of public libraries, we have from his pen several catalogues of collections brought together by bookdealers who turned to the great master of bibliography for their description. Among these the full description of a hundred and forty-six codices from the library of the scholarly Italian rabbi, M. S. Ghirondi, published for S. Schönblum in Steinschneider's own clear handwriting, is of particular importance.

Steinschneider's catalogues always contain a brief account of the history of the pertinent collection and some appendices offering important texts and detailed contents of especially valuable codices. Those of the Berlin catalogue are of unusual importance. The plates, with specimens of different handwritings, were of great value for the study of Hebrew palaeography for which the material was at that time almost entirely lacking. Steinschneider, naturally, was deeply interested in this neglected branch of study.

His tremendous erudition and enormous industry made Steinschneider's catalogues repositories of rich and often unexpected information on every branch of Jewish literature. To him, however, these catalogues were not ultimate aims, but merely tools and starting points for further research by himself and others. In all his work he never lost sight of the grandiose scheme of his youth — to investigate the relations of the Jews to their surrounding world in science and literature and, in particular, the points of contact between Arabic and Jewish literature and culture.

While gathering material about the Jewish translators, he collected information on the Arabic authors of importance whose works were known to the Jews, thus incidentally enriching the study of Arabic literature from Hebrew and other hitherto neglected sources. These studies also contributed to an elucidation of the influence of oriental on occidental literature. His first larger work, which was a ripe fruit of such investigations, was his comprehensive book: *Al-Farabi, the Life and Work of the Arabic Philosopher with Special Regard to the History of Greek Science among the Arabs.* It was published among the *Memoires* of the St. Petersburg

Academy (1869), a volume of over two hundred and seventy folio pages. What started him on this investigation was the discovery in some Hebrew manuscripts of a short account of Platonic philosophy which he traced back to Al-Farabi.

Shortly after starting on the Bodleian catalogue (1849), he prepared a prospectus of the work which he had submitted to the Culturverein in Berlin a few years earlier and which occupied him for the next half century. Its first part was to be a record of "the Arabic literature of the Jews"; the second was to give an account of "the Jewish translators from the Arabic"; the third was to deal with the religious relations between Islam and Judaism. As it happened, the task was to be carried out in the reverse order. The third part was centered around the only comprehensive criticism of Islam by a Jewish author, Simon Duran (composed in 1423), which had been printed but once, and in a careless manner. Steinschneider published a German translation of that criticism on the basis of a carefully corrected text (in 1879); it was followed two years later by the edition of the text itself. But the copious notes which were to elucidate the subject matter in all its aspects were never organized for publication, though rich material for these notes is found among his literary remains. As an introduction, he collected materials on the polemics between Islam and other religions; this grew into a volume of over four hundred and fifty pages: *Polemical and Apologetic Literature in Arabic between Muslims, Christians and Jews* (1877). Jewish polemics against Islam, which is found almost exclusively in Hebrew texts, is exhaustively treated in an appendix of some hundred and forty pages. References to Arabs and Islam in Talmud and Midrash, in legal and cabalistic literature and in liturgical compositions are enumerated, names and epithets given to Arabs and

Islam in Jewish literature are collected and the subjects of controversy are indicated.

Right after Steinschneider published these parts of the third volume of his planned work, an external stimulus caused him to take up the second. In 1880 the Académie Française offered a prize for a complete bibliography of the Hebrew translations of the Middle Ages. The prize was offered under the influence of Renan, whom Neubauer had approached in this matter, and was meant to encourage Steinschneider to carry out this task to which he had paid so much attention for decades. Four years later he presented a French *Memoire* containing a full discussion of the translations in the fields of philosophy, mathematics and medicine, with an outline of minor subjects. He was awarded the prize in 1885.

In the meantime the Académie had offered the *Prix Brunet* for a treatment of Arabic translations from the Greek (1882). After an essay submitted by another scholar, in 1884, had been judged inadequate, Steinschneider approached this task also. Since a considerable portion of the medieval Hebrew translations were in turn based on Arabic translations from the Greek, Steinschneider had necessarily given careful attention to them and had made various contributions to this field even as he had investigated the "Arabic translations from the Indian." Thus the theme of the second prize of the Académie had been close to his studies and naturally attracted him after he had handed in his work on the Hebrew translations. He submitted his *Memoire* in 1886 and was granted the prize in the following year. "The Arabic Translations from the Greek" appeared, in the author's German translation of the French original, in eight issues of five different publications during the next decade. Twenty-four copies of the reprints were combined with a special title page in 1897 to form a volume of about four hundred pages.

The Hebrew Translations of the Middle Ages and the Jews as Interpreters: A Contribution to the Literary History of the Middle Ages, mostly from Manuscript Sources is, as the title indicates, a much more ambitious undertaking. Excepting the Bodleian catalogue, it is to be considered Steinschneider's greatest work. The printing of the volume of over eleven hundred pages extended over four years; and it appeared in an edition of three hundred copies, at the author's expense, in 1893. Steinschneider had condensed his language to the utmost and had printed the nearly seven thousand footnotes continuously in unbroken lines. This achieved his aim of reducing the size of the volume, but it proved to be a great inconvenience for the reader.

It is impossible to give a popular account of this fruit of half a century's concentrated research in all possible literatures. Hardly anything escaped the indefatigable scholar, who made use of everything written on his subject, even in the remotest sources, even in out-of-the-way periodicals, in every modern language except the Slavic and Hungarian. The first half of the book gives a brief account of the few Hebrew encyclopedic works and then deals with the various branches of philosophy; the second treats of mathematics, astronomy and medicine, and finally with *Varia*, viz., philology, law, different types of folk-literature and superstition in scientific garb. In each class the works of the Greeks, the Arabs, the Jews and the Christians are successively discussed. More than a thousand Hebrew manuscripts, besides many Arabic and Latin ones, are recorded, the data about the lives of the translators are collected and their style and language aptly characterized. Incidentally, the book contains much information on the scientific Hebrew terminology created by the mediaeval translators.

In view of its overwhelming profusion of details and notes, the book obviously was not intended for continuous reading; it is again a work of reference, to be consulted for a particular problem which concerns the scholar at the time. It is a reliable guide to all the mediaeval authors in its fields of interest, almost never found wanting, a bureau of information, a universal catalogue, an inexhaustible mine of knowledge. The material gathered in this work offers to generations of scholars an abundance of subjects for original research in the sources. As in the case of many of Steinschneider's writings, the reading of this book requires hard work and strict concentration. But the interested scholar finds in it rich compensation for his efforts. One wonders how a single man could succeed in so gigantic an undertaking. Yet how many other important books and articles came from his pen while he was gathering the material for this one!

Among the compact general remarks preceding the book, we find many a characteristic and incisive observation. "No Ghetto exists for the spirit," he remarks in connection with the many Hebrew translations from the Latin of the scholastics. "A great knight might boast that he could neither read not write; among Jews an illiterate was considered as belonging to the rabble." "Anything may be said about the Jews that makes them appear contemptible. To this day historians apply different measure and weight when speaking of Jews." "I have undertaken my researches for myself in the first place; there have always been men who considered research an end in itself, as other people do with other enjoyments." He disclaimed all responsibility for eventual excerpts from and popularization of his work; what is offered to the "people" is often nothing more than water poured over bare bones stripped of all meat. "He who does not work himself can gain nothing by mere reading (of my book), nor does he deserve it." "I am writing about Jews, not for them, not *pro domo* . . . . One cannot enlighten antisemites, least of all by history. To emphasize the culture of the ancient Jews in order to require justice for those of the present would be treason against inalienable human rights .... The history of the daughter-religions is one of incessant murderous attacks against their own mother; if ever one of them should succeed, the evil-doers will perish with the deed."

"Parting from this book," he concludes, "which has claimed the greater half of a long life, is like taking leave from life itself; every end makes us realize how puny the individual is as against the whole of mankind. This very thought, however, stimulates us to explore the relationship between the individual and the universe; it teaches us that the finite is merged in the infinite, not destroyed." This leave-taking from life was premature; another fourteen years of incessant, fruitful work were still to follow.

The impression made by this masterpiece was such that even the Prussian ministry felt compelled to recognize the merits of the great scholar by conferring on him the honorary title of "Professor." The diploma was handed to him privately by Wilmans, the *Generaldirektor* of the Royal Library, on February 2, 1894. Any other scholar of such achievements would have received a full professorship at one of the great universities decades ago, and would have been elected member of the Royal Academy. But Steinschneider was a Jew and therefore was honored at the age of seventy-seven with the empty title of professor!

The last chapter of the *Hebrew Translations* deals with the translators from Hebrew into other languages and with the interpreters who, through oral explanations in the vernacular, enabled Christian scholars, ignorant of Hebrew, to prepare Latin translations of Arabic or Hebrew works. Such collaboration was of frequent occurrence during the Middle Ages. A decade later he rounded out his work on the translators by his *European Translations from the Arabic up to the Middle of the Seventeenth Century*. It appeared (1904–1905) among the publications of the Vienna Academy which shortly before had elected him to membership and thus given him another medium of publication for his tireless pen.

Of his tripartite work, the scheme of which had accompanied him through almost the whole of his life, the first part, the *Arabic Literature of the Jews*, was still unpublished. When it finally appeared (in 1902), the scanty material which he had thought ready for publication in 1845 had grown to fill a volume of over four hundred pages. It deals, in chronological and geographical order, with the Arabic literary productions of the Jews of the East and West down to writers of modern times and discusses the Samaritan-Arabic works in an appendix. As in the Bodleian catalogue, the paragraphs devoted to Saadia and Maimonides are the longest. The life and works of every author are exhaustively dealt with, as one might have expected, and the extant manuscripts are fully recorded. The introduction contains some general remarks and points to some of the considerations and conclusions for the history of culture to be derived from the details with which the book is concerned. Here again Steinschneider declares that he does not offer a history of literature for the general reader but a book of reference for the scholar.

For many years Steinschneider had lectured to his students at the Veitel-Heine-Ephraim Institute on "An Introduction to the Arabic Literature of the Jews." While engaged in the preparation of his *Arabic Literature of the Jews*, he decided to publish these lectures in the *Jewish Quarterly Review*. They were distributed over five volumes and were translated into English by his devoted secretary, Miss Adeline Goldberg. The original lectures were preceded by an essay, written in English, on the Arabic names of the Jews. The detailed list of these Arabic names fills over two hundred of the three hundred and eighty-six pages of the volume of which twenty reprints appeared with a title page a year before the *Arabic Literature* (1901).

Steinschneider's interest was not limited to the Arabic writings of the Jews; it embraced all the different languages in which the Jews had produced a literature of their own.

In one of his earliest publications — *The Foreign Elements in the Neo-Hebrew and their Utilization for Linguistics* (Prague, 1845), a lecture delivered at the first gathering of orientalists at Dresden — he dealt with these foreign elements from the point of view of their interest for the philology and the linguistics of the languages from which they were derived. The importance of Jewish works in foreign languages for the history of the culture of the Jews occupied him during all his life and he often took occasion to discuss this subject in his writings. He paid special attention to it in his "General Introduction to the Jewish Literature of the Middle Ages," where he discussed all of these languages — from Aramaic, Greek and Persian to those of Western Europe. The latter especially interested him. At his instigation, his friend, M. Kayserling, published his *Biblioteca Española-Portugueza Judaica*. He himself prepared a bibliographical list of the Judaeo-German publications up to 1740 on the basis of the manuscript catalogue of the Oppenheim collection mentioned above (1848–1849; 378 numbers). Upon examining the books themselves in Oxford, he found that he had overestimated the reliability of the catalogue which had served him as source, and he corrected his list in the Bodleian catalogue. Characteristically, as sharply critical of his own works as of those of others, he stated that his list was teeming with errors and deficiencies. He therefore gave up the idea of correcting and completing it, but he added a list of nearly eighty

Judaeo-German manuscripts known to him (1864–1869). The general remarks about the importance, origin and growth of this literature, which he had contemplated, were never written, though he discussed some phases of the subject in his paper on the "Folk-Literature of the Jews."

We are also indebted to him for a bibliography of the Italian literature of the Jews. He published several more detailed articles in Italian in the 1870s and treated the subject exhaustively in German in a series of instalments in three volumes of a German periodical (1898–1900). While his discussion of Judaeo-German literature, as far as the printed books are concerned, is a dry bibliographical list, his "Italian Literature of the Jews" up to the end of the seventeenth century is a valuable contribution to the history and culture of the Italian Jews, containing much information culled from Jewish and non-Jewish sources alike. For the eighteenth century, he limited his treatment to a mere bibliographical list. Italian Jewish literature appealed to Steinschneider because its writers were educated and cultured persons and their language showed no influence of the ghetto. The Italian Jews have shown, he states, that Church and Inquisition can build ghettos and destroy and mutilate books, but that they cannot shut off the spirit by imprisoning it within walls.

A very useful record of the literature on the Hebrew language up to 1850 was compiled as a preparation for a projected new edition of Gesenius' *History of the Hebrew Language* to which it was to serve as an independent appendix. The *Bibliographical Handbook of the Theoretical and Practical Literature on Hebrew Linguistics*, preceded by a lengthy introduction on the sources for the bibliography and history of the Hebrew language, was dedicated to the memory of the author's mother who had died in the beginning of its publication year (1859). The book contained some sharp attacks on two contemporary Jewish scholars and involved Steinschneider in a bitter controversy with the famous orientalist, Johannes Gildemeister, who wrote a very unfair review of it. Many decades later, Steinschneider published more than eighty pages of "Additions and Corrections" (1896).

While these "Additions" were going through the press, Steinschneider organized his accumulated notes on "Christian Hebraists," a record of over four hundred scholars from the Middle Ages to the end of the eighteenth century who had devoted their attention to post-biblical Hebrew literature. Spread over five years of a bibliographical periodical (1896–1901), this list gives us information on all contributions by Christians, mostly theologians, to the study of the later Jewish literature, a curious chapter in Jewish bibliography.

Of far greater significance are Steinschneider's contributions to the investigation of the Jewish share in the fields of mathematics and medicine. The fact that much of the work by Jews is based on Arabic predecessors induced Steinschneider to devote considerable attention to Arabic works in these subjects. As a matter of fact, as far as medicine is concerned, Steinschneider's contribution to the Arabic field is greater than to the Jewish. At the same time, some of his studies on medicine among the Jews, especially that dealing with the earliest European Jewish author of the Middle Ages, Sabbatai Donnolo, are of fundamental importance. Even the lengthy articles about Donnolo, which extend to about two hundred and forty pages, contain more about general history of medicine than about its Jewish representatives. He dedicated this work to his uncle, Dr. Gideon Brecher, on his seventieth birthday.

A translation of Maimonides' famous *Treatise on Poisons* — advice for first aid before a physician can be consulted — is preceded by a bibliographical essay on the "Toxological Writings of the Arabs." It is followed by appendices on Indian and Persian sources used by the Arabs and exceeds in size the annotated translation of Maimonides.

Most of Steinschneider's contributions to the history of medicine among the Jews consist of descriptions of medical manuscripts. The only exception is that part of his *Hebrew Translations* which deals with medicine. Here he discusses not only the Arabic writings of the Jews, but, besides the direct translations from Arabic and Latin, also a few Hebrew medical compilations based on non-Jewish predecessors. As far as we know, he did not plan an all-embracing treatment of this subject, yet no one could have handled it with equal mastery.

A list of "Jewish Physicians" — over two thousand — was published (1914–1915), a few years after Steinschneider's death, by A. Freimann in his bibliographical periodical. The list records the period of every physician and the known sources about his life and work. It is extremely useful for reference in spite of its incompleteness — other scholars added nearly a thousand names in the following years. Like all his publications of the kind, this one is a monument to his untiring industry in the methodical collection of information on all kinds of subjects over a period of six or seven decades.

How deeply interested he became in Arabic medicine is evident from his contributions to the terminology used by the authors in their original works and in their Latin translations, corrupted as they often were. His studies in this particular subject, based on the examination of rare books and manuscripts in Arabic and Latin, culminated in his "Heilmittelnamen der Araber," over two thousand pharmacological terms, which fill nearly a hundred and fifty pages of a series of articles (1897–1899). Yet Steinschneider was a layman in this field.

In "Mathematics among the Jews," on the other hand, we are indebted to him for an extensive treatment from the early Middle Ages down to 1840. A series of articles was begun in a mathematical journal in 1893 and was continued in various periodicals for fourteen years, till the end of his life. The concluding instalment was in press at the time of his death. In these we have the record of a millennium of Jewish studies in the various branches of mathematics, in astronomy and astrology, in chronology and the computation of the calendar, written in Hebrew, Arabic, Latin, and modern languages, dealing to a large extent with unpublished works. It is a bibliographical compilation, but the historian of mathematics will find here rich material and many a helpful hint.

Steinschneider's contributions to the study of Arabic mathematics are even more extensive. Community of interest had brought him into contact with the Roman prince, Don Baldassarre Boncompagni, who had established a printing press mainly devoted to works dealing with the history and bibliography of mathematics and who published, for twenty years, a periodical devoted to his hobby. Boncompagni provided his friend with tracings and copies of portions of manuscripts in Rome and Paris which he needed for his researches and encouraged him to pursue his studies in this field. Steinschneider published a number of lengthy papers in the periodical, several in the form of "Letters to D. B. Boncompagni." They amount to about five hundred folio pages (1859–1884). His final contribution, "Arabic Mathematicians and Astronomers" (1901–1908), although not completed, fills over a hundred folio pages. It was interrupted by his death, the last instalment being published posthumously. He wrote besides numerous studies in German periodicals devoted to mathematical research.

In the last decade of his life Steinschneider began to prepare for publication the lectures which he had delivered for many years to his students at the Veitel-Heine-Ephraim Institute. I have already mentioned his "Introduction to the Arabic Literature of the Jews" and his "General Introduction to the Jewish Literature of the Middle Ages" (1905), which Elbogen characterized, on account of its methodological importance, as the scholarly legacy of the author.

The publication of these lectures was inaugurated by a volume which marked the first step in the cultivation of a field never attempted by any predecessor. No one else was so well prepared to deal with this subject. Steinschneider expected the *Lectures on the Lore of Hebrew Manuscripts, their Collections and their Catalogues* (1897), to be the first and probably the last of his lectures to appear in print. He decided to publish them more or less in their original form, since, in view of his eighty years, it would have involved too much work to recast them into a handbook. They were to serve for others as an outline for a future monograph. Here he dealt with a subject in which great ignorance had masqueraded in the cloak of erudition for centuries without a protest; catalogues teemed with amusing misunderstandings and misinterpretations. Nowhere could one find any guidance for the proper description of Hebrew manuscripts, in itself a very difficult subject. Now, for the first time, the nestor of Jewish scholars, who had examined more Hebrew manuscripts than any other contemporary, gave the rich fruits of his experience in this modest volume in which the thousands of details are so well organized that it has become a most useful guide and instructor for all those interested in the subject.

The last of his lectures to be published, *The Historical Literature of the Jews*, Part I, "Bibliography of the Hebrew Works," also appeared as an independent volume (1905). The plan for this book, as for many of his other works, originated at the time when his *Jewish Literature* made him survey all its branches. For sixty years he had paid attention to the historical Jewish writings; since 1865 he had lectured on the subject twelve times, mostly limiting himself to the Middle Ages, only rarely and cursorily going down to the eighteenth century. Steinschneider himself prepared this book for the press down to the end of the Middle Ages; he also separated the Hebrew sources from those in other languages. Dr. A. Freimann completed the volume, although the author carefully revised the work of his collaborator. The two thousand cards covering the non-Hebrew sources were never published. For the mediaeval works, he gives not a mere bibliography but a critical account of the narrative sources and a discussion of their contents. The book is dedicated to "the tried friend, Miss Adeline Goldberg," who for many years assisted him in his work, helped with proofreading and index-making and in every way did her best to lighten his tasks for the master whom she revered like a father. It was the last book he published.

It is probable that he intended to make another one of these lecture series available to the public. Israel Abrahams recorded in his necrology that, a few weeks before Steinschneider's death, the nonagenarian wrote to him offering a series of articles which were to run in the *Jewish Quarterly Review* during the next two years. Even at that advanced age, he looked forward to years of further scholarly activity.

It would be easy to continue this description of Steinschneider's work almost indefinitely. I have passed over the biographical articles which fill over six hundred pages

of the first (and only) volume of his *Gesammelte Schriften;* I
have not mentioned his *Hebraeische Bibliographie*, a bi-
monthly edited by him for twenty-one years, in which he
reviewed most of the books sent to the editor and to which
he contributed some hundred and twenty articles of a
bibliographical nature, some sixty more extensive reviews
and over three hundred miscellaneous notes of different
size. I left out some series of articles dealing with lighter
subjects, like those on "Purim and Parody" (1881–1884;
1902–1903; over a hundred pages), "Chess among the
Jews" and many others. Suffice it to say that he contributed
to some eighty periodicals, encyclopedias and similar
collections and that his bibliography records some fourteen
hundred items. Joseph Jacobs once figured out that, if one
would put all the books and articles written by Steinschneider flat on top of one another, they would be taller
than the author himself. That was about twenty-five years
before Steinschneider's death, and the output of his later
years was very considerable. About four books and a
hundred and fifty articles were added to his bibliography
after his eightieth birthday. Thus it was possible to speak
in this essay of only a very small part of his work. Those
mentioned in the course of this paper would fill a bookshelf
of three and a half feet.

Besides his direct contributions to Jewish learning, Steinschneider indirectly furthered research by helping others
by his oral advice and his correspondence. Miss Goldberg
made a list of a thousand persons whose letters to him he
had preserved, and which are now in the Library of the
Jewish Theological Seminary. "His scientific correspondence took up a great deal of his time," Joseph Jacobs
records; "he could manage to get more canned learning on
a postal card than any man in Europe." Among his
correspondents we find relatives, friends of his youth, pupils,

students in general and outstanding scholars who appealed to the Berlin oracle when they were in need of some information on a point of mediaeval literature in any of the spheres of which he was absolute master.

Most of his writings were purely technical and dry. He avoided every superfluous word and I remember that, when I was working for a short time at his *Geschichtsliteratur*, he asked me: "Why do you use two words when one would serve the purpose?" On another occasion, he said that it was his task to publish as much of his accumulated material as possible, since others did not have access to all his sources. Only in the introductions to some of his later books did he permit himself some general remarks, which showed either his appreciation of the broader problems involved in the subjects with which his books dealt or his concern with the questions of the day. As a rule, he would not permit such matters to distract him from his concentrated work in solving literary problems and making his materials available to the small circle of scholars who shared his devotion to true scholarship.

In his early years he was not averse to belletristic writing. Under the influence of Rückert's translations from the Arabic, he tried his hand at rendering some of the lighter kind of mediaeval Jewish literature into verse or rhymed prose, and he dedicated a little volume of such translations, *Manna*, to his fiancée. Later on he referred to this dedication of 1847 as the official announcement of his engagement. Even here he could not resist the temptation to add learned notes and parallels at the end. He wrote some lighter articles and verses for various periodicals and newspapers, mainly in his early years, probably for financial reasons. Thus we find the serious scholar as collaborator of the *Pesther Tageblatt*, Freund's *Bild und Leben* and even Gerson's *Modezeitung*. He also gave to a society of young merchants a few lectures about culture (*Bildung*) and the influence of travel, on superstition and similar general subjects. Some of these he published in his late years in a series of popular lectures of which his friend, the eminent pathologist and anthropologist, Professor Virchow, was one of the editors. In earlier decades he had published many of his researches in the history of medicine in the *Archiv* edited by the same scholar.

In the revealing fragments of a diary from his student days, which he fortunately preserved, he relates that one evening (in 1839), on coming home, he burned his belletristic writings and thus broke down the bridge to journalism and frivolous literature. Having atoned by this sacrifice of his vanity for the youthful offence of wasting time, he vowed that henceforth his pen would be dedicated exclusively to serious pursuits and the search of truth. Frivolity was certainly not one of his faults; on the contrary, the search for truth and exact knowledge was the characteristic, life-long watchword. With inexorable sternness towards himself and others he strove for objective research.

He never tired of fighting shallowness and superficiality, sham and charlatanery among those working in the field of Jewish scholarship, and he would never countenance the suppression of facts for apologetic reasons. In the hundreds of reviews he wrote, he was the conscience of Jewish scholarship, encouraging beginners where he observed serious effort and condemning superficiality, dilettantism and pseudo-learning. Fraud he would never forgive and he therefore took every opportunity to censure an Eljakim Carmoly, who claimed to have discovered in his manuscripts new facts which actually were the products of his imagination. Incidentally, Carmoly had repeatedly and in an unpardonable manner attacked Zunz, the revered master. Steinschneider missed no opportunity to chastise the fabrications and forgeries of this otherwise industrious and learned man. He calls his French *History of Jewish Physicians* a "rich source of plagiarisms, embellishments, inventions and forgeries" which had transmitted grave errors unto the third generation. On Carmoly's death, Steinschneider wrote a necrology which began: "On February 15th, the former Rabbi of Brussels, Eljakim Carmoly, entered into the eternal 'Truth,' after he had denied and maltreated it by all kinds of forgeries and impudent plagiarisms in numerous books and articles . . . ." He remarked in one of his lectures that he had been charged with persecuting Carmoly beyond the grave. He denied this; he had nothing personal against Carmoly; for his part Carmoly could enjoy the best place in *Gan Eden*; but his forgeries still mislead scholars and it is for this reason that he still must protest and warn against him.

Two years before this he had written a necrology of the bibliographer and philologian, Julius Fürst, in a similar ironic and bitter vein. Fürst had attacked him very rudely and undeservedly in his student days and had omitted his name and writings from his *Bibliotheca Judaica*. "Reverence for the irreverent would be misunderstood," said Steinschneider, adding ironically "The departed has deserved well for his introduction of literary industry into Jewish circles . . . ." He devoted a long appendix to the introduction of his *Bibliographical Handbook* to a sharp polemic the orientalist Gildemeister of Bonn. The prevailing polemical tone among Jewish scholars in the middle of the last century was anything but dignified and Steinschneider's sharp pen was ever ready to answer his opponents in kind. Among his brief necrologies, however, the two on Carmoly and Fürst stand by themselves.

Among his pet aversions was also the historian of Judaism, Heinrich Grätz. He, too, had attacked Zunz and had made ample use of Steinschneider's researches without giving him credit, stating only occasionally, "the bibliographers say." Having no appreciation for the popular, subjective way in which Grätz wrote his great work, Steinschneider strongly objected to occasional careless slips. The two scholars were too different in their whole make-up and their conception of Judaism to understand and to do justice to each other.

For many years Steinschneider and Neubauer, assistant librarian of the Bodleian Library, were bitter enemies and attacked each other in the sharpest terms. The fact that Neubauer was charged (1868) with the cataloguing of the Oxford manuscripts may have influenced Steinschneider's judgment. When, however, Neubauer, on a mission from the French Academy, visited the Berlin library in 1877 to investigate the manuscripts by French authors, Professor Stern, the head of the manuscript department, introduced the two and they soon found that they had enough in common to cooperate rather than to fight each other. Neubauer told me that when they made peace, Steinschneider then and there said to him that he had in press an article against him which would have to appear unchanged; but he promised to add a note at the conclusion announcing the end of their literary feud. We read, in fact, at the end of a sharp five-page article, "On Criticism and Method," a footnote saying: "A personal meeting which recently took place makes me expect confidently that possible future controversies between us will be confined to the subject matter." The rather cynical Neubauer, who was much less sensitive than Steinschneider, readily agreed and the two great bibliographers became fast friends. Steinschneider, in the introduction to his *Hebrew Translations of the Middle Ages*, made this statement: "Dr. Adolf Neubauer has contributed to my work more than all the others put together" (by giving information on numerous manuscripts in different libraries). Neubauer proudly drew my attention to this passage when he told me the story of their reconciliation.

Steinschneider had made very important discoveries among the Judaeo-Arabic manuscripts which he examined during his stay in Oxford in 1851. The most important of these was the identification of an incomplete volume, lacking author's name or title, as the long lost *Siddur* of Saadia. He had various important compositions of the manuscript transcribed at his own expense, intending to have them published with an adequate description of the hitherto unknown manuscript. When he gave the copies to one of the itinerant publishers who at that period used to print old texts and peddle them around as a means of earning a livelihood, he made the condition that the publication should include his introduction. The publisher, however, sent back Steinschneider's introduction and refrained from mentioning his name altogether. The unpleasant affair led to a break in the old friendship with David Cassel who had served as intermediary between Steinschneider and the publisher and had prepared the texts for publication. Steinschneider, in a four page pamphlet, exposed the action of the publisher and printed a letter of Cassel's expressing the hope that their long-standing friendship would not be affected by this unpleasantness. Cassel, however, was mistaken; thenceforth all connection between the two was broken off. Cassel no longer read proof of the Bodleian catalogue as he had done theretofore, and in a work of Cassel's on which he had collaborated and which had been printed a decade earlier, Steinschneider wrote over the personal dedication "To my dear friend M. St." the words "only up to 1856!" (By a slip of the pen he actually wrote 1865, but such slips were not unusual with Steinschneider.)

In all his critical evaluations, Steinschneider aimed at absolute objectivity, no matter who was involved. Even in necrologies of friends the personal element was generally suppressed and an effort made to give a fair appraisal of the merits of the departed. In his reviews also, praise or condemnation were pronounced regardless of personal relations. Sometimes his blunt pronouncements wounded a dear friend without his fully realizing it. For example, a review of his — I heard this from his own mouth — made an end of his forty years' friendship with Dr. Meyer Kayserling. The latter had published a biography of the famous rabbi and journalist, Ludwig Philippson, founder and editor of the *Allgemeine Zeitung des Judentums*. He did not indicate that Philippson also happened to be his father-in-law. We can easily understand that he overestimated the importance of his hero. Now Steinschneider did not like Philippson and was opposed on principle to his entire journalistic activity. Some of his statements may be of interest: "P. undoubtedly has the dubious merit of having reared modern journalism, with its lights and shadows, on Jewish soil, of having promoted an amalgamation of religion and science, Judaism and politics, community and personalities, of having given a forum to autodidactic presumption in preference to expert learning. The *"allgemeine" Zeitung*, in the course of half a century, has begotten nearly two hundred daughters in all countries, languages and jargons which tried to draw adherents away from their own mother; except for a few, they all fell into deserved oblivion . . . . It is understood that the abuse of a medium does not make it objectionable in itself. These remarks are in no way intended to find fault with P.'s honesty, the integrity of his endeavours and their partial success . . . . I must energetically oppose the concluding remark that P. directly or indirectly promoted, to any degree worth mentioning, 'the thorough scientific study of Judaism' if scientific is understood in the proper sense of the word. The best-known representatives of learning in the Jewish field say nothing of any promotion by him, nor does the author of the biography in his own valuable scholarly writings over a period of forty years . . . . It would have been better not to refer to P.'s attitude to Jewish learning and its representatives." He concludes that "It is a thankless job to add the necessary shadows to a dazzling picture, but if a respected scholar appears somewhat blinded, it is the unavoidable duty of a friend of long standing, who had no relationship to the person discussed, to adhere to the well-known dictum, *Amicus Plato sed magis amica veritas.*" He did not see that here his own prejudice against journalism and popularization was as one-sided as Kayserling's admiration for Philippson and he could not understand the reaction of the latter to his review.

A long feud with another former friend, A. E. Harkavy, was ended when the latter was invited to contribute to the *Jubilee Volume* on Steinschneider's eightieth birthday and in his paper expressed his admiration for the master and assured him that, in all their bitter controversies, both equally had been striving to find the truth.

Though Steinschneider carried on many literary controversies and did not easily forgive an opponent, there was one man to whom he always looked up and whom he considered beyond reproach—Leopold Zunz. Zunz was the fatherly friend whom he revered and worshipped even though he occasionally, on the basis of new sources, had to correct some of his statements. An attack on Zunz he resented, I think, even more than one against himself. In preparing a bibliography of the Master of Masters: *The Writings of Dr. L. Zunz, the Founder of the Science of Judaism, Listed for His Sixty-Third Birthday,* he accompanied the entries with a severe censure of his critics, especially Carmoly and Philippson. In the dedication he states that Zunz's writings and personal information had served him innumerable times, directly and indirectly, as guides and signposts. When he reprinted this bibliography for the eightieth birthday, he omitted these "shards" (*Scherben*) so as not to immortalize the names of these critics together with Zunz.

Zunz had immediately recognized the unusual qualities of the young student when he came to Berlin in 1839 and had drawn him to his house. Most of the group of younger students, all of whom looked up to Zunz as their idol, were rather afraid of the great man, but Steinschneider soon became his personal friend as well as the friend of his gracious wife, Adelheid. He played piano for her and acquainted her with Italian music and even gave her music lessons. From her and her husband's letters to Steinschneider after the latter had gone to Prague, we learn how intimate their relations had been and how anxious both were to see their younger friend back in Berlin. Zunz paid him the great compliment of recommending him to his publisher for preparing a new edition of Zunz's first important essay, *Something About Rabbinic Literature*, in which he had given an outline of the work to be done in this field. But nothing came of this plan. Zunz criticized the shortcomings of Steinschneider's early articles in kindly terms, at the same time encouraging him by recognition and friendly advice. Repeatedly he expressed the wish for the younger man's return to Berlin to have his assistance in his work.

About the same time Geiger wrote to Zunz that "Steinschneider gives great promise for the future; his articles are somewhat overloaded and drowned in the accumulation of petty details; once he learns to organize his material, he will achieve excellent work." That prophecy of 1841 certainly came true. Though Steinschneider continued to crowd his publications with a profusion of references and details, they show a remarkable talent for organization.

In spite of fundamental differences in their attitude towards Judaism, a warm friendship united Steinschneider and Geiger which was later extended to Geiger's scholarly son, Ludwig Geiger. Steinschneider furnished Geiger with valuable material, drawn from manuscripts, for his work on mediaeval scholars, and he is one of the few to whom Steinschneider set up a literary monument by a more extended article after his death.

Only two other friends were thus distinguished, Rapoport and Zedner. The personal relations to the former during his stay in Prague had been temporary, but the literary relationship between the two continued. The article gives a warm appreciation of Rapoport's work and an account of the difficulties of various kinds during the years of his Prague rabbinate which prevented Rapoport from fulfilling the great expectations for Jewish scholarship which had been reposed in him. It shows a warm interest and keen insight on the part of the younger friend. He concludes with the statement: "It took the Prague rabbinate twenty-seven years to consume a rare genius; this the history of Jewish literature will inscribe on his tomb."

The most personal of these necrologies is that of the modest author of the incomparable *Catalogue of the Hebrew Books in the Library of the British Museum*, Joseph Zedner. It is the only biography of this rarely gifted but retiring and little known scholar. Steinschneider had met him in the house of the bookseller, A. Asher, where Zedner had acted as tutor and literary adviser. Through Asher's recommendation, he had received an appointment at the British Museum and there, after the acquisition of the printed books of the Heimann J. Michael library, he had built up the wonderful Hebrew collection of that great institution. Though personally not interested in bibliographical details, he had answered Steinschneider's numberless inquiries in connection with his work on the Bodleian catalogue and had supplied him with information which he could not get from the staff of that library in spite of their good will. The loving picture Steinschneider drew of the unusual personality is a touching tribute to their warm friendship.

Steinschneider, in fact, had a rare talent for friendship. Even if in the course of his busy life he could not keep up a regular correspondence with all the friends of his youth, a warm attachment remained and most of the friendships formed during his student days accompanied him through life. It was so with A. Benish, M. A. Levy, Albert Loewy of London, the well-known *Sanitätsrat*, S. Neumann, and many others. He even kept up friendly relations with David Cassel's older brother, Selig, in spite of his conversion to Christianity and his becoming Paulus. In this case, however, the old intimacy was no longer evident. The story is told that when Cassel informed him that the spirit had overpowered (*übermannt*) him, Steinschneider retorted with one of his quick puns which are untranslatable: *Was, übermannt, überweibt hat er Dich.*

In addition to numerous Jewish friends, Steinschneider, through his work in cataloguing the treasures of various libraries as well as his researches in old science and mediaeval literature, was thrown into close contact with many non-Jewish scholars, contacts which sometimes ripened into friendships. His intimate relations to Dr. Bandinel, the chief librarian of the Bodleian, have already been discussed. The famous orientalist and authority on comparative religion, Professor Max Müller, offered him, on one of his visits to Oxford, his hospitality until he could procure adequate quarters. He maintained an intimate correspondence with the brilliant Arabist, William Wright. He also became friendly with the scholarly Prussian ambas-

sador to England, von Bunsen, famous for his Egyptological
and biblical studies. In Leiden he became very intimate
with the orientalist Juynboll and friendly with Kuenen and
Dozy. His researches in Greek philosophy among the Arabs
and Jews brought him into contact with scholars like
Valentin Rose, to whose edition of a volume of the Academic Edition of Aristotle's works he contributed the translation of an Arabic text, even as he furnished a translation
from the Hebrew for Bruns' edition of Alexander Aphro-
disias' commentary on *De Anima*. He corresponded on
texts of Greek philosophy with Diels, a third member of the
Berlin Academy. There were numerous scholars in other
fields who expressed their gratitude to the modest Jewish
scholar for rich information. Through Prince Boncompagni
he became acquainted with various Italian and French
students of the history of mathematics.

No German university was liberal enough to honor itself
by offering the eminent scholar a chair for research in the
Jewish past. Any expectations he may have had in this
respect were to be disappointed. His indefatigable, fruitful
activity, however, found warm recognition in Jewish and
non-Jewish circles. The University of Leipzig conferred on
him the degree of Doctor of Philosophy without the usual
formality of requiring the submission of a thesis and an
oral examination (1851). His *Jewish Literature* evidently
was considered a sufficient *specimen eruditionis*. After the
appearance of his article on Juda Romano in an Italian
periodical (1870), the Roman Jewish community sent him
a formal vote of thanks with the request that he continue
his researches in the intellectual history of its past. In 1885
and 1886, he received the two prizes by the French Academy for his works on the mediaeval translators. The Ruma-
nian Société Historique Juliu Barasch, founded in memory
of a friend of his student days with whom he had under-

taken an unpublished German translation of Saadia's philosophic work, made him an honorary member in 1887. In the same year, Columbia College of New York, in connection with its centennial anniversary, conferred on him the honorary degree of Doctor of Laws. Hebrew Union College gave him the honorary degree of Doctor of Divinity on his eightieth birthday (1896). He received the honorary title of "Professor" from the Prussian ministry (1894) and on August 3, 1903, the Vienna Kaiserliche Akademie der Wissenschaften elected him to membership. He welcomed this distinction because it gave him a new medium for his publications; it would have been more appreciated at an earlier period of his life. For his ninetieth birthday he received the congratulatory letter of Harnack signed by his colleagues on the staff of the Royal Library and the *Seniores scientiarum mathematicarum* announced that they *Mauritio Steinschneider, Professor celeberrimo, doctissimo, illustrissimo . . . Nonaginta Annis Feliciter Glorioseque Peractis Gratulantur.* On the attached leaf the names of forty-four mathematicians, beginning with Thales and Demokritos and going down to the end of the nineteenth century, are printed with their dates. The names of the Berlin admirers who had the pages printed are not indicated, and Steinschneider made no annotations on the sheets.

For his eightieth birthday, at Neubauer's suggestion, two of his younger pupils, George A. Kohut and Samuel Poznanski, published a *Festschrift* which contains thirty contributions in German, French, Italian and Hebrew. One of the two non-Jewish contributors refers to his acquaintance with the celebrant since the days of his work on the Bodleian catalogue at Oxford.

Being averse to any public demonstration, Steinschneider avoided any celebration of these anniversaries by leaving the city for the days involved. "I vanished without leaving a trace," he told his admirer, Kohut, who inquired where he had been on his eightieth birthday. It was an expression of his deep inner modesty which was characteristic of the great scholar. "I desire no title and honors, no large sphere of activity, nothing but bread and inner independence. My vanity has become very indifferent to wounds," he writes to his fiancée in 1846 as a man of thirty, and in the following year: "I do not care at all for the so-called honor, e. g., to be a professor, which imposes sacrifices and brings no returns. My position in life must be as free as possible, but it must be integrated with life, and that requires character, not a mere mask."

This great modesty and unpretentious simplicity, free of any vanity, were characteristic of the great master during his whole long life. With true heroism he resisted all temptations, which were bound to come to a man of his prominence and fame, to be diverted from his work by activity in politics or society. He never permitted himself to be used or abused for any purpose. During a scholarly career which extended over three generations he never for a moment lost sight of his aim to bring the intellectual activity of his people during the Middle Ages to the ken of modern scholarship and to claim for it its proper share in the strivings for human progress. With all his power he fought the old notion that Jewish literature was purely theological, to be dealt with by theologians; theology was merely one of its branches, but by no means the most important one. He often emphasized that he was not a theologian. It is noteworthy that, despite his objection to Jewish national movements, he did not hesitate to state that the Jews are a nation in the original meaning of the term, united by an ideal fatherland, by a book which dates back to the most ancient history and by a language derived from it. They have no cause to deny their race or to be ashamed of the close ideal bond. It was a great,

though somewhat hidden, love for his people which gave
him the impulse to devote himself so exclusively to the
exploration of all the branches of its literature. A child of
the period of rationalism and averse to any kind of mysticism, he still was the first to make invaluable contributions
to the literature of Cabala. Only against the legal literature
did he seem to feel a certain dislike, perhaps because he
had devoted so much time to its practical study in his youth.

Unequalled in erudition and creative power, he was a
supreme master of the whole mediaeval Jewish literature
and of general literature as far as it had any relation to
it. The most universal Jewish scholar of the last century,
unique and incomparable in the manysidedness of his
scientific researches and in the mastery of foreign languages,
his range was as vast as his learning was deep. Pure
intellectuality prevails in his writings and absolute veracity
and rare justice were the mottos of his work. He was
impartial in his judgment of men, of things and of subjects.

Most of his work was dry and was meant for a small
circle of serious and devoted scholars. His great book on
Hebrew Translations was published in only three hundred
copies; that was characteristic of Steinschneider. But behind the amazingly industrious scholar was a man of rich
and deep sentiment, a man who was greatly interested in
the events of the day, in world politics and especially in
everything that affected the Jews. "How can your Jewish
bankers grant a credit to the Czar?" was the first question
he directed to the French bibliographer, Moise Schwab,
when he visited him. And then they turned to a discussion
of Zionism which both opposed. In this connection a
remark of his from an earlier period may be recorded: "For
a long time now there exists for me no Jewish question, but
only a human question."

It was indeed surprising — when one came with a certain
awe and trepidation to the very simple and old-fashioned

study out of which for decades such streams of learned publications had issued — to see the same friendly reception accorded by this giant of learning to insignificant young students, to scholars of reputation or to old friends. He knew how to put his visitors quickly at ease and to chat with them amiably with his ever-ready wit. His everyday conversation was stimulating and animated and showed how far his knowledge and his interests went beyond his special sphere. This apparently crusty scholar, who guarded every moment for his research, readily gave of his precious time to his young pupils and took an abiding interest in their scholarly as well as in their personal concerns. He gave them fatherly advice based on the manifold experiences of a long life and the rare wisdom of his keen intellect. Those of his pupils in whom he recognized true zeal and promise for Jewish learning had free access to his home and were treated as friends. Some of them he even helped out of financial difficulties from his own moderate means. It was for his kind and noble personality as much as for his invaluable instruction that these younger men loved and revered him, looked up to him like a father and cherished, long after his death, the memory of the hours spent with the great teacher. By his sharp polemics he made many enemies, but the number of his friends and admirers was infinitely larger. By word and example he taught his students method and thoroughness. He made them realize that before the time comes for comprehensive general surveys, an infinite amount of detailed research will have to be done. The bricks will have to be prepared before the majestic structure of Jewish literature through the ages can be successfully erected. It was the greatness of Steinschneider that he devoted an unusually long life to establishing a massive, sound foundation for such a future building — that he shirked no difficulty, no menial tasks to gather the bricks. At the same time, he never lost sight of the ultimate structure for which they were intended. His erudition, his acumen, his power of combination, which he applied to every subject, created a long series of works which will always serve as examples of scholarly objectivity, integrity of research free of tendenciousness and a striving for truth for truth's sake. This, too, is part of the rich heritage which Steinschneider left to Jewish scholarship.

6

David Hoffmann

TRADITIONAL Judaism in Germany in the middle of the nineteenth century was in desperate straits. The vigorous Reform movement was making constant inroads into its ranks, and it lacked the leadership of men possessing the ability and training to fight the tendencies of the Reformers. It was only when two great leaders arose who took up the cause of Orthodoxy and, equipped with all the weapons of modern thought along with a mastery of the ancient tradition, threw themselves into the controversy, that a change came about. These two men, Samson Raphael Hirsch and Israel Hildesheimer, though quite dissimilar in their attitude towards the questions of the day, were great personalities. Both had been thoroughly steeped in Bible and Talmud before acquiring the scientific method taught to students at the universities. Both were endowed with keen minds and unusual energy. Hirsch was of a philosophic turn of mind; Hildesheimer was a man of action. Hirsch was a man of unbending character who would never compromise; Hildesheimer was a practical man who, though never yielding on any question involving his principles, would try to carry his point without acrimony. While Hirsch attempted to give a philosophical basis to Orthodoxy, Hildesheimer aimed to spread it by training teachers who would propagate his principles in their congregations. Consequently, while Hirsch's great works became the gospel of the Jews of southern Germany who shared his uncompromising attitude, the seminary founded by Hildesheimer exerted greater influence in strengthening Orthodoxy, not only in all parts of the country, but also beyond its borders.

Hildesheimer was a great talmudic authority, and in the rabbinical school which he established in Eisenstadt, Hungary, he instructed his pupils in the talmudic sources. At the same time, he trained his students in the elements of general culture: in mathematics, the classical languages and other subjects which in his opinion were indispensable to a rabbi. In Hungary he found himself in an untenable position, being attacked by both Reformers and Hasidim. The latter, in that country, refused to realize that in modern times it was necessary to combine a general education with proficiency in the Talmud. When Hildesheimer finally gave up the struggle and left Hungary to accept a call to Berlin, many of the well-trained talmudic students whom he had gathered around himself followed him to his new sphere of activity and attended his *shiurim* in Berlin. Hungary, however, had left its mark on Hildesheimer. For, though a native of Halberstadt, Germany, he had been deeply influenced by the pilpulistic method of interpreting the Talmud which prevailed in Hungary, and he consequently modified the more direct approach which had been prevalent in the last great rabbinic schools of Germany, in Altona, Fuerth and elsewhere, and which he had acquired in his youth.

In Berlin he became more convinced than ever of the necessity of establishing a modern school for rabbis, where the young men would find guidance in meeting the perplexing problems raised by their studies at the universities, and be trained in the various branches of Jewish learning in conformity with their background of Western culture. Looking about for a faculty for the newly-founded Rabbinical Seminary for Orthodox Judaism, Hildesheimer immediately invited Dr. David Hoffmann, one of the most gifted of his former students at the Eisenstadt *yeshiva*, who had joined him in Berlin.

The personal life of this great scholar was not eventful. He was born on the first of Kislev, 5604 (November 24, 1843), in Verbó, Czechoslovakia, the son of R. Moshe Juda, the *dayyan* of that city, who died when his son was only five years old. Hoffmann revered his father as a saint and maintained that he himself never attained his father's pre-eminence as a talmudic scholar. The boy began to study the Bible at the age of three, Rashi at four, and Talmud at five. By his tenth year there was nothing more he could learn in his home town. He once told me that, at that age, he could deliver a talmudic discourse as well as the local rabbi and did not see in what respect the latter was superior to him. The Verbó community then sent the prodigy to a neighboring *yeshiva*. When Hoffmann was twelve, Rabbi Samuel Sommer accepted the rabbinate of Verbó, and it was he whom Hoffmann considered his first real teacher; he followed him when he left for Papa. Rabbi Sommer must have realized his pupil's unusual gifts at that early period, for he had him instructed in secular subjects at his own expense.

When ill health compelled the rabbi to close his *yeshiva*, Hoffmann went to the *yeshiva* of the eminent Rabbi Moses Schick at St. Georgen, which he attended for a year (about 1859). This great talmudic authority grew very fond of his young pupil and took him into his home. The influence he exerted on the grateful boy was evident to Hoffmann's last days. He always followed his teacher's practices as he had observed them in his daily life and frequently quoted his opinions. In 1860 he went to Eisenstadt to enter the rabbinical school which Dr. Hildesheimer had founded and there he also continued his secular studies. Thence he went to Pressburg, in 1863, and became the pupil of R. Abraham Samuel Benjamin Schreiber, the *Ketab Sofer*.

After graduating from the Evangelical Gymnasium of that city, in 1865, Hoffmann went to the University of Vienna and came in contact with the Jewish scholars of that city. Once, at a lecture there, he pointed out that the *Midrash Tanhuma* understood a Mishna in a sense opposed to the explanation of the Babylonian Talmud. Because of this remark, Isaac Hirsch Weiss asked him why he generally objected to such independent interpretations. His answer was that, though the Midrash had the right to disagree with the Amoraim, this did not justify us in taking the same liberty. Evidently the young man was already, at that time, combining acute critical observations with rugged adherence to the traditional point of view. Dr. Solomon Schechter, however, told me that Hoffmann did not leave in Vienna the reputation of assuming so unyielding an attitude.

In order to help support his mother, Hoffmann interrupted his studies at the university to accept a position as teacher at the *Lehrer-Praeparanden-Anstalt* at Höchberg, Bavaria. He was to spend the following fifty-five years or so in Germany. The stay in Höchberg, near Würzburg, brought him into contact with the famous rabbi of the latter city, Rabbi Seligmann Bär Bamberger, and his circle. Here he became acquainted with the German method of studying the Talmud which was very different from that current in Hungary. Their thoroughness and exactness in evolving the plain meaning of the text, while giving constant attention to the application of this meaning to the practical legal decisions, deeply influenced him and he gradually developed a way of study of his own by blending the methods of his Hungarian teachers, including Dr. Hildesheimer, and the Würzburg circle. In Würzburg, too, he became a frequent visitor at the home of a well-known businessman and Talmud scholar, R. Jona Rosenbaum at Zell, a pupil of the famous R. Mendel Kargau of Fürth, whose work, *Giddule Tahara*, he had edited after the author's death in 1845. Rosenbaum kept up his talmudic studies and was an intimate friend of the *Würzburger Raw*, as Bamberger was called. A few years later Hoffman married his daughter, Zerline, who became the devoted companion of his life and who was to survive him many years. She made it her life's task to take care of all practical problems and permit him to pursue undisturbed his lifework as teacher and scholar.

About two years later, in 1869, when Dr. Hildesheimer was called to Berlin, Hoffmann followed him to the Prussian capital to continue his studies at the university and attend the talmudic lectures of his great master. In 1871 he was offered a position as teacher at the school founded by Rabbi S. R. Hirsch in Frankfort, and he settled there for some time. · In 1873, when Hildesheimer founded his Seminary, Hoffmann was appointed immediately to teach Talmud and Codes to the younger students, while the rector himself instructed the upper class in these subjects. Hoffmann was destined to teach the same subjects for the next forty-eight years, in addition to lecturing on the Pentateuch and giving a few other courses of which I shall speak later.

The rest of his life, insofar as it was not touched by the wars of 1866, 1870–71, 1914–19, and their repercussions, was uneventful and devoted to the quiet pursuits of a teacher and scholar. To fulfill a promise he had made to his father-in-law, that never a day would pass without his giving some time to the study of the Talmud, he accepted in 1874 the position of lecturer at the *Shass-Hevra*. Here his daily *shiur* was attended by a group of scholarly *ba'ale battim* and a number of his students. He covered the

Talmud several times. The last *siyyum* for the complete
Talmud was celebrated on Purim, 1908. It happened once
that, on closing his eyes during a lecture to consider a
difficult question raised by one of those present, he fell
asleep for a moment. Though nobody noticed this momen-
tary lapse, he felt mortified and decided that he must take
a rest before the *shiur*, which he read in the early afternoon.
He called this his "preparation" and used the expression
as an excuse when anybody wanted to see him at that time.

In the *Shass-Hevra* he read the text with Rashi's commentary and, where necessary, with *Tosafot*, laying emphasis
only on the *peshat*, the plain meaning. His instruction at
the Seminary was of a higher order. Here the *Tosafot* were
studied very intensively and he drew on all the parallel
passages to clarify the subject to the last degree. He added
frequently remarks showing the students the true way to a
critical understanding of the Talmud and to research in
this field. He required careful preparation on the part of
the students and he would occasionally make sarcastic
remarks to those who came ill-prepared to an examination
(*hazara*). His manifold duties did not leave him much
time for preparation, but thanks to his wonderful memory
he had a complete grasp of every passage of the Talmud.
I remember that once, when he expected a learned visitor,
he did prepare a *shiur* (in Ketubot). In half an hour he
looked over some ten leaves in the bulky compilation of
R. Bezalel Ashkenazi, and I was struck by his mastery of
the text and his quick perception which enabled him to
follow at so rapid a pace all the different interpretations
collected in that book.

In teaching Codes he would go back to first sources; but
he realized that the time at the disposal of the Seminary
was not sufficient to cover the entire ground even for the
sections he taught. He therefore prepared an abstract of
all the codifiers, to the latest important collections of

responsa, and dictated this to the students, always adding the injunction that they were never to make decisions on the basis of this dictation without first looking up the original sources. This compilation on various parts of the *Shulhan Aruk* was arranged with the clarity, the excellent organization of the material and the emphasis on the essential so characteristic of Hoffmann. It was superior to all modern works of the kind, so far as it went, and it is unfortunate that this abstract has remained unpublished.

Hoffmann was a splendid teacher of Talmud and Codes, but fell short as a lecturer on the Pentateuch and other subjects, since he read his manuscript too rapidly for his students to follow his arguments and take notes. He always prepared more material than he could possibly cover during a term, and his hurried reading was an attempt to give his students as much as was humanly possible.

In 1895, when his revered master, Dr. Hildesheimer, had to give up his teaching owing to his advanced age, Hoffmann took over the instruction of the upper class and continued to instruct it up to June, 1921. When Hildesheimer passed away, in 1899, the general wish was for Hoffmann to succeed the great leader as the head of the institution he had been serving so successfully for over a quarter of a century. But Hoffmann was somewhat reluctant to take over this heavy burden and responsibility; he favored the appointment of the prominent Rabbi of Halberstadt, Dr. Siegmund Auerbach. His friends and colleagues, however, prevailed upon him and he was appointed acting rector in 1899, an appointment which was made permanent in 1902. Under his stewardship the institution continued to develop as a rallying point for Orthodox Judaism in Germany.

The great merits of his scholarly and educational activities were accorded public recognition on his seventy-fifth birthday, in 1918, when the German government conferred on him the title of Professor, a distinction granted to only a handful of Jewish scholars.

It was characteristic of Germany that this great scholar was twice refused naturalization when he applied for it: in the Bismarkian era, some years after his appointment at the Seminary, and again in 1900 after he had become rector of the institution. Hoffmann bitterly resented this refusal by the police commissioner of Berlin and was indignant over the antisemitic attitude implied in this action.

In his last year he suffered from increasing weakness; the climbing of stairs became a great strain for him. To spare him, a door was broken through from his apartment to the adjoining lecture hall of the Seminary. During the last months of his life the students came there for the daily prayers to enable him to carry on his practice of attending services every morning. I was privileged to participate in these services on his last Yom Kippur and Succot and to see his joy in having his grandson sitting before him. When we were departing from Berlin, it was early in the morning, and he happened to be in that synagogue; he came out during the repetition of the Eighteen Benedictions, blessed his children and grandchildren, but would not say a word to us, even at this last farewell, in order not to interrupt the prayers. That was characteristic of his minute observance of every law. Four weeks later he passed away in his sleep, on the 19th of Heshvan — November 20, 1921.

I was present, shortly before our departure, at what was probably his last session with the *Bet Din* of the congregation Adass Yisroel on which he had served gratis, first as a member and then as its head. A complicated question was to be discussed and the other members had studied the subject and set forth the results of their investigations. But he was able to draw their attention to several important sources that had escaped them, giving them the exact references to the numbers of the responsa without consulting the volumes, since he found it hard to take the heavy tomes from the shelves.

His mental vigor and his memory remained unimpaired to the last day, and only an hour before his death he made a note on the margin of the small octavo Talmud which he had used exclusively for his studies for half a century. A fellow student in the early days in Berlin had sold it to him at a reasonable price. As he found out later, it had been bought on credit from a bookseller at a higher price and sold to him as a not very scrupulous means of obtaining ready cash. Only on his seventieth birthday did he come into the possession of the great Vilna Talmud edition which the *Shass-Hevra* presented to him.

Deeply religious and meticulously observant of all Jewish laws, he was very exacting towards himself and yet lenient towards others. In his mode of life he has been justly compared with the saintly, medieval German scholars, the *Haside Ashkenaz*.

When Herzl started the Zionist movement, Hoffmann felt very sympathetic towards it though his official position did not permit him to express himself publicly. The Seminary was dependent on the support of the Orthodox, and the teachers had to be very careful in all their utterances not to give offense to some extreme fanatics of Frankfort and other parts of southern Germany. But in a letter to one of his sons who had written to him in an unfriendly vein about the movement, he gave expression to his sympathy with Zionism which, so he wrote, meant giving up the aping of foreign religious customs and the denial of Judaism. Even if they were not observant now, he said, the Zionists would vote with the conservatives against organ and modern prayer books in the Synagogue. Though he considered their ultimate aim a utopia, he felt that they

would join the Orthodox in the work of Palestinian colonization and of spreading the love of Judaism among wider
circles. We ought to leave the fight against Zionism, he
asserted, to those who remove references to Jerusalem from
the prayer book and who have their children baptized.

Hoffmann was compelled to shift for himself at a very
early age and this gave his mind a practical turn. He displayed a lively interest in the political affairs of the day
and always read the financial page of the newspaper. He
was quite handy with tools and in his younger years he
would himself make necessary repairs in the house; he
rather enjoyed such diversions from his intellectual work.
His personal needs were more than modest; he liked to
speak of the time when the middle part of a herring was
a delectable dish to be indulged in only on the Sabbath.
Only twice in his life, as a young student, had he gone to
the theater; his only recreation was an occasional walk,
and he had to be coaxed to indulge even in this.

His industry was prodigious; otherwise he would never
have been able to accomplish so much literary work in
addition to his extensive teaching program. In the systematic regularity of his life he turned every minute to good
account. Once he started on one of his books or papers,
he followed the principle *nulla dies sine linea*, not to let a
single day pass without devoting some time to his work.
Sometimes he would jump up from the table at mealtime,
while waiting for the next course, to snatch a few minutes
for writing. During such periods of literary preoccupation,
he did not permit visitors to encroach on his time beyond
what was absolutely necessary. He was, however, genuinely
fond of people, friendly to everybody and would occasionally entertain a large gathering with his ready wit and keen
sense of humor, relating good stories or singing Jewish
folksongs.

The long academic vacations did not exist for him. As

a rule he tore himself away from his studies for only a few weeks and, as soon as he returned, took up his lectures at the *Shass-Hevra* and announced a *Ferien Schiur* for those of the Seminary students who had remained in Berlin.

Dr. Hoffmann loved his teaching, which he considered his most important activity. He never considered the number of lectures allotted to him too large. He was always ready to add an extra lecture on some special subject as a *privatissimum*, to be attended voluntarily by those of the students who were interested. He started the two hours of his Talmud *Shiur* in the early morning, in the summer at half past seven, right after the services in the Seminary synagogue and a frugal breakfast; then there followed an hour of Codes and, twice or three times a week, as a fourth hour, his lectures on the Pentateuch and other subjects.

He repeatedly told me in later years that he wished to be pensioned so that he might have more time for his literary work. But this did not mean that he wished to give up his teaching; he merely wanted to be relieved of the administrative work connected with the rectorate, a desire which we can the better understand if we consider that he had to attend to all official matters personally, without the help of a secretary. In the last years his colleagues spared him the greater part of such work.

Hoffmann had a beautiful voice and he often read the prayers at the early Sabbath services in the *Shass-Hevra*, where he always functioned as reader for the *Musaf* prayer on the holidays. He was also an accomplished reader of the Torah. He preached occasionally on the High Holidays in the *Shass-Hevra*. Though he followed the old method of *maggidut*, his sermons were modern and found hearty appreciation.

His childlike simplicity struck everyone who came in contact with him and won him every heart. This simplicity also found expression in his lucid style and his clear presentation of any subject he chose to write on, even of those dealing with the most complicated problems. Although he was conscious of the value of his contributions to Jewish learning and of his mastery of the field of rabbinic literature, modesty was his outstanding characteristic. He was entirely free from any ambition, except that of serving the cause of Judaism to the best of his abilities.

Hoffmann was of a very retiring nature, reluctant to give expression to his innermost feelings. Many might have thought him cold and lacking in personal sympathy, and yet their worries might have caused him sleepless nights. Students might consider him distant and not realize how glad he was to discuss with them any scholarly or personal problem if they but approached him. He might have appeared severe because he was always engrossed in his studies, while as a matter of fact he was of an unusually mild disposition. He would never utter a harsh judgment against anybody nor would he allow people to indulge in gossip in his presence. I had the rare good fortune, as a young student, to live for a year in his home and thus had the opportunity to see his inherent kindness hidden behind the external, serious appearance. I think that in the last years of his life the relationship of his young students to the revered and beloved master became more intimate.

The range of his knowledge was very wide and by no means limited to the subjects of his teaching and to his main scholarly activity. We are surprised, when looking through his bibliography, to see what books he reviewed. Many of them were far removed from his special field, and yet he never limited himself to empty phrases but always had something worthwhile to say about them.

He had a genius for mathematics even to the point of once arriving at a new and interesting solution of a problem which a professor at the University of Berlin had assigned to his advanced students. His solution greatly impressed the professor when it was shown him. In one of his note-books, among his researches in tannaitic literature, I came across thirty or forty pages of complicated mathematical calculations dealing with the problem of squaring the circle. He also enjoyed playing chess and liked watching the game, but he could not refrain from interfering when he noticed that a good move escaped one of the players.

His scholarly method was thoroughly scientific and modern. He was a master of textual criticism, adhering rather to the old critical canon that the difficult wording was more likely to be correct than the easier reading which obviates the difficulties. His researches have pointed new directions and are indeed epoch-making for the critical study of tannaitic literature. No scientific study of this literature is possible without starting from the foundations which he laid. His fine critical mind and his rare acumen were most fruitful and led him to unexpected results which were generally accepted. For Hoffmann was not only critical towards his texts and his predecessors, but equally so towards himself. He could never be dazzled by a clever hypothesis. All his works show sound method and careful attention to every point involved and they therefore contain lasting contributions to Jewish learning. To these we shall now turn.

One of the fields in which Dr. Hoffmann's works were of outstanding significance was the study of the Pentateuch. Scientific research on the book which is the foundation stone of Judaism had been left entirely to the Protestant theologians. They approached the Jewish Scriptures with very little reverence; they subjected it to hypercritical investigation, which cut the books into several, in their opinion irreconcilable, sources; and they permitted their prejudices and their acumen to play havoc with the faith of many Jewish students. These could nowhere find an

answer to the dazzling hypotheses of higher criticism which
were paraded as the irrefutable results of modern science.
Dr. Solomon Schechter once pointed out that higher criticism was actually higher antisemitism. But this was not
clear to the young men three-quarters of a century ago.
An interpretation of the Pentateuch, in accordance with
modern scholarship, but with proper regard to Jewish
tradition, was a crying need which was widely felt but from
which the handful of Jewish scholars shied away. Hoffmann was the first and most outstanding scholar who
successfully tried to fight the opponents with their own
weapons.

In appointing Dr. Hoffmann as teacher of the Pentateuch
at the Berlin Seminary, Dr. Hildesheimer felt that he was
fulfilling the obligation of the new institution to equip the
future rabbis with the ability to answer the constant attacks
on the authenticity of our holiest book. Even a man like
Samson Raphael Hirsch, who in his own writings avoided
this subject, asked Hoffmann during the first year of his
incumbency whether he paid attention to biblical criticism
in his lectures, and, glad to learn that this was the case,
strongly encouraged him to continue along these lines.
From the beginning of his activity as teacher at the Seminary, Hoffmann devoted special lectures to this field.
Characteristically, he would begin with the book of Leviticus, since olden times the first book of instruction for the
young. To this book he always paid special attention and
in nine of the first twenty-five years his Pentateuch lectures
were devoted to it. In the second year he took up Deuteronomy with an evidently elaborate introduction. He paid
less attention to the other books. None of the books was
apparently interpreted completely.

The first report (1874) of the newly established institution, was accompanied by a scientific study from his pen, a
thorough discussion of the meaning of ממחרת השבת in

connection with the '*Omer* sacrifice and the Feast of Weeks. In fifty-six quarto pages, he refuted the views of the ancient Jewish sectarians and of some contemporary Christian scholars and concluded with the evidence for the correctness of the traditional explanation. In the following years he published shorter biblical studies in Jewish periodicals, some of them collected in *Abhandlungen über die Pentateuch-ischen Gesetze*, I, 1878. Another long paper, "The Highest Court in Jerusalem," published with the report of the Seminary in 1878, dealt with both biblical and talmudic problems. The author revised it seven years later for inclusion in a second part of the *Abhandlungen*, but this part never appeared. A longer paper, on "The Age of the Day of Atonement," took issue with various Jewish and non-Jewish critics.

Of much greater importance were his articles against the greatest of the Bible critics of the time, Julius Wellhausen. In a series of articles, covering a hundred pages, he took up various chapters of the famous *Prolegomena* of that eminent theologian and showed up the weakness of many of his arguments (1879–1880). A quarter of a century later (in 1904) Hoffmann once more went over this ground and published his objections to Wellhausen's theories in book form as *The Principal Arguments against the Graf-Wellhausen Hypothesis*. It is perhaps the most important criticism against the validity of Wellhausen's dating of the various supposed components of the Pentateuch. Though Hoffmann was absolutely convinced of the unity of the Pentateuch, he approached the problem in these investigations from the critic's point of view and laid bare Wellhausen's inconsistencies and the deficiencies of his arguments. Hoffmann's aim in this work was entirely negative. He did not try to replace the theory he refuted with a positive one of his own, since he did not believe in the modern approach to Pentateuchal criticism.

In Wohlgemuth's *Jeschurun* he published, in 1914–1919, a series of studies, "Problems of Pentateuchal Exegesis," on selected passages of Genesis and the first half of Exodus, in which he was mainly concerned with the refutation of the arguments against the unity of the Pentateuch.

The ten studies on Genesis are included, partly in shorter form, in a more comprehensive treatment of the critical problems of that book and appeared in the second instalment of his *The Principal Arguments against the Graf-Wellhausen Hypothesis* (1916). He promised to continue his studies also on the other parts of the Pentateuch and the book of Joshua. But, except for the above-mentioned six articles on Exodus in *Jeschurun*, nothing of these was written.

Since these two parts of the book appeared originally as appendices to the *Annual Reports* of the Seminary, they did not receive much attention among non-Jewish Bible scholars. The author was only concerned with undoing the harm and destroying the influence of the modern theories on the Pentateuch in Jewish and, particularly, religious Jewish circles. It is nevertheless very regrettable that his strictures against Wellhausen did not find a wider circulation. The clear arguments of the author and his very acute observations still deserve the full attention of those interested in the problems of the Bible. A translation of the book into Hebrew, by Eliezer Barishansky (Jerusalem, 1928), may have this desirable result.

The efforts to refute the Christian criticisms of the Pentateuch occupy considerable space in Hoffmann's more comprehensive works in this field, namely, his commentaries on Leviticus and Deuteronomy. But here the chief aim is a positive one, to give the reader a clear and constructive interpretation of these books, with special emphasis on their legal portions. The commentary on Leviticus (1905–1906) devotes nearly 900 pages to the thorough interpretation of this, from the legal point of view the most important, part of the Pentateuch. The clear translation and explanation of the various sections is always preceded by elaborate introductions. In these, into which some of his earlier papers are incorporated, the unity and authenticity of the biblical passages is defended against the critical onslaughts of the modern science of the Bible and, at the same time, the reader is offered a lucid presentation of the structure and contents of each part. Hoffmann made use of the wealth of information contained in traditional literature which is completely neglected by the non-Jewish commentators, who deny the continuity of Judaism and consider the post-exilic literature as a new creation of the rabbis of the talmudic period. Hoffmann showed convincingly how much this traditional literature contributes to the correct understanding of many a biblical law, since many of these traditions are as old as the biblical literature itself. Time and again he refutes the results of Christian Bible scholarship and shows the errors of its theories.

Christian Bible scholars have produced frequently worthless hypotheses. They have looked for parallels in anthropology for the explanation of biblical laws which are satisfactorily interpreted in the rabbinic sources to which they had no access and which they, therefore, simply declared worthless utterances of rabbinic sophistry — an easy method of avoiding difficult studies. Hoffmann's commentary, on the other hand, is an important link in the chain of Jewish interpretations of our Bible, prepared, as it was, after consulting the ancient versions, the classical works of the Middle Ages as well as the few modern efforts to contribute to a proper understanding of Scriptures. It is a monumental work, and an orientalist of the rank of Joseph Halévy declared that, since Rashi, no such thorough commentary on Leviticus has been produced by rabbinic scholarship

In his general preliminary remarks, the author gives a

clear exposition of the orthodox Jewish attitude with which
he approaches his text. This attitude is one which he
shares with all his Jewish predecessors, who had no reason
or occasion to specify their views, since these were accepted
in their times by all their coreligionists. Objections have
been raised against this confession of faith which perhaps
contributed to prevent the spread of so learned and important a work in non-Jewish circles. But Hoffmann's sole aim
was to help his own people to gain a better understanding
of their Bible and he did not make any effort to reach
others.

I know of only one review of the book by a Protestant
Bible scholar, Professor B. Baentsch. He wrote in 1908, two
years after the publication of the second volume, but he
only knew of the first. A perusal of the eight columns of
this review is instructive. The reviewer, it begins, read
the preface and the preliminary remarks about the author's
dogmatic point of view and his belief in the Mosaic authorship of the Pentateuch with a slight feeling of ghostly
horror. He excuses himself for proceeding in spite of that
because, he confesses, he had derived a certain amount of
new information from this commentary and he thinks it
would be quite useful if biblical scholarship would not pass
the book by, but be reminded by it of various shortcomings
of modern criticism and exegesis. He admits that the
author, in his discussion of modern criticism, proceeds with
acumen and skill and succeeds in invalidating some arguments and showing that some proposed textual emendations
are untenable. He praises various points of the work,
especially the application of the traditional halaka to the
interpretation of the laws, the conscientious weighing of all
aspects when different interpretations of a passage are
possible; the decision in such cases seems always well
founded. But he criticizes the efforts at harmonization of
the text as well as the symbolical interpretation of sacrifices,

of laws of purity and similar matters. This is actually the weakest part of the book, and here the author follows Samson Raphael Hirsch. Considering the gulf that divides the reviewer from the author, the former's judgment is distinctly favorable.

Before leaving the book, I want to mention one highly characteristic remark of the author in the preface. As to his interpretations of the difficult phenomena of the book, he states that, if his apology appears weak and insufficient, it is due to his own inadequacy; whenever, on the other hand, his argument will be found strong and convincing, it is only the truth of the revealed Torah which speaks for itself and is victorious. In the former case, he hopes that his commentary will stimulate others, gifted with richer mental equipment, to obtain better results.

Hoffman had contemplated continuing his work soon with the publication of a commentary on Deuteronomy. But the first volume of this appeared seven years later, in 1913. In the meantime, he had edited the tannaitic interpretations on that book contained in an unpublished Yemenite compilation, the *Midrash ha-Gadol*. This text served to correct the *Sifre*, the tannaitic Midrash on Deuteronomy, in numerous passages and made available a great amount of other tannaitic material on the book which had not been known theretofore. Since his own commentary laid such stress on the ancient traditional interpretation, he considered this an indispensable preliminary task. The commentary itself has the same characteristics as its predecessor. It covers the first twenty-one chapters.

World War I interrupted the work, which was resumed after peace was re-established. Up to the last weeks of Hoffmann's life, the author worked on its completion. At the time of his death, one hundred and sixty pages were printed and the manuscript of six more pages was ready. It was his custom not to complete his works, but to prepare

enough of the manuscript for a signature, that is, sixteen
pages, and give it to the printer. The press of his friend,
Itzkowski, was only a few doors away from his home, and
its owner was a regular attendant of his Talmud lectures
in the *Shass-Hevra*. Thus, there was no difficulty in publishing the fragment of the second volume, which reaches
to the end of chapter 31. The commentaries on the song
and the last blessing of Moses, which had never been treated
by Hoffmann in his lectures, were still to be written, and
the comprehensive introduction to Deuteronomy, which
had been composed in 1878, was to be completely recast
with due attention to the later literature. This second
half of the second volume, which was to be of the same
size as the first half, was missing. The completed part was
published shortly after Hoffmann's death, in 1922, by his
oldest son, Dr. Moses Hoffmann.

From the works on the Bible, we turn to those in the
other most important field cultivated by Dr. Hoffmann,
the talmudic literature.

Hoffmann started his literary activity with his *Mar
Samuel, Rector of the Jewish Academy of Nahardea in Babylonia*,
an excellent and interestingly written biography of that
great Babylonian scholar of the third century. The modern
title of the position held by the *Amora* is a curious concession
to the times. This treatise was submitted as a doctoral
thesis to the University of Tübingen, and on the basis of
it the author received his doctor's diploma on December 17,
1870. In the same and the following year, it was published
in a Jewish weekly and appeared in book form in 1873.

This contribution to the historical research of the talmudic period was one of the first to be written by a partisan
of Orthodoxy. Though generally acclaimed, it aroused an-
tagonism in certain circles. These circles objected to any
human approach to the worthies of the past, to any treat-

ment which tried to present them as human beings with
human emotions, whose actions and opinions were influenced by their character and their environment. These
objections found expression in an unpublished correspondence between a relative of Dr. Hoffmann's, Rabbi
Hile Wechsler, a saintly hyper-orthodox South-German
Talmudist, and Rabbi Samson Raphael Hirsch of Frankfort,
the great representative of uncompromising Orthodoxy.
While the latter approved Hoffmann's efforts to come to
grips with Protestant Bible criticism, he considered such
an historical approach to the heroes of the talmudic period
not only dangerous, but directly irreligious. When Wechsler's private appeal to the author was of no avail, he sent
the book and his correspondence to the Frankfort champion
of Orthodoxy. The latter pronounced the book plainly
heretical and a denial of the fundamental truth of Judaism
as he understood it. He advised his correspondent to show
up the sentences which proved the charge without taking
the trouble to refute details. The author should be made
to realize his lack of maturity and to promise to abstain
from any publication for the next ten or, at least, five
years.

Hirsch objected to quotations from the works of Frankel,
Graetz, Rappoport and similar scholars, who, in his
opinion, contradicted the tenets of traditional Judaism.
By quoting them the author had attracted the attention of
his pupils to their works. He had warned Hildesheimer
repeatedly, Hirsch wrote, that if he would open a "critical"
Rabbinical Seminary, with immature teachers, he would
cause a greater *Hillul ha-Shem* than Frankel had with the
Breslau Seminary. Hirsch had bitterly attacked Frankel
and Graetz some two decades earlier. Both correspondents
recognized the strict personal piety of Hoffmann, which,
however, could not excuse this work. The planned public
attack did not materialize, but the correspondence was

sent to Hoffmann whose copy of these letters is before me. It must have been a great shock for him to read those utterances of men whom he respected highly.

Hoffmann thereupon wrote to the Chief Rabbi of England, Dr. Nathan Adler, whom he had met some time before, and asked his opinion whether the book in any way contradicted the principles of Orthodox Judaism and whether the Orthodox point of view of the author were not evident to the unbiased reader; also he hoped to hear that the publication of such writings would not be injurious to Orthodox Judaism even if they quote anti-Jewish works. As was to be expected, he received a very encouraging reply from Adler. His revered teacher, Dr. Hildesheimer, also staunchly upheld his great pupil; on the margin of his copy of *Mar Samuel*, which I own, he added some sharp remarks against Wechsler's criticism which he found to be based on misunderstanding.

For some reason, the attacks on the book were not published, but it seemed to me interesting to refer to them since they showed what difficulties the newly-established Seminary had to contend with from the side of extreme Orthodoxy which it was meant to serve. The attitude of certain circles, especially in Frankfurt, caused the institution difficulties for many years.

During the first decade of his activity at the Seminary, Hoffmann occasionally gave public lectures on subjects drawn from talmudic literature, such as his biographies of Simon ben Shetah, Rabbi Joshua ben Hananya, the members of the royal family of Adiabene in Babylonia who had accepted Judaism, or the synagogues in antiquity. He also wrote some reviews on books in his fields of interest.

In 1882 he gave, for the first time, his lecture on the "Introduction to the Mishna" which I heard in 1897. He mapped out an ambitious plan for this subject. Of the two parts into which he divided it, the first dealt with the origin of the Mishna of Rabbi Judah ha-Nasi; the second was to treat of its later history.

He started with a general discussion of the Oral Law and its relation to the Written Law. He then took up the rabbinic enactments, the *geserot* and *takkanot* of the old authorities and the *minhagim*, the two forms of oral tradition, the Midrash deriving the laws from Scripture, and the abstract *Halaka*. Finally he discussed the tannaim, the teachers of the first two centuries, who transmitted the Mishna to their successors. A discussion of the controversies of the tannaim, which was to conclude this part, was never written, nor was the second part, which was to deal with the Mishna in Babylonia and Palestine, the treatment of the Mishna in the two Talmudim by the amoraim, the sages of the Talmud; the relationship of the Tosefta to the Mishna was also to have been taken up in this connection. The exegesis of the Mishna in post-talmudic times was to have been followed by remarks on the criticism of the Mishna. Though he repeated this lecture from time to time and added references to more recent literature, he never went any farther in working out his theme.

In 1881 he had started a series of critical studies on the Mishna in the *Magazin für die Wissenschaft des Judentums*. Out of these grew his pioneering investigation on *The First Mishna and the Controversies of the Tannaim* (1882). Here, he demonstrated that some of the earliest parts of the Mishna can be traced back to the beginnings of the Common Era and showed that there are entire passages in our Mishna which had been composed before the destruction of the Temple and been incorporated with slight modifications by the final redactor at the beginning of the third century. He tested his results by an analysis of the treatise Abot and then showed that, often, controversies of later authorities in the Mishna were based on different traditions of statements made by their predecessors.

It is out of place here to follow these acute investigations in detail. Suffice it to state that the main results of Hoffmann's research have been generally accepted and that they represent very important progress beyond his predecessors in the critical examination of this fundamental source of rabbinic literature.

The complicated problem of the relationship between Mishna and Tosefta was never made the subject of a complete study by Hoffmann; he did examine, in one of his above-mentioned critical studies, a series of short Toseftas quoted in the Babylonian Talmud with the formula *Tna* or *Tni aloh*, which some early methodologists had declared to be the real Tosefta. Hoffmann had copied all these, about two hundred and fifty passages, and submitted them to a searching investigation, throwing much new light on the subject.

The last of his critical studies he devoted to the Tannaitic Midrashim. Here he gave, for the first time, a brief exposition of the ideas which he fully elaborated four years later, in 1887, in his famous *Contributions to an Introduction to the Halakic Midrashim*. Since 1885 he frequently read one of these Midrashim in class, though sometimes only for one term and only for one or two hours a week. His research in this field led to his most important and original contribution to the critical investigation of talmudic literature.

The phenomenon, that in these Midrashim we frequently find teachings which are in disagreement with the accepted legal decisions as incorporated in the Mishna and in other sources, had been noticed before. Geiger, especially, had based on it some of his theories about the existence of an old halaka which had been overthrown by the later authorities. Hoffmann pointed out that these Midrashim came from two contemporary schools which differed fundamentally in certain rules and methods of interpretation — those of R. Akiba and R. Ishmael, two of the great tannaim of the first half of the second century. Both developed their exegesis of the legal sections of the Pentateuch in independent Midrashim on Exodus, Leviticus, Numbers, and Deuteronomy, which showed marked differences in their interpretations and their derivation of the Oral from the Written Law. They frequently disagreed not so much in their results as in their derivations of the laws from the biblical texts.

Once there existed two sets of Midrashim on the four books, but, curiously, the Midrash of R. Ishmael has been preserved for Exodus and Numbers, that of R. Akiba for Leviticus and Deuteronomy. Hoffmann proved the existence of the lost parts of both sets and pointed to some remnants of these which are to be found in talmudic literature and were still known to mediaeval scholars. Some parts of R. Ishmael's Midrashim were inserted in those of R. Akiba's school.

It is impossible in this essay to give a fuller account of the great discoveries incorporated in the ninety-two pages of this work which is full of information compressed into the smallest possible space. David Kaufmann said of this book that Hoffmann often hid his most significant discoveries in his footnotes.

His most important result, that there once existed two independent sets of Midrashim to the four later books of the Pentateuch, was to find a most unexpected verification. A year after the publication of the work, Israel Lewy, that great critic of talmudic literature whose treatise on the Mishna of Abba Saul had been Hoffmann's only predecessor in a searching investigation of the Mishna, discovered large extracts from the *Mekilta of R. Simon* (a Midrash on Exodus from the Akiba school) in the *Midrash ha-Gadol* on Exodus, a hitherto unknown midrashic compilation from Yemen. Hoffmann himself found, in another volume of the same work, remnants of the *Sifre Zutta*, of the Akiba Midrash on Numbers and of the Midrash of R. Ishmael on Deuteronomy. Subsequently, Schechter discovered a few fragments of the *Mekilta of R. Simon*, the *Sifre Zutta*, and the *Mekilta of R. Ishmael* on Deuteronomy among the fragments of the Cairo *Geniza*, and Hoffmann published the *Mekilta of R. Simon* in a rabbinical monthly in 1901–1903 and later, with use of *Geniza* fragments put at his disposal by Schechter, as a volume in 1905. In 1908–9, he edited the tannaitic Midrash on Deuteronomy as it is found in the *Midrash ha-Gadol*, a combination of our *Sifre* with the lost *Mekilta of R. Ishmael*; again he could use for the latter some fragments of the original turned over to him by Schechter. He also had copied the remnants of *Sifre Zutta* from the Yemenite compilation; but since one of his pupils started with an edition of these fragments, he desisted from editing it. It was later edited by Horowitz. The discovery of the *Mekilta of R. Ishmael* on Deuteronomy was announced by Hoffmann in 1889; he published some specimens with an introduction in the following year and in 1897, and he supplemented the statements of his Hebrew introductions with special papers, written after his edition of the two texts, in which he modified his results in some details. His general conclusions had been fully verified by the new discoveries.

All the researches of Hoffmann in the tannaitic literature showed a combination of great learning, remarkable acumen and sound modern scientific method together with an untiring industry. At the outset, he had collected all the quotations from the works of R. Akiba and R. Ishmael in talmudic and midrashic literature, whether transmitted with the name of the authorities or anonymously, copying them in full so as to have the basic material at hand for his critical examination. His work is a remark-

able example of unbiased critical examination and reveals
how much our understanding of the whole talmudic and
midrashic literature stands to gain from the application of
similar methods. In detail his work has been carried
farther by later scholars, but no literary investigation of our
tannaitic works is possible without due attention to his
pioneering researches.

At the request of the Mekitze Nirdamim Society, Hoffmann undertook an edition of the whole of the *Midrash
ha-Gadol* on Exodus, a large part of which he had excerpted
for his *Mekilta of Rabbi Simon*. About half of the book was
published, the first instalment in 1913; the second, though
printed in 1915, was issued only in 1921, after the end of the
world war. But then, at the age of 78, he was not in a
position to continue his work. It will have to be completed
by other hands. In his notes, he showed that he was
familiar with the midrashic literature as well as with the
talmudic, and though a specialist like Dr. Ginzberg was
able to trace a few of the sources which had escaped him,
Hoffmann's edition, based on four manuscripts, remains an
excellent piece of work.

Speaking of his contribution to these studies, we must
not pass over his translation of parts of the Mishna. His
translation of Nezikin was published in 1893–98, and seven
parts of his Taharot appeared in 1910–16. These were
followed by another part published posthumously in 1922.
Only two complete treatises and the beginning of the third
were prepared by him; the rest of the volume was completed
by two of his pupils. His translation was strictly literal,
though occasionally a few words were added in brackets to
make the sense clearer.

The real value of the work is the excellent commentary
which elucidates the text in masterly fashion, interpreting
the etymology of the various terms and their sense in their

context, pointing to the biblical basis of the contradictory opinions of the tannaim and adding everything the reader may require for a proper understanding of the text. After the volume on Nezikin was finished, he wrote a short introduction to all its treatises. For the much more difficult order of Taharot, he added preliminary remarks to every treatise, summing up the complicated subject matter in masterly fashion and enabling the student to find his way in a field so foreign to most modern scholars. His commentary is filled with important information gathered from the work of all his predecessors with critical appraisal and cast in the shortest possible form. The work is of equal value to the scholar and to the lay reader who ventures into the study of the Mishna, which at that time was still indulged in by many *ba῾ale battim* as a religious duty.

In his commentary to the Mishna, as in various other studies and in reviews, Hoffmann made valuable contributions to talmudic lexicography, for which his knowledge of the classical languages, as well as of Semitics, served him in good stead. He used the Samaritan *Targum*, the *Peshitto*, and the Arabic dictionary to solve difficult lexicographical problems. He read in these occasionally to find parallels and explanations for passages of rabbinic literature. His interpretations of difficult words are often unexpected and revealing. To give one example: A passage of the *Sifre* enumerates the various good qualities for which a man might be appointed judge; two of these seem surprising: This man lent me money; this man is a relative of mine. Hoffmann found a corrupt foreign word in the *Midrash ha-Gadol*; and as a result he emended *Helleniston* (a student of Greek) in place of *hilvani mamon* (he lent me money) and suggested the translation "poet" and "good preacher," for *kerobi*, in place of "my relative." An index at the end of the volumes of his Mishna commentary — that for Nezikin was the first publication of mine — lists these linguistic remarks. A collection of all of them would form a useful contribution to neo-Hebrew lexicography.

Similarly, his occasional critical remarks on passages of the tannaitic and talmudic literature are of the highest value; but they are mostly spread over the pages of various periodicals and footnotes to his books and articles. They all give further evidence of his immense learning, his sure method and his great acumen. But it is not possible to say more about these subjects here.

Through the influence of one of his colleagues, Dr. Hirsch Hildesheimer, the gifted son of the founder of the Seminary, Hoffmann was prevailed upon to use his vast stores of knowledge for the defense of his people against the antisemitic attacks which, in the 1880s, took a new and vicious turn. Hildesheimer, the editor of one of the German Jewish weeklies, the *Jüdische Presse*, played a very prominent part in the apologetic activity during that period.

In 1883, there appeared the *Judenspiegel* by Dr. Justus, a pseudonym for the convert, Aaron Briman, who had been a Talmudist of some standing. He had started his literary career with a Hebrew work on a talmudic subject and subsequently had become converted, first to Protestantism and later to Catholicism. This unprincipled fellow, with a prison record, had forged quotations from Talmud and *Shulhan Aruk* in order to place the Jews in a very unfavorable light. A German daily had printed extracts from the *Judenspiegel*, and its editor was brought to court on the charge of inciting classes of the population against each other and imperilling public peace. An instructor of the Münster Academy, Dr. Ecker, asked by the court for an expert opinion, published *The Judenspiegel in the Light of Truth*, a pamphlet which gave scholarly sanction to the lying attacks of "Justus."

In the following year, another antisemitic pamphlet was

brought to court at Bonn, and the famous orientalist of the university of that city, Dr. Johannes Gildemeister, was called as an expert; his *Gutachten* also contained bitter attacks on the *Shulhan Aruk*. Against these various publications, Hoffmann wrote a series of twenty articles in the *Jüdische Presse* in 1884 which appeared in book form in 1885 and, in a much enlarged second edition, in 1894. *The Shulhan Aruk and the Rabbis about the Relations of the Jews to the non-Jews* was intended, in the first place, for those Jews whom these pamphlets might have confused in their attitude towards the Jewish codes which they knew only through these attacks; it was intended, in the second place, for Christian theologians and orientalists whom it would enable to check the references and form a fair judgment of the works containing the condemned opinions. The aim was accomplished and the book played an important part in the defense against antisemitic attacks in the following years.

One of the outstanding theologians, the Leiden professor, A. Kuenen, with whom Hoffmann had had scientific discussions on other topics, wrote to him that the book had entirely convinced him of the truth of its main thesis and given him valuable information on many details. Every page, he said, gives evidence of the admirable erudition and acumen which the author applied with happy results. Only a man who had devoted his whole life to the study of the extensive rabbinic literature was able to discover the errors which, in special cases, might become a danger in practical life. He referred to Hoffmann's statement that divine laws cannot be cast aside by the faithful, but have to be interpreted to make them applicable; he liked the clear way in which the author had shown how such interpretive activity had been successfully carried on.

Hoffmann exposed a series of falsifications in Justus's *Judenspiegel* and compiled a genuine "mirror of Judaism,"

in 111 paragraphs, to show the real attitude of the Jewish
authorities towards the relationship of the Jews to their
Christian neighbors. He laid as much emphasis on this
positive side as on the criticism of the errors of his opponents. One of the main points of contention was the claim
that the term *Akum*, an abbreviation for "those who wor-
ship the stars and the zodiac," always refers to Christians, since, in one instance, an "akum with a cross"
occurs.

Against this charge, Hoffmann showed that the term
Akum was created by Christian censorship and introduced,
in the sixteenth century, by a convert who compiled a
Canon Purificationis for Hebrew books. It is never found in
the earliest editions of the *Shulhan Aruk* published during
its author's lifetime, and thus the "akum with the
cross" is an evidence of the ignorance and thoughtless-
ness of Christian censors, not of the intolerance of the
Jews.

At the age of 70, Hoffmann was called upon to write
an opinion for the court concerning the blasphemies in a
bitter attack against the God of the Jews by another in-
famous antisemite, Theodor Fritzsche. For several months,
he worked day and night, often till three in the morning,
on his very elaborate expert opinion of which only a few
chapters have been published. The Leipzig court, having
received five such opinions from Jewish and Christian
scholars which partly contradicted one another, turned
them over to Professor Rudolf Kittel, who was to render
a final recommendation to the court. Kittel did not have
the unbiased attitude of a Kuenen and, by an artificial
construction, differentiated between the God of the Pentateuch and that worshipped by Jews and Christians at
present. In additional notes to some of the published parts
of his own opinion, Hoffmann called attention to the
prejudiced and one-sided interpretations which had caused

Kittel's criticism of his statements. Written on the eve of World War I, this case was a prelude to the "new" Germany that was to arise two decades later.

Hoffmann's activities in fighting antisemitism were of great practical value and made the name of the retiring scholar known among wider circles; nevertheless, they did not play a large part in his life. The same applies to his polemics against Reform. Reviewing a voluminous work, *The Dietary Laws*, by Rabbi A. Wiener, Hoffmann wrote a series of twelve articles in the *Jüdische Presse* in 1895 and republished them fifteen years later in revised form in a jubilee volume for an Orthodox rabbi, since the subject had retained its relevancy. Wiener had absolutely denied the validity of the Oral Law and Hoffmann took the opportunity to formulate the arguments for the authority and authenticity of the *Torah she-be'al Pe*. He traced the descent of the theories of the modern ̄Reform rabbi to those of the ancient sect of the Sadducees and later the Karaites and describes it as a neo-Sadducean attitude. He was mainly concerned with the fundamental principles involved and devoted little space to errors in detail. This paper is perhaps the best formulation and defense of the traditional point of view in respect to the Oral Law.

Another controversy in which Hoffmann took part concerned a new Reform prayer book by the *Oberrat der Israeliten* of Baden, the official representative body of the Jews of that duchy. This prayer book had caused an uproar among the traditional Jews of Baden, and their indignation decided the *Oberrat* to publish a lengthy memorial in defense of the changes made in the ancient Jewish prayer book. The defense was prepared by one of its members, Dr. Steckelmacher.

At the request of the Society for the Preservation of Traditional Judaism in Baden, Hoffmann wrote an "Epistle" addressed to this Society, to enlighten them about the reform of the *siddur*. After some general remarks, he turned to the important points of dogma with which the new edition had tampered: the omission of the laws of sacrifice, the dogma of resurrection, and the messianic hopes and the promise of the restoration of Israel.

The tone of these controversial treatises which deal with the fundamental attitude towards the great principles of traditional Judaism, so close to the writer's heart, is, as can be readily understood, quite sharp though always dignified. But the arguments are clearly formulated so as to strengthen the adherents of Jewish tradition in their views. They are important contributions to the controversies between Reform and Orthodoxy and naturally give evidence of the great learning and the mature thought of Orthodoxy's outstanding leader.

Hoffmann considered the subjects important enough to interrupt his scholarly work for their sake in order to raise his voice against those who endeavored to destroy the principles which he had spent his whole life upholding and instilling into the minds of his pupils. His works in this field of Jewish polemics show the scholar in his relation to the religious life of his time; he felt he had to leave his ivory tower to strengthen the adherents of the Torah against those whom he considered its detractors.

Actually, Hoffmann's official duties did not permit him to turn away from the problems of the present. As teacher of Codes at the Seminary and head of the *Bet Din* of the Orthodox community of Berlin, the Adass Yisroel, he had to render religious decisions continually. Besides, the large number of his former students, as well as many scholars in Germany and even in Russia, frequently turned to him, especially in his later years, as the greatest living talmudic authority in Germany. Some of the inquiries of former pupils were very simple and required only brief answers not involving serious study. When, however, complex questions were involved, he would sometimes spend every free minute for weeks looking up all the authorities and studying the matter from the first sources to the latest responsa. In 1892 his oldest son gave him a large folio ledger to preserve such responsa and other results of his research in a more permanent form. He filled four such large volumes — one of which was unfortunately stolen after his death — with answers to legal questions and halakic *derashot* which he delivered twice a year in the synagogue in place of his revered master, Dr. Hildesheimer, and at the opening of every term in the Seminary. He also entered therein critical discussions of talmudic passages and similar matters. He himself did not intend to publish them; but, in his introduction to this collection, he expressed the wish that his son, who had given the impetus for this collection of his *hiddushim* and responsa, would organize and publish the material after his death. He gave the collection the title *Melamed le-Hoil* and wrote a very characteristic preface. He pointed out that the old method of acute discussion of talmudic problems to stimulate the student had its full justification as much as the modern method of critical science. Only very few of those who had abandoned the old-fashioned study of the Talmud and restricted themselves to mere criticism had been successful in their endeavors.

He himself, he wrote, had done much work in critical study of the literary problems of talmudic literature, had published an interpretation of a *seder* of the Mishna and had tried to interpret the Torah scientifically, in the spirit of our tradition; but at the same time, he had always cultivated the love of his youth, the method of his revered teachers, the talmudic *pilpul*. In his discussions of the topics, however, he often combined the older method with critical remarks on the subject. Even if it was customary in *pilpul* to ride roughshod over the laws of logic, there was no harm in that, since there was now greater need than ever to stimulate the students to incisive thinking. This was the more desirable since the study of the Talmud was so neglected, especially in Germany, and the scholarly young Talmudists could find rabbinical positions only in small communities, while the important and large congregations merely looked for a talented speaker, even if he be utterly ignorant.

Hoffmann would enter into his notebook critical remarks, legal responsa and *pilpul*, as each came to hand. He would also copy in it responsa of scholars of the previous generation which he had in his possession. (He entered especially a number of responsa of R. Mendel Kargau, the teacher of his father-in-law, which had come into his hands after the latter's death.) He expressed the hope, again in the introduction mentioned above, that his children and descendants would study these notebooks.

He concludes this statement with a very striking, almost prophetic observation. Most of his other publications were written in German; who could tell whether they would not perish and be forgotten shortly; a Hebrew book, however, would remain and preserve his name for the future. He prays that he be granted life and strength to translate his other works into Hebrew. That would give him the greatest satisfaction. This remarkable statement may have been written in 1892, when its author was forty-eight years old. His son, Moses, began carrying out his wish and in 1926, 1927 and 1932 published a selection of his responsa, including some by Kargau and others, arranged in the order of the *Shulhan Aruk*. The third volume also contains an appendix of scientific notes and remarks on the Talmud and its commentators, clothed equally in the form of responsa, following classical precedent in this respect. But the bulk of this work still remains unpublished.

Hoffmann's responsa deal frequently with problems caused by the modern conditions of life and social changes. They are based on his unusual mastery of the first sources and the opinions of the early authorities, but they are replete with references to the great Talmudists of his own century. His decisions are always well founded and pay proper regard to the spirit of the time and the special situations, but they naturally do so entirely in the traditional spirit. Especially in the third volume, dealing with questions on marriage law, one meets occasional references to the confusion brought into Jewish family life by the Reformers.

It would be out of place here to go into further details, but it may not be without interest to refer to one responsum published by the author himself in German. The question had arisen whether women were to be permitted to participate in elections in the Jewish communities. Hoffmann decided that they may be given the active right to vote, but should be denied the passive right of being elected to the boards of the community. He defended this decision against the objections of a Dutch rabbi who would not permit them to participate in any way, even in an election.

I have endeavored to sketch in broad outline the contributions of Dr. Hoffmann to various fields of Jewish learning. It is impossible to exhaust the subject within the limits of an essay. A glance through the bibliography of his writings included in the *Jubilee Volume* published for his seventieth birthday in 1913 shows a considerable number of articles and reviews dealing with subjects which seem remote from the main fields of his studies. Looking

through the bibliography, we realize the manysidedness of the eminent Talmudist who actually was at home
in almost every branch of Jewish literature. Incidentally,
it may be observed that a few of his reviews were
signed I. T. — *Ish Tikva*, the Hebrew translation of his
name.

In spite of his numerous duties, Hoffmann was the
editor of learned periodicals. In 1876–1893 he published,
together with his friend and colleague, Dr. Berliner, the
Magazin für die Wissenschaft des Judentums and in 1884–1895
the *Israelitische Monatsschrift*, a scholarly monthly supplement to the weekly *Jüdische Presse*. In both he wrote
numerous original contributions and reviews. In the
Magazin he occasionally added comments of his own to
papers of his collaborators, and I know of one instance in
which the contributor resented this to such an extent that
he did not continue his article. On the other hand, the
enthusiasm for Halevy's *Dorot Harishonim* induced a later
editor of the *Israelitische Monattsschrift* to add to the first
instalment of Hoffmann's review of that work, the heading
"A Masterpiece"; this heading, which he considered an
exaggeration, did not appear again in the sequel.

To sum up the picture of the life and work of Professor
David Hoffmann, I may state that his was a rarely har-
monious personality. His whole life was a complete unit,
free of dissonance. In spite of early privations and ines-
capable blows of fate, his was a distinctly happy life. A
continuous rise in accomplishment found its end in a peace-
ful death, a *Mitat Neshika*, as our sages call it. His deep-
rooted piety guided him through the severest trials and
he always remained true to himself. His modern method
of scientific thinking and research, and his thorough
acquaintance with the literature of Bible criticism never

interfered with his faith. There was no division between different departments of his mind and soul as we sometimes observe in our days. The old and the new were beautifully blended in him. David Hoffmann may serve as an example of unassuming piety and wholehearted devotion to the cause of Judaism and Jewish learning.

7

Mayer Sulzberger

MAYER SULZBERGER was one of the foremost leaders and one of the most outstanding personalities of American Jewry at the turn of the twentieth century.

Sulzberger was born in Heidelsheim, Baden, June 22, 1843. His father was *hazzan* and teacher in that community. In consequence of the anti-Jewish movement in the wake of the revolution of 1848, in which the Jews of Heidelsheim had had to suffer, the Sulzberger family decided to emigrate to America. Mayer Sulzberger retained a vivid recollection of the events preceding this step, when the cry, *Die Juden müssen aus dem Wald*, and the *Hep! Hep!* of the mob, made life uncertain and when Prussian soldiers who came to suppress the uprising were stationed in his father's house and befriended the children. In 1849, the family came to America and at once settled in Philadelphia. Here the studious youth passed through the public school and the Central High School, from which he graduated in 1859, just after he had reached the age of sixteen. At the same time he received his Hebrew education from his father who laid the foundation for his knowledge of Bible and post-biblical Jewish literature in which he remained deeply interested all his life. Since he was too young to begin his studies for the legal career for which his father had destined him, he spent two years in business, gaining experience and insight which proved invaluable in later life.

In 1862 he entered the law office of Moses A. Dropsie, under whom he studied, and was introduced to the practice of law. He was admitted to the bar in 1865 and, after being associated with Mr. Dropsie for another ten years, opened an office for himself in 1876. He became one of the leading lawyers of Philadelphia, enjoying a very lucrative practice. In 1894, he was elected judge in the Court of Common Pleas on the Republican ticket. When he came up for re-election, in 1904, his reputation was such as to bring about his nomination by both parties without any opposition. He became the President Judge of this court, from which he retired in 1915 at the age of seventy-two. His public career, however, did not end with his retirement. In the last year of his life he was a member of the committee to revise the constitution of the Commonwealth of Pennsylvania. He attended the meetings of that body as far as his health permitted him to do so and threw himself with youthful enthusiasm into this work which greatly appealed to him and engrossed his attention.

The example of his father and the great influence of his revered master and friend, the Reverend Mr. Isaac Leeser, led Sulzberger at an early period to take an active part in the Jewish communal life of his beloved home city which he always refused to leave, however tempting might be the offers made to him at various times to settle elsewhere. It is not my intention to enumerate all the local and national institutions with which Judge Sulzberger was connected, such as the Jewish Hospital in the foundation of which his father had had a most prominent part, the Young Men's Hebrew Association of which he was the first president, the Baron de Hirsch Fund of which he was a trustee from its inception, and many others. When the American Jewish Committee was established, in 1906, it was only natural that Judge Sulzberger, with his wide vision and statesmanship, should be chosen its president, a position he held for several years. In this capacity he addressed the Committee on Foreign Affairs of the United States House of Representatives on the question of the Russian passport in a memorable speech which had much to do with the success of the movement to abrogate the Russian treaty.

While every institution could count on his wholehearted support and cooperation, his efforts were largely concentrated on the furtherance of Jewish education. He was secretary of the Maimonides College (the first rabbinical college in this country), took a leading part in the reorganization of the Jewish Theological Seminary, was trustee of Gratz College and of Dropsie College. His inspiration was potent in all these institutions of learning.

His personal influence was most pronounced in the Jewish Publication Society where, as chairman of the Publication Committee, he more than anybody else helped to shape its policies. He was to a large extent responsible for the splendid work this Society has done.

When the American Jewish Historical Society was founded, Judge Sulzberger naturally was one of the original members and from the second year of its existence until his death belonged to its council. He contributed to its sixth meeting a paper on Jacob Henry and the Gratz family, probably based on the interesting collection of Judeo-German letters which he presented in 1915 to the Historical Society. While this paper was not published, he contributed to the *Publications* of that Society an admirable necrology on his friend, Joseph Jacobs, with a fine appreciation and a full bibliography of his many-sided literary activities. Another necrology he devoted to his lifelong associate in public activities, William B. Hackenburg. His deep interest in the Historical Society, however, cannot by any means be gauged by these few contributions; it was due to the fact that he fully realized the enormous importance of a careful study of the history of the Jews in our own country based on the original sources.

Sulzberger's literary activity began with his collaboration in Leeser's *Occident*, to which he contributed, among other things, a partial translation of Maimonides' *Guide of the Perplexed* and of de Rossi's dictionary of Jewish authors. True to a promise made to his dying teacher, he edited this periodical for one year after Leeser's death. The wide range and great significance of the articles which he himself contributed to this volume have been pointed out in Dr. Solomon Solis-Cohen's remarkable address delivered at the memorial meeting and included in his volume, *Judaism and Science*. In that address copious extracts from these articles are given. It is to be hoped that a collective volume will make these and some other papers of the brilliant judge more accessible. Unfortunately, their number is not very large, since his very active life gave Sulzberger but scant leisure for literary work. They consist mostly of public addresses which this master-orator was called upon to deliver. In many instances, however, he spoke extemporaneously, since he could offer original ideas on any subject in the attractive garb of the choicest English. As Joseph Jacobs once remarked, he never met a man with as rich an English vocabulary at his command as Mayer Sulzberger. While he wrote little, he was an omnivorous reader in various languages and on the greatest variety of subjects. It is interesting to come across an article of his in the *Revue des Etudes Juives* occasioned by a paper of Bacher on a passage of the Midrash. From an out-of-the-way book on the Jews of China, Sulzberger throws new light on the passage in question. Similarly, we learn from an article by Brann, in the *Monatsschrift*, on the descendants of Maimonides, that Sulzberger sent him additional information from a manuscript in his possession correcting some of Brann's statements. We thus get an idea of the attention with which he followed even the publications of the technical journals of Jewish learning in which one might hardly have expected him to be interested.

How vitally he was concerned with Jewish studies became

evident when, in the last two decades of his life, he special-
ized in an independent and very original study of various
aspects of biblical antiquities. Four most stimulating
volumes are the result of this labor of love: *The Am-Haarez,
the Ancient Hebrew Parliament, a chapter in the constitutional
history of Ancient Israel* (Philadelphia, 1909); *The Polity of
the Ancient Hebrews* (ibid.,1912); *The Ancient Hebrew Law of
Homicide* (ibid., 1915); and *The Status of Labor in Ancient
Israel* (ibid., 1923). In these books he considered difficult
problems of biblical law and constitution from a new angle.
He brought the keen mind of the expert lawyer and experienced statesman to bear on these questions. He cross-
examined his texts as he was wont to do with his witnesses
in his legal practice and read between the lines as he did
with the evidence in court proceedings. His results are
often striking and surprising and reveal to us the unusual
mental equipment and the penetrating method of the
author. They manifest a vigor and freshness of mind which
would never permit the reader to suspect the age of the
writer.

While his own learned writings mainly date from the
later years of his life, he always was eager to stimulate and
encourage all Jewish scholarly work, particularly in this
country. He realized at an early period that for a healthy
development of Jewish scholarship in America a great
library was indispensable. He therefore began to bring
together a most remarkable collection of rare books and
manuscripts, which became the nucleus of the present
Library of the Jewish Theological Seminary. He directly
and indirectly influenced the growth of Jewish libraries of
other institutions, especially that of the Dropsie College,
so that he may rightly be called the father of Jewish
libraries in this country. He presented his splendid law
library to his court when he resigned from the bench.

Judge Sulzberger's long and active life left a rich harvest

which the coming generations of American Jewry will gather. His powerful personality and his mighty intellect left a strong impress not only on his home community but on the whole of American Jewry. He always upheld traditional Judaism as transmitted to him by his father and his teacher, Isaac Leeser. He lent his voice to the oppressed and always stood for justice tempered by mercy, for he had uncommon insight into human nature and could find the good in every human being. His rare sense of humor illuminated his speech and the sparkle of his wit made every conversation with him a delight. With the quickness of a flash he could grasp any problem and throw new light on it from the rich store of his knowledge and his experience. He was fully alive to the advance of modern civilization, but at the same time extremely conservative in his personal habits. It is curious, for example, that this extremely busy man always wrote his letters and papers and even the preliminary material for his books in longhand, not even availing himself of the convenience of a fountain pen. His beautiful library was a Mecca for many visitors in the most varied walks of life.

It was touching to observe how patiently he often listened to the abstruse exposition of some scholar from Eastern Europe who might be uncouth in appearance as well as in method of argumentation. Sulzberger's broadmindedness was one of his outstanding characteristics.

He died in Philadelphia on April 20, 1923. To those of us who were privileged to come into closer association with him and to enjoy his personal friendship, the memory of Judge Sulzberger's radiant personality will forever remain a source of inspiration.

8

Solomon Schechter

A REMARK once made by Adolf Jellinek to an English
visitor, that the date of Schechter's arrival in England should be marked as epoch-making for Jewish
learning in that country, applies with even greater force to
his arrival in America. Here, however, his activity and influence were not limited to the fields of scholarship. A
brilliant exponent of Historical Judaism, he gave it a powerful impetus in this country by the school he established and
greatly extended its influence. Only a later generation
will be able to gauge objectively the degree to which
Schechter's conception of Judaism has moulded American
Jewish life.

Solomon Schechter was born in Focsani, Roumania,
probably in December (ר"ח טבת), 1850. He received his
early education from his father, who had emigrated from
Lukasch, Russia, and exercised the function of a *shohet* in
Focsani. Dr. Schechter was fond of speaking of this
self-denying, saintly and scholarly man. The respect he
felt for him proved a blessing to the son even in the
periods of greatest storm and stress. He felt that it was his
father's influence which had kept him within the fold of
conservative Judaism.

The unusually gifted boy, who learned to read Hebrew
at the age of three and knew the Pentateuch at five, was to
devote his life from his early youth to the study of the Torah.
At the age of ten he began to attend the *yeshiva* in Piatra, a
nearby town, and when about thirteen years old he was
sent to one of the greatest talmudic authorities of the time,
R. Joseph Saul Nathanson, of Lemberg. After a year of

assiduous study, he returned home with a highly compli-
mentary certificate from his great teacher for his zeal and
for the originality displayed in his studies, the more remarkable when we consider the boy's age. In 1875, he went to
Vienna. His first contact with European culture naturally
made a very deep impression on the mind of the young
Talmudist. The upheaval which such contacts produce
in young men of this type may be observed even at the
present time. It is impossible to estimate how great a loss
Judaism is suffering through the numerous defections from
its ranks caused by the sudden removal of its most gifted
sons from the Eastern ghetto into the university life of the
West. It requires great inner strength to withstand the
influence of the new surroundings and to continue to value
the heritage of the Jewish past so little esteemed in those
circles.

Schechter ascribed his escape from the dangers of the new
environment to his respect for his father and to the friendship of two men in Vienna, Adolf Jellinek and particularly
Meir Friedmann. Jellinek recognized at once the unusual
gifts of the new arrival and did everything in his power to
help him in his struggle for a living. He charged him with
cataloguing his library and procured stipends for him.
What was even more appreciated, he favored him with his
personal friendship; Schechter never forgot the stimulating
discussions carried on with him during long walks through
the streets of Vienna. One of the prize essays, "The Library
of R. Bezallel Ashkenazi, traced from his Responsa and his
Novellae," announced by Dr. Schechter for the students of
the Jewish Theological Seminary for the scholastic year
1915–1916, goes back to a suggestion received from Jellinek
at that time. During his stay in Vienna, Schechter was a
regular pupil of the *Beth ha-Midrash*, a modernized talmud-
ical high school in which Jellinek took great interest. Here
he enjoyed the instruction of Meir Friedmann and Isaac

Hirsch Weiss, the two scholars who, in different ways, showed a happy blending of old-time talmudic scholarship with modern methods. Weiss, who had devoted himself to the presentation of the historical development of the halaka or, rather, the halakists, wished his pupil to follow in his footsteps; but it was Friedmann, with his lovable personality and depth of feeling, who gained the deeper influence over Schechter. Friedmann had shown his mastery in his editions of the oldest midrashim and their interpretation in the true spirit of their authors. As a teacher of Midrash he was unsurpassed. Along this line Schechter followed him in his first great book, to the displeasure of Weiss, who did not fully appreciate the value of such editorial work and whose own editions were therefore not his highest accomplishments. Friedmann, who entrusted the instruction of his sons to Schechter, was, I think, in Schechter's own opinion, the man who had exercised the greatest influence on him, and Schechter always remained fondly attached to him. From Weiss, who liked to exercise rabbinical functions, from which Friedmann refrained, Schechter received the rabbinical diploma when he left Vienna for Germany, in 1879. The document bears testimony, not only to Schechter's unusual acquaintance with Bible, Talmud and Midrash, as well as later Jewish literature, but also refers expressly to his high moral character, which shrank from all hypocrisy and disdained all sham.

His old friends accompanied Schechter with their good wishes and their fatherly care. I had the opportunity to read a touching letter written by Weiss in answer to the first letter his pupil sent him from his new place of residence. A father could hardly have shown more solicitude for the welfare of his son than this master displayed for his pupil. He expected him to make new friends easily, for Schechter had always possessed this gift. But he advised him particularly to cultivate the friendship of Dr. P. F. Frankl, whose

acceptance of the rabbinate of the Berlin community had
been the real reason for Schechter's leaving Vienna. Since
he had followed this old friend to his new sphere of activity,
Schechter needed no advice on that score; his deep feeling
of friendship for Frankl did not end even with the latter's
death.

In Berlin, Schechter came in contact with all the great
scholars of the city. The only one who had a lasting influence on him was Israel Lewy, one of the foremost talmudic
critics, whose method he followed in the introduction to
his *Abot de-Rabbi Nathan.* He also enjoyed the instruction
of the great Steinschneider and, although in later years he
showed a certain aversion to bibliographical research of
which Steinschneider was the foremost exponent, he
expressed his indebtedness to the great bibliographer in his
first article in the *Beth Talmud* and paid him a fine tribute
in his *Seminary Addresses.*

Due to his friend Frankl, Schechter's years of study were
brought to a close and he began to make use of the enormous store of learning he had accumulated. In 1882, Claude
G. Montefiore, who was studying in Berlin, wished to continue in England the studies he had auspiciously started in
Germany. Strangely enough, it was not possible to find a
proper teacher in the country that harbors the greatest
treasures of the Jewish past. It was necessary to import one,
and at Frankl's recommendation of Schechter as the man he
was looking for, Montefiore invited him to go with him to
England. Thus Schechter joined the small band of Jewish
scholars that had immigrated to England — Adolf Neubauer, Michael Friedlaender, and S. M. Schiller-Szinessy
— and soon secured access to the wonderful collections of
the British Museum. Of these he had heard legends current
in his native place, as he tells us in the first volume of his
Studies in Judaism. His studies had only sharpened his
curiosity about them. To his rambles among the manu-

scripts of the Museum and the Bodleian Library we owe the discovery of Saadia's commentary on the rules of interpretation and the testaments of the two sons of Rabbi Asher ben Yehiel which strongly appealed to a mind like Schechter's who was constantly seeking the soul in the scholar.

In London, Schechter finished his first great book, an exhaustive edition of the *Abot de-Rabbi Nathan*, an important and interesting talmudic book of ethical content, which was included in all the Talmud editions but the text of which had suffered very much at the hands of ignorant copyists. Here for the first time a Hebrew text was published on the basis of all extant manuscripts and with the painstaking conscientiousness one was used to see applied to Greek and Latin texts but which was almost a *novum in Hebraicis*. The learned author had discovered a second version of the book and he published this for the first time side by side with the well-known text. He had read through numberless volumes, both in print and in manuscript, to collect quotations which in some way might help to elucidate the difficulties of the text, and all the wealth of his own knowledge and acumen were brought to bear on the interpretation of the book. Even after text and commentary were printed, the author was not yet satisfied; he continued his labors, the results of which he incorporated into appendices. The publication of this volume, in 1887, put Schechter in the front rank of Jewish scholars, and for over fifty years *Abot de-Rabbi Nathan* has been quoted only according to Schechter's edition (which recently was republished in New York).

In the same year his essay on "The Chassidim" appeared, translated by Montefiore from the German original. Many years later it was retranslated into German and from that into Roumanian. For the first time, a sympathetic picture of the Hasidic movement had been painted showing the underlying beauty of many of its teachings as well as the idealism of its founders and early representatives. The essay marked an epoch in Schechter's development. He had now entirely passed his *Sturm und Drangperiode* and could do justice to the associations of his early youth, which on his first contact with Western life had become so repulsive to him. As a matter of fact, the respect for his father, a devoted adherent of Hasidism, had much to do with this defense of the movement. Ten years earlier, under the fresh influence of the great change he had undergone, Schechter had published a biting and very clever satire on hasidic life in the form of letters by Hasidim. This first article of Schechter's, written in Hebrew, had appeared in a periodical anonymously, but he always felt that he owed an apology to his father for having ridiculed what the latter held in such veneration. The result was the essay on the Hasidim which now appears as the first of his "Studies."

In London Schechter for a time was connected with Jews' College, at that time under the presidency of Dr. Michael Friedlaender, one of the most modest and saintly of Jewish scholars who always manifested the warmest friendship for Schechter. In his house Schechter also met Mathilde Roth, who, as his wife, was to exercise so great an influence on his life, and without whose constant and unselfish care, which removed every obstacle from his path at the cost of the greatest personal sacrifices, he never could have done his work as he did.

That he did not neglect the primary object of his coming to England was testified to abundantly by Montefiore, in 1892, in the introduction to his Hibbert Lectures, his first important scientific publication. In 1890, Schechter was appointed Lecturer in Rabbinics at Cambridge University, and here his influence soon asserted itself, not only among the Jewish students, who always were welcome and felt at home in his house, but also in the circle of the Cambridge scholars, whatever their specialty. Here he became the intimate friend of the famous folklorist, Sir James George Frazer, of W. W. Buckland, the Regius Professor of Law, of the Icelandic scholar Eiriker Magnusson, and many others who found it profitable to discuss with him complicated questions connected with their own subjects. These ties of friendship persisted even after Schechter came to the United States. Whenever he returned to England he was greeted with the greatest enthusiasm by his numerous friends.

In 1893 a travelling scholarship enabled Schechter to visit the great Jewish collections of Italy and to gather material in two fields: the history of the biblical canon and the textual criticism of the treatise *Abot* in which he had been interested since his work on *Abot de-Rabbi Nathan* had brought him face to face with its problems. In Cambridge, Dr. Charles Taylor had naturally kindled this interest in the treatise to which he had himself devoted many years of labor. The material on *Abot* collected by Dr. Schechter is being prepared for publication by one of his former pupils, Rabbi Jacob Kohn, whom he had entrusted with this task some time before his death. But his notes dealing with the history of the canon have not been utilized yet. Though he did not, at the outset, exploit the material which attracted him, the Italian trip brought some important literary discoveries in the line of midrashic literature, such as the *Aggadath Shir ha-Shirim*. It is to be hoped that more of the material collected by him may in time become accessible. About the same time, Schechter was engaged in editing a voluminous Midrash on the Pentateuch, which had reached Europe from Yemen a few years previously and which for the first time had been utilized by Schechter to whom Mr. Montefiore had presented a copy of it for his *Abot de-Rabbi Nathan*. His uncommon mastery of the whole of the midrash literature, with its most obscure

quotations, enabled Schechter to discern at once that this
Yemen compilation had made use of many an unknown
midrash and also offered important variations in the texts
of the known books. In 1902, after ten years' work, the
first volume of the *Midrash ha-Gadol* appeared, on the eve
of the editor's departure to the United States. The notes
and references to this interesting book show once more the
master of Midrash, who could trace the great majority of
the sources of the compiler even though the latter had
combined the various texts into a more or less continuous
work without any mention of the origin of the sentences.
As Schechter states in the preface, he had read the proofs of
this volume partly in some German city, partly in Rome,
in Cairo, and in Jerusalem; that is to say, not only the visit
to the Italian libraries had fallen into the period of printing
this Midrash, but also the great turning point in his life —
the discovery of the *Geniza*.

The existence of the *Geniza* at Cairo had been known
before, and from time to time dealers in antiquities had
stealthily abstracted old parchments from their centuries-
old resting place and sold them to European or American
collectors and tourists. Dr. Schechter himself told me the
story of his visit to his friends, Mrs. Lewis and Mrs. Gibson,
who had just returned from a trip to the East and showed
him some old Hebrew leaves which the learned ladies had
acquired on their journey. One of these leaves attracted
his special attention, and he at once conceived the idea that
it contained a piece of the original of Ben Sira, in which he
had long been especially interested, as is shown by an
article published a few years previously, enumerating all
the Hebrew quotations from this book occurring in Jewish
literature. To test the correctness of his idea he had to go
home, for the ladies, being strict Presbyterians, had no copy
of the Apocrypha in their house. I need not dwell on the

universal stir produced by the discovery of the original of
the book looked upon as part of the Bible by the Christian
world. It had a sequel quite unique in the annals of Jewish
science. Dr. Schechter was enabled — not through Jewish
liberality, it should be added parenthetically — to start
immediately for Egypt in order to search the *Geniza* at first
hand for further parts of Ben Sira. With his wonderfully
magnetic personality, he succeeded far beyond all expec-
tation and was permitted by the Jewish community of
Cairo to take with him all the treasures he unearthed.
Together with Dr. Taylor, who had made it possible for
Dr. Schechter to go to Egypt, he presented the priceless
treasures to the university whose teaching staff he adorned.
From that time on his scientific activity was centered on
the fragments he had discovered. One must have seen him
in the midst of these dusty, crumpled bits of paper to
realize fully the amount of learning and quickness of
perception required to separate documents of one class
from another and bring some kind of order into that chaos.
It may be said without exaggeration that hardly any other
single scholar has enlarged our knowledge of our past to the
same degree as Dr. Schechter. He has changed our entire
view of conditions in Babylonia, Palestine and Egypt in the
tenth and eleventh centuries. Various *Geniza* publications
in the *Jewish Quarterly Review*, his *Saadyana* and other writings will always remain first-class sources of Jewish history.
By no stretch of the imagination can the importance of the
discovery of the *Geniza* be overestimated or the further
discoveries be foretold that may be made in this collection
which, unfortunately, but for casual visits of foreign scholars, has been lying idle since Dr. Schechter left Cambridge.

Besides his volume of Ben Sira, published in collaboration
with Taylor, the publication of the *Documents of Jewish
Sectaries* has made the greatest impression. The former
brought him public recognition in the professorship of

Hebrew at the University of London, without his application for the post, and in the honorary Doctor's degree by Cambridge University; the second was similarly recognized by Harvard. It is characteristic of Schechter, and deserves the greatest credit, that he at once recognized the importance of this puzzling and enigmatical sectarian text which, in so rich a collection of unknown fragments, would have been neglected by almost every other scholar.

Between the two publications, a most important change had taken place in Schechter's life. He had given up the pleasant associations, the intimate friendships, and the quiet life of Cambridge University, to devote his great powers to his own people. The change was largely prompted also by the desire to bring up his children in Jewish surroundings. It was mainly through the efforts of some of the most farsighted leaders of American Jewry that Dr. Schechter was invited to take charge of the reorganized Jewish Theological Seminary. Having come to New York on April 17, 1902, he threw himself into his work with all his youthful enthusiasm, with all the resources of his rich personality. The Seminary became the center of all his thoughts; he absolutely identified himself with it to the exclusion of anything else and looked at every question from the angle of the Seminary. How would this or that fact or action influence the institution to which his loyalty so completely belonged, was the test he constantly applied. And the thought of it occupied him not only in office hours or during the scholastic term; it accompanied him on his vacations and on his travels; it even took precedence over his scientific work. Outside of the terrible world war, from which he suffered mental agonies, nothing gave him so much concern as the many problems connected with the maintenance of the institution the building up of which he considered the crowning achievement of his life.

Rabbinic Theology was one of the favorite subjects taught by Doctor Schechter at the Seminary, while formerly it had received but scant attention in similar institutions. I cannot speak from personal knowledge about Dr. Schechter as a teacher, but I know how carefully he prepared all his lectures, how much conscientious labor he bestowed upon them. For him lectures were on a plane with his literary activity; his scientific conscience would not permit him to discuss a topic in the classroom unless he had satisfied himself that he had covered all the sources on the subject. This does not of course mean that he would incorporate them all in his lectures. Only the results of his researches were put before the students. I often saw him going over the entire haggadic literature in order to mark the passages dealing with a theological point he was going to take up with his class. These passages he then had copied out and put on large sheets. He studied this source material with the greatest care to select the most important and striking passages and to bring the whole into systematic order. In the same way he went through the talmudic passages and the entire bodies of codes and all the different rites for his lectures on liturgy.

Painstaking accuracy was one of Dr. Schechter's characteristics. While his deep erudition and his marvelous memory would have enabled him to speak on many subjects with very little preparation, while his brilliancy would have allowed him to hold the attention of his students — and to instruct them — under all circumstances, he would rather not lecture at all than speak without what he considered adequate preparation. And yet I fancy that it was not so much the solid foundation of all his statements but the way he expressed them, the remarkable personality of the master, which so strongly influenced his pupils and made an everlasting impression on all those who came under his sway. He never tried to show off by artificially

swelling the number of his references and by dragging in
learned notes. His ideal was to convert the results of his
painstaking investigation into clear and easy language,
obliterating even in his lectures as much as possible the
labor which had preceded the writing. This accuracy he
wished to implant in his pupils as well, and he always used
to recommend that the beginner start by editing a text,
for in such work the most minute exactness is required and
thus an excellent schooling is given for scientific work.

As a teacher Dr. Schechter had gained a great deal of
experience in Cambridge, where it often was his task to
introduce Christian theologians with inadequate preparation into the mysteries of rabbinic literature. There he had
had occasion to find out how matters, which to most teachers might seem too evident to require commenting upon,
were causing considerable trouble to some of the students.
As a result of his Cambridge experience, Dr. Schechter had
learned to have consideration even for the ignorant beginners, and he often showed much more patience with them
than one might have expected from a scholar of his eminence and temper.

He was free of scholarly haugntiness and would give his
friendship to men of affairs as readily as to the learned, but
his objection to sham culture and education was inveterate.
He had no use for what he called the "encyclopedic ignorance" of the "highly uneducated" who tried to impress
people with their superficial knowledge. In the Seminary
he used every occasion to emphasize the need of thorough
Jewish learning for the rabbi and he looked forward, to use
his own words, to the time when even in this country we
would have a sprinkling at least of learned men among our
rabbis who would now and then favor us with real contributions to scholarship. That this was not the only aim of
rabbinical training he fully realized, and many of the
Seminary's alumni can testify to the warm personal interest

he took in the success of their practical duties. But he felt that the limited time at his disposal was needed to give his pupils a Jewish scientific foundation on which they could build afterwards, while the experience of life would teach them the rest. The Seminary therefore had to underscore the vital importance of scholarly attainments and to raise the standard of Jewish knowledge.

Dr. Schechter's relations to his pupils were by no means limited to the classroom. He took a genuine interest in their well being and did his best to free them from material cares. He always liked to see them in his home and was ready to listen to their troubles and wishes. Through that especial gift of his to make friends with the young and his remarkable understanding of youth with its advantages and shortcomings, there developed a beautiful attitude of real friendship between him and some of his pupils which started in their student days and continued ever after. There were many who looked up to him as to a father and, like a father, he was always ready to take a charitable view of the students and to let mercy prevail over justice. When a student had given serious cause for complaint, Dr. Schechter often took his side and tried to excuse him. It was very hard for him to be rigorous and usually he decided at the last moment to be lenient once more. The students appreciated his great kindness and reciprocated with love and admiration, and even after they had left the Seminary they always turned to him for help and advice in the difficulties which confronted them in their communal work.

In his activity in this country Dr. Schechter combined to an astonishing degree true scholarship and wholehearted interest in practical Judaism. If we look upon his work as a whole, we find that it was eminently constructive. He was very clever in polemics, and a happy phrase was always at his disposal in writing, as it was in his conversation. Dr. Schechter rightly maintained that the best apology for

Judaism was a clear historical analysis of its teachings, and he never thought that much good could be accomplished by controversial pamphlets. When a book or an utterance annoyed him, he was wont to sit down and write a review or an answer in caustic style and full of irony; but later he would revise it again and again until all polemical bitterness would be removed, or else he would suppress it altogether. Thus I know of two reviews of his, one of which was already set up in type, which he withheld from publication after having come in personal contact with the authors whose books he had reviewed. With his broad sympathies he could understand the other side, if he wanted to, and he did not wish to jeopardize his activities by personal controversies to which such criticism might have led.

In his masterly *Aspects of Rabbinic Theology*, he carefully abstained from refuting or even mentioning the innumerable false conceptions set forth by Jewish and non-Jewish writers as teachings of the rabbis. His book, with its clear exposition of the rabbinic views of various theological concepts, is certainly the more effective for it. Of his literary activity, his *Studies in Judaism* and his *Aspects of Rabbinic Theology* made him well known to the educated public. He shows in these works a wonderful combination of most thorough scientific research with an admirably lucid presentation, in a style entirely his own, which nowhere suggests to the reader that the author not only was not born an Englishman but became acquainted with English as a mature man. The casual reader cannot surmise what painstaking work lies behind the elegant, characteristic sentences, or what untiring research was required to establish the facts offered to the public without claim to original investigation, with the air almost that they may be found in any handbook. I shall never forget the number of books he consulted for the essay on Safed, the responsa volumes searched from cover to cover for some stray reference that might possibly occur there, but often did not, and his happiness in finding the statutes of the Safed saints in a newly-acquired manuscript of the Seminary Library. Dr. Schechter, like no other modern Jewish scholar, could put his own rich personality in the place of the mediaeval author who attracted his interest, be he a Talmudist pure and simple, a "liberal" philosopher, or, *horribile dictu,* a cabalist. For him the rationalistic prejudice against the mystic did not exist. A man did not need the excuse that he had, besides cabalistic writings, also a medical or mathematical work to his credit. It is largely due to Dr. Schechter that historical justice has been done to the Jewish saints and mystics of the Middle Ages.

It would be entirely wrong to consider Dr. Schechter a dry scholar who spent his time among his books, removed from the questions of the day. Although in England, in his official activity, he was out of direct touch with the affairs of the community, his interest in all matters Jewish was very strong. In accordance with his nature, he was in opposition to the ruling powers in Jewry. Opposition to the customary and the mechanical routine of organization with its deadening effects was one of his characteristic traits. His "Epistles to the Jews of England" manifest his interest in that Jewry. In America his position brought him face to face with the problems of our time and compelled him to address the public regularly at the commencements of the Seminary, occasions which a man like Schechter would naturally utilize to give expression to his own views on the burning questions of the day in his characteristic fashion. By a stroke of good fortune, he himself, a few months before his death, carried out a plan that had occupied him since the end of the first decade after the reorganization of the Seminary—that of publishing a collection of his *Seminary Addresses and Other Papers,* giving permanent form to the addresses he had prepared with infinite care and setting forth his views on the most important problems of present-day Jewry. The volume, ending with his last public address, therefore is of great value for an understanding of the ideas for which he had assiduously labored.

In characterizing Schechter's scientific work, one finds great difficulty in stating which branch was his specialty. The progress of biblical science he had always followed with keen interest, if frequently with serious doubts as to the correctness of the results accepted by the modern school. He had occasion but rarely to occupy himself with these questions in his books, but the introduction to his *Ben Sira* registers his protest against the prevailing school of thought and offers documentary evidence. Such evidence — again characteristic of our time — has been taken into consideration by non-Jewish scholars abroad, while most Jewish scholars fight shy of biblical studies.

Schechter had been, since his early youth, a master of talmudic studies and for many years taught the Palestinian Talmud in the Seminary. His last two years were devoted to the preparation of an exhaustive treatise on Jewish charities, a subject with which he was better equipped to deal than anyone else. (Alas, it was not destined to be written by him!) He intended to give special attention to the halakic aspects of Jewish philanthropy. He was occupied in the last weeks of his life with reviewing the relevant talmudic passages and the early commentaries upon them. The enactment passed in the middle of the second century by the rabbinic authorities at Usha concerning tithes, of which the Babylonian and the Palestinian Talmuds give diametrically different accounts, was the last scientific subject he discussed with me. He kept track of the modern scientific literature on talmudic subjects and complained, shortly before his death, that a recent dissertation on the

laws of *Hazaka*, a new acquisition of the Seminary library,
had not been brought to his attention. His article, "Talmud," in the extra volume of Hasting's *Dictionary of the
Bible* may be mentioned in this connection as a masterpiece
of lucid presentation of a difficult subject.

To liturgy also he refers only rarely in his publications
outside of his treatment of its theological aspects. Nevertheless, he was very deeply interested in this branch of
Jewish study, lectured on it in the Seminary and intended
to write a comprehensive review of all the recent publications in this field.

I have spoken already of his marvelous acquaintance
with the whole midrashic literature. If the discovery of the
Geniza had not intervened, Dr. Schechter would probably
have finished the edition of the five volumes of the *Midrash
ha-Gadol* and would have contributed much to the study of
the history of that branch of literature.

While his work on theology has always attracted great
interest, Schechter himself had to be urged by outsiders to
put his material on the subject into shape. His clear
insight into the theological concepts of the rabbis has always
been admired, but somehow Schechter seemed to prefer to
devote his leisure to other matters. Still, the reception
accorded to his *Aspects* made him think of a second volume
for the discussion of some other problems of rabbinic
theology, but the plan never went beyond his casual
thought.

What made him most popular were his historical or, to
be more definite, his biographical essays. He possessed the
remarkable ability of putting before the reader the historical setting as a frame for the picture drawn by him with
incomparable skill. It made no difference whether he
wished to portray an individual or a body of scholars or
saints. It is very much to be regretted that we do not have
more of these masterly sketches from the hand of this

literary artist, which incidentally throw much light on the conditions prevailing in various periods. His interest in Jewish history was most comprehensive; perhaps he was more attracted by the pious Jews of mediaeval Germany than by those of Spain with their secular culture. He took very little interest in the Jewish Historical Society of England, objecting to "provincial Judaism" on principle, and he was very glad when the American Jewish Historical Society, whose corresponding member he was since 1896, widened its scope to include the whole of Jewish history.

Dr. Schechter's great interest in the questions of practical Jewish life was most clearly evidenced in the establishment of the United Synagogue and the immense importance attributed to it by its founder. "This will be the greatest bequest which I shall leave to American Israel," he wrote to Dr. Cyrus Adler years before his idea was translated into action. To this institution he devoted his wholehearted interest and solicitude in the last years of his life, for in the United Synagogue he saw a powerful instrument for the propagation and perpetuation of historical Judaism, of which he was the foremost exponent in this country.

He worked all his life for the ideal of Conservative Judaism. His ideal found expression in the phrase "Catholic Israel" which he coined, representing Jewish traditions as they had developed from Sinai to the present day. This position of Dr. Schechter's was the result of his scientific conviction as well as of his fervent religiosity. The latter found striking expression when Dr. Schechter took the place of the *Ba'al Tefillah* to read the *Neilah* prayer in the Seminary synagogue. All those present could feel the religious enthusiasm of his soul as he recited his favorite prayers and everyone was under his spell as he stood there before us. He was very fond of the tune of *Neilah* and he liked to sing the *Yisgadal* in that *niggun* all year round when he was in a particularly happy mood. An interesting selection indeed for a favorite song! Perhaps this was somewhat akin to his unusual understanding of the mediaeval mystics and the Hasidim who found in him so warm a defender and expounder.

The aim which Dr. Schechter had put before himself for his old age was to settle in Palestine and to devote his last years to a quiet life in the land of our forefathers, occupying himself again mainly with talmudic studies to which his youth had been given. This was by no means the result of his Zionist affiliations; he had discussed this plan with his fiancée before his marriage and always liked to think of it. For a man with such an ideal it was only natural to join a movement which tended towards the re-establishment of a home for our people in Eretz Yisrael; but with him it was very much a religious matter, as he clearly pointed out in his statement when he publicly declared his allegiance to Zionism.

In conclusion, a few words must be said about Schechter the man who, "higher than any of the people from the shoulder and upward," attracted attention in any gathering in which he appeared. His striking head, with the beautiful blue eyes which looked so straight and piercingly at everybody, expressed the man's personality. His magnetism, his happy flashes of humor, brought everyone under his spell. The brilliant expressions of his genius, uttered as unexpectedly as lightning, often made his friends wish for a Boswell to collect his utterances. His breadth of mind made possible a circle of friends and admirers unusually large and diversified. Nothing was foreign to the interests of this man, who had read the masterpieces of every literature but did not refrain from indulging freely in the lighter novel to rest his mind. When his interest in a subject was roused, he sought all possible information upon it by reading almost everything written on it. For a time Japan was

the center of his reading appetite. In certain phases of
American history he always showed deep interest. He ever
appreciated it if his friends drew his attention to a book
worth reading on the Civil War or on Lincoln; on both
subjects few people have read more extensively than he.
This unusually wide reading enabled him, in writing as in
conversation, to illustrate his statements by apt quotations
from all kinds of sources. He was a master in the use of such
quotations and very fond of them; sometimes he even put
his own words in the mouth of an indefinite somebody. He
found common ground for conversation with everyone, and
it was very touching to observe Dr. Schechter among children. Whatever their age, they all looked to him as a friend
and he made it his business to cultivate their friendship.
Perhaps he always attracted children because he was himself childlike in many respects.

I may be permitted to give a personal reminiscence of
my first meeting with Dr. Schechter, when in 1898 I came
to England as a young student to collate the manuscripts
of a book, *Seder Olam*, in which I understood Dr. Schechter
to be interested. Having with some difficulty made an
appointment with him for a certain Sunday, I came to his
home in Cambridge, a total stranger, without any letter of
introduction, and asked him whether he could give me some
material for the book in question. He told me he had given
up the idea of editing the book, though he had made copies
of some important manuscripts with his own hand and had
begun to write notes on the text. Without hesitation he
presented all his material, the result of considerable work,
to the young stranger of whom he knew nothing. I always
thought this a remarkable expression of generosity, characteristic of his impulsive nature, which would form a predilection or an aversion in a moment and be guided by it
in his actions. In the same measure, he had his prejudices
which he was wont to express in even stronger language

than they were felt. A violent diatribe by Schechter against a person did not preclude his otherwise having great respect for the man's character or abilities. His friends knew how much to deduct when Schechter relieved his feelings by such an explosion. In personal relations he went to extremes; a person was wholly good or wholly bad, he was no friend of lukewarm feelings. If he felt that he had offended a friend, he would try at once to straighten the matter again, and never was Schechter more human than in such moments of reconciliation.

Considering Schechter's life as a whole, we may without hesitation say that it was happy in personal experience as it was in achievements. His sudden, unexpected death (on November 19, 1915), without antecedent suffering which his impetuous temperament could ill have borne, formed a fitting climax.

I have tried to give a few glimpses of this powerful personality; but a writer of quite different gifts is required to do justice to the departed master. I was favored with his intimate friendship for many a year and our relations will always be a cherished and sacred memory to me. To quote one of his old Cambridge friends,

> He was one of the few — the very few — men I have known who were real leaders of thought, enlighteners of the world.

We who were privileged to be his friends could not find a better expression of what we felt when he was taken from us than the words of a lifelong friend, Sir James G. Frazer, of Cambridge, who at the news of his death, wrote, in a private letter, the following tribute to his beloved confrère:

> In him we have lost one of our truest friends and one of the finest and most remarkable men we have ever known. It would be difficult to say whether he was more admirable for the brilliance of his intellect and

the readiness of his wit, or for the warmth of his affection and the generosity and nobility of his character, but I think it was the latter qualities even more than his genius which endeared him to his friends. It was a wonderful combination of intellectual and moral excellence, and the longer and the more intimately one knew him the more deeply did one feel the impression of his greatness and goodness. I reckon it among the good fortunes of my life to have had the privilege and honor of his friendship, and I am sure that very many who knew him must feel as I do. His memory — the memory of his intellectual honesty, his generous enthusiasm for everything that was noble and beautiful, and his unmeasured contempt for everything that was base and ignoble — the memory of this will abide with us and be an inspiration to us to the end of our lives.

9

The Jewish Scholarship of Joseph Jacobs

JOSEPH JACOBS' scholarly gifts were so varied and manifold as to constitute a rare combination in one person. This wonderfully talented man would have been an ornament in a chair of English literature or of folklore at some great university, and it is a pity that circumstances did not permit him to concentrate his unusual abilities in either of these fields. While his greatest powers were shown in the subjects mentioned, I wish to dwell on his achievements in the field of Jewish scholarship in which I am better able to appreciate his merits. To some extent this was only a by-path in the intellectual journeying of the versatile man, but he himself stated in the dedication of his essays that his Jewish studies "have engaged his deepest thought and sincerest feelings."

His interest was chiefly centered in Jewish history, and for several years it was his ambition to write a work on this subject which was to give a picture of the political and social position of the Jews, omitting the literary history which fills so large a place in all our books of this kind. For the purpose of this history, for which he thought he had found the key in the Church legislation of the Middle Ages, Jacobs began to compile, in chronological arrangement, "Annals of Jewish History," which he hoped would be completed and published some day by a pupil of his. Jacobs drew largely on secondary sources, not going back to the originals from lack of time. For, like Neubauer and others, he maintained that there was still so much to be

251

done in the field of Jewish history and literature that it was more important to make the materials accessible rather than spend too much time on minute details. In his historical conception Jacobs was entirely free from all prejudice; at times it even seemed that, in order not to show any Jewish bias, he went too far in his effort to understand and defend the Church and its representatives in their treatment of the Jews.

His most important contributions were in all likelihood in the field of the early history of the English Jews. He had been one of those most active in rousing interest in that subject; he had taken a prominent part in the arrangement of the Anglo-Jewish Historical Exhibition of 1887, for which he and Lucien Wolf compiled a very useful bibliography. For the history down to 1206, his *Jews of Angevin England* offers an almost complete collection of the sources gathered with the greatest industry from printed and, to a considerable extent, from manuscript material. This he made interesting by his ingenious remarks, of which the appendices in particular bear striking evidence. From unpublished sources he also reconstructed the "London Jewry" of the time of the expulsion, tracing by a novel method of his own the location of many of the houses owned at that time by Jews. In the early volumes of the *Jewish Quarterly Review* and the *Transactions of the Jewish Historical Society of England*, many original and stimulating contributions of his are found, and his pioneer work in this field will always be gratefully remembered.

He gave a remarkable exhibition, during his trip through the Spanish archives, of his ability to discover the essential point at a glance and of his working capacity. As the result of twenty-eight working days, he brought back a record of over 1,700 single records and 19 copies of important documents which threw new light on the conditions of the Jews in Spain. These are incorporated in his *Sources of Spanish-*

Jewish History, which remains an indispensable source book even now, after the great addition to our knowledge resulting from the important publications of Fritz Baer.

Jacobs showed in his "Glossary of Jewish Terms," in the *Jewish Yearbooks* he published in London, evidence of his wide reading and his practical sense of what is useful and needed; he never carried out his intention to enlarge and publish it in book form, but the headings are probably all included in the *Jewish Encyclopedia*. Here his wonderful versatility, which enabled him to take up any subject at short notice and present it in a comprehensive, interesting and mostly original form (take for instance his *History of Geographical Discovery*), was of the greatest assistance to him and to the whole undertaking. Not to speak of the archaeological articles in which he had always been interested — he had coined the term institutional archaeology — I will only mention two articles of the last volume which were entirely outside of the sphere of Jacobs' studies. Under "Triennial Cycle" he put before us in a clear form, illustrated by a very clever diagram, the results of Buechler's complicated investigation; under "Typography" he gathered in very small compass a lot of information from various not readily accessible sources, adding some observations of his own, e. g., the statistical tables on the contents of Hebrew literature. I think it was to his work in preparing this article that I owe my acquaintance with Joseph Jacobs which soon grew into a warm friendship.

Statistics was one of Jacobs' pet subjects, and his *Studies in Jewish Statistics, Social, Vital and Anthropometric* was perhaps the first modern effort in this field which dealt with the subject comprehensively in all its different aspects. Various articles in the *Jewish Encyclopedia* and elsewhere contain valuable contributions to this branch of knowledge.

Even in his books on general subjects, Jacobs liked to discuss matters of Jewish interest; thus, in his remarkable introduction to Aesop, one of his best books, he has a chapter on the Indian origin of Proverbs 30, reprinted in his *Studies on Biblical Archaeology*, and one on the fables in the Talmud in which, through the clever change of the last letter, he turns the fables of the *Kobsim* (washermen) into those of the Greek fabulist Kybisses.

We learn from his valuable bibliography, *The Jewish Question*, that he was the author of the famous articles in the *Times*, in January, 1882, for the first time denouncing the Russian persecution of the Jews, which brought about the Mansion House Meeting.

These brief notes are not meant to exhaust the labor of Joseph Jacobs in the field of Judaism; they are only the very inadequate tribute of a friend who had the privilege of close association with Jacobs for the last ten years of his life and who often had occasion to be thankful to him for his ever ready help and advice. For years we used to talk over the scientific questions which occupied us. We discussed at length his ambitious "European Ideals," which were to remain a mere outline, and our last meetings were devoted to the various chapters of his book on the *Jewish Contributions to Civilization: An Estimate* [1919], of which I saw all but the concluding chapter in almost final form.

I know of no one who was more ready to put the full store of his encyclopedic knowledge at the disposal of anybody who wanted it and who was freer from all egotism and self-consciousness. He was a man of a beautiful, sweet disposition, of an unusual modesty which never gave the outsider an idea of his eminence in many respects, a staunch friend and one who bore malice to no one, not even if attacked. His name will live in the annals of Jewish scholarship.

10

Henry Malter

IT is not easy to give an account of the life of a scholar like Henry Malter. There are no high lights in the story of his life, no great events of general interest. He was a quiet, unostentatious devotee of Jewish learning who shunned publicity. He was permeated with lofty idealism and fervent devotion to learning. It would require a literary artist to write an adequate sketch of the silent martyrdom undergone by this sensitive personality in his struggle with the needs of daily life. In such trials he had numberless predecessors in many generations of Jewish scholars. But he felt that he was deprived of the compensation they received through the general recognition of their labors in the vineyard of the Torah. In our country, we are too much concerned with the problem of economic adjustment to give proper attention to those who spend their lives in the unprofitable business of reconstructing our people's past and in trying to bring the spiritual treasures of former generations nearer to our contemporaries. We have not yet learned to appreciate spiritual values in their proper perspective and we lack laymen with a background of Jewish learning who share to some extent the interests of the scholar and follow his efforts with sympathetic understanding. The Jewish scholar is a lonely man in the United States, and there are few places where he can find companionship and encouragement. Dr. Malter suffered from this loneliness, yet he could not get himself to associate with men whose materialistic view of life prevented them from appreciating that intellectual aspect of Judaism which was so dear to him.

255

There is no record of Dr. Malter's early life, though he occasionally referred to the hardships of his student years. Of his early childhood we have a very characteristic account from his own pen in a Hebrew autobiography of which, unfortunately, only two short chapters were written. Consequently, we can give only a brief outline of the years preceding his arrival in this country.

Malter was born in a small village, Banse, near Zabno, Galicia. His autobiography gives a vivid sketch of the life there. It is characteristic of his early surroundings that he was not quite sure of the year of his birth, his father adding or subtracting a few years in order to excite his ambition for progress in his Hebrew studies, or to boast to others of his accomplishments. The probable date of his birth was March 23 (Shushan Purim) 1864.

He devoted his youth to talmudic studies under the guidance of his scholarly father and early acquired a mastery of this vast literature. But these studies did not satisfy the very gifted young man to whom articles in the Hebrew weekly, *Ha-Maggid*, had brought the tidings of other fields of Jewish learning and of the combination of Jewish studies with modern culture. Since this paper was published in Lyck, he directed his steps to that small town in Eastern Prussia, which he reached after great hardships, walking much of the way.

Further wanderings led him to Berlin, where he lived for over a decade, adapting himself completely to Western standards, though originally many of the German customs seemed very strange to him. He earned his living by teaching Hebrew, meanwhile acquiring the secular education which enabled him to qualify for admission to the university in 1889. At the same time, he continued his Jewish studies and enlarged their scope under Stein-schneider at the *Veitel-Heine-Ephraimsche Lehranstalt*, 1890–1898. He came very close to the famous master, whose favorite pupils he and Poznanski became at this period. The influence of Steinschneider very largely shaped Malter's scientific career. At his suggestion, the latter selected as the subject of his doctoral dissertation a philosophic treatise by the famous Mohammedan theologian Al-Gazzali in Hebrew translation. He tried to reconstruct the lost Arabic original on the basis of other works by the same writer, and in this first essay displayed his thorough familiarity with Arabic philosophic literature, as well as with the mediaeval Hebrew terminology of the translators. He received his doctor's degree from the University of Heidelberg, in 1894, and his rabbinical diploma, in 1898, from the *Lehranstalt für die Wissenschaft des Judentums*, which he had attended for five years. At the latter institution it was Martin Schreiner who particularly attracted the young scholar, as he shared his interest in mediaeval philosophy.

During his student years, Malter, although of a retiring nature and of a pessimistic frame of mind, gained the respect and friendship of the best and most serious of his fellow students. The bonds between him and such men as Samuel Poznanski, David Neumark and especially Micah Joseph Berdyczewsky lasted throughout their lives.

Malter took a deep interest in the publishing society *Ahiasaph*, which at that time printed its publications in Berlin, and for this society he translated one of Steinschneider's chief works, his *Jewish Literature*. In this book, Steinschneider had for the first time given an outline of the vast literary pursuits of the Jewish people in its thousand years of dispersion, classifying it by periods and subjects. In the Hebrew translation by Malter the book became accessible to much larger circles and exerted a great influence. Malter's translation is remarkable for his Hebrew style which showed his pronounced purism, avoiding Germanisms and foreign words as far as possible and replacing them largely with terms he had gathered from

mediaeval literature which had been forgotten by modern
writers. He also frequently coined new terms which have
since been generally accepted. The basis of his work was
an authorized English translation which had appeared
forty years earlier; but he added notes, taking account of
the progress made in the various fields since that time.
Steinschneider's longer notes were left for an appendix
which never appeared, though in 1908 and 1909 Malter
translated and supplemented these additional notes in
collaboration with the present writer. If he had been
informed beforehand that the book would be reprinted
in 1923, we should probably possess this standard work in
a complete and up-to-date edition. It is to be hoped that,
with the new interest in Hebrew publications, a publisher
will be found for these additions to his work on which he
spent much time and effort.

A common devotion to our great teacher ripened in
Malter and the present writer the plan for an edition
of Steinschneider's collected works, the first volume
of which appeared after Malter's death. It contains a
fine, comprehensive sketch of the master from Malter's
pen.

Malter's writings show a wide range and a remarkable
versatility. His interest in bibliography found an early
expression in his contribution to Glassberg's book on
Circumcision (1896). Later (1899), at Steinschneider's
suggestion, he was charged with the very difficult task of
cataloguing the books and manuscripts left by the well-
known bookdealer, Fischel Hirsch. The collection included
many fragments of very rare, and even unknown, books
and leaves of manuscripts, the identification of which
required an unusually wide acquaintance with obscure
branches of Jewish literature. It was probably his extensive
bibliographical knowledge which led to Malter's appointment as librarian of the then recently-established communal

library of the Berlin community, a position which he held only one year.

In January, 1900, Malter was appointed Instructor in Mediaeval Philosophy and Arabic at the Hebrew Union College, Cincinnati, and in September of the same year he married Bertha Freund, of Saaz, Bohemia. He remained in Cincinnati till 1907. During these years he taught not only the subjects for which he was appointed, but also Bible, Mishna, Talmud, *Shulhan Aruk* and Ethiopic. For a while he also filled the office of rabbi of Shearith Israel Congregation. Malter did not feel happy in his new surroundings and resented the attacks on the works of the Jewish past made by writers who, in his opinion, were not competent to deal with such matters. Though hardly an admirer of the *Shulhan Aruk* himself, we find him defending it against aspersions in one of the Jewish weeklies. As a convinced nationalist, he could not reconcile himself to the philosophy of Reform Judaism and he tried to expound his personal views on this question in a series of articles in the *Hebrew Union College Journal*, 1902–03, under the characteristic title "Backward, then Forward." In this series, he tried to show that, without the idea of Jewish nationalism and culture, Judaism could not endure as a religion pure and simple. Neither Orthodoxy nor — much less — Reform would be able to carry on the old struggle for survival successfully. The final article which was to give the author's own solution of the inner Jewish problem was not permitted to appear.

Being at variance with the leaders of the institution as to the fundamentals of the theology of Reform Judaism which the Hebrew Union College represented, Malter could not long remain a member of its faculty. In 1907, he resigned and came to New York where he devoted himself to literary work, collaborating for a while on J. D. Eisenstein's Hebrew encyclopedia, to which he contributed a number of articles, including a comprehensive one on Aristotle in Jewish literature.

Two years later (1909), Dropsie College was opened and Professor Malter was given the chair of Talmudic Literature, which he filled to the time of his death, April 4, 1925. His teaching was by no means limited to the interpretation of the Talmud and to the discussion of literary and introductory questions connected with it. Besides interpreting chapters of the Babylonian and Palestinian Talmud and various Midrashim, we find him reading the chief philosophic works of the Judeo-Arabic period. At the same time he lectured on bibliography, on mediaeval Jewish literature in general, as well as on its various branches, such as talmudic, halakic, philosophical, ethical, historical, exegetical, poetical and liturgical.

With the conscientiousness which was characteristic of Malter in everything he did, he took his teaching very seriously and tried to give his students the best possible training. Where only incorrect texts were available, he did not hesitate to procure manuscripts, in order to be able to get as close to the exact wording as possible and to introduce his students into the secrets of textual criticism. He had great pedagogic gifts and I have heard him praised by his pupils, particularly as a most excellent teacher of Talmud. He paid attention to philological accuracy as well as to clear understanding of the subject matter and never left a passage until every aspect had been clarified.

The same painstaking exactness characterized all his literary work from the very beginning. Before writing on any topic he made himself familiar with the entire literature, no matter whether he was working on an article for an encyclopedia, a review, or an original paper.

His favorite subject was Judeo-Arabic philosophy. He started a series of articles on the influence of Arabic philosophy on Judaism, of which only the general introduction and the article "Al-Kindi" have appeared (*Ha-Shiloah*, VI, 38–52, and XV, 99–115). In his dissertation he announced the plan of publishing the most important work of the Arabic philosopher Gazzali, *The Intentions of the Philosophers*, in the Arabic original, utilizing the various Hebrew translations for fixing the text. He had procured photographs of the two Arabic manuscripts, but I do not know whether he proceeded far with the actual work.

The book which was to crown his labor in this field was to be an adequate edition of Judah ibn Tibbon's Hebrew translation of Saadia's great philosophic work, *Emunot we-Deot*, which tried to reconcile Judaism with Arabic philosophy. He had prepared a very elaborate commentary on this book, some twenty years before, and had revised the text on the basis of the Arabic original. He realized, however, the necessity of obtaining access to the manuscripts of the Hebrew translation in order to be sure to put the text before us in the form in which it had actually come from the hands of the translator and in which it had made its mark on Jewish literature. Having chosen this task, he never lost sight of it, even while he was engaged on other commissions given him by various bodies. In the last year of his life he finally had his material collected and felt free to revise his earlier work and to prepare the edition of which he had always dreamt. He told me a few days before his premature death — at the age of sixty-one — that he had covered 240 of the 320 pages of the Arabic text, when a malignant disease began to sap his vitality. While suffering unbearable pain, he managed to go over another sixty pages, and only twenty were awaiting final revision when his power of resistance was broken. He died on April 4, 1925. Near the goal of his dreams, a cruel fate wrested the pen out of his hand; and his last thoughts were undoubtedly of this and other projected works which he had to leave unpublished.

The most important of Malter's published works is his exhaustive volume, *Saadia Gaon, His Life and Works*, opening the Morris Loeb Series issued by the Jewish Publication Society. This volume is regarded by many critics as the best and most scholarly biography of a Jewish worthy we possess in the English language. Here the originally scanty material on the life and personality of the greatest gaon, later greatly enriched by the new material found in the *Geniza*, was subjected to searching criticism in copious footnotes. On the basis of this body of information an interesting and well-written sketch of Saadia's life was made. The works of the many-sided scholar are classified and described in the second part of the volume. Their influence on later generations is illustrated in a special chapter, showing how they spread to all lands of the Diaspora. The bibliography of these works is discussed separately in a third part of the book, covering over a hundred pages. Here the author, with uncommon thoroughness, compiled a large corpus of references from the widely scattered literature of the subject, so that the comprehensiveness of his work is amazing even to the specialist. He bestowed a great deal of care on the literary form of his presentation and, in spite of his 660 footnotes, Malter succeeded in producing an attractive and readable volume.

Another of Malter's special interests was Shem Tob Palquera, a later philosopher of less originality, but in many ways an interesting personality, who lived in southern France in the thirteenth century and whom Malter regarded as a representative of the wide culture of his country and period. He appealed to the scholar also as an excellent stylist. Malter sketched the life and activity of this "enthusiastic champion of learning and enlightenment," in a very interesting essay (*Jewish Quarterly Review*, New Series, I, 151–81), and published his "Treatise on Dreams" with a lengthy introduction (ibid., 451–501). Several notes to this text developed into short essays, such as "Dreams as a Cause of Literary Compositions" (in the *Studies in Jewish Literature in Honor of K. Kohler*). One of his students, at his suggestion, selected another work of Palquera as a thesis, while Malter himself intended to edit a third of the smaller unpublished writings of the same philosopher.

During his last seven years, Malter was engaged in the task of establishing, on the basis of all the extant manuscripts, the correct text of the treatise Ta'anit of the Babylonian Talmud. His text, and English translation, appeared posthumously in 1928 in the Schiff Library of the Jewish Classics. But the full significance of his tremendous work became manifest only when his complete notes were published with all the various readings and his critical remarks. The American Academy for Jewish Research, of which he was the secretary, published it in 1930 as Volume I of its special publications under the title: *The Treatise Ta'anit of the Babylonian Talmud critically edited on the basis of twenty-four manuscripts, quotations by old authorities and early editions, and provided with notes containing the critical apparatus as well as discussions and explanations of the text*. This work of patient labor and critical acumen, which led him back to the talmudic studies of his youth, for the first time shows what liberties the copyists took with the wording of their Talmud texts and what critical method is required in order to fix the original version.

Malter contributed many articles to the *Jewish Quarterly Review* and to various German and Hebrew scientific journals and popular periodicals.

One may dwell, in conclusion, upon the personality of this remarkable scholar. He was most painstaking in his work and shirked no labor in order to reach reliable results. He was very regular and systematic in his working hours as in his habits of life, and this made it possible for him to accomplish so much. His scholarship was of a very high order. He always tried to give his best and to present the results of his researches in pleasing form. While he disliked to rewrite what he had written, he took great pains to formulate his sentences properly before putting them on paper. His style was lucid and even elegant. He wrote German and English equally well, but his fine Hebrew style was more characteristic than either.

Malter had a pronounced sense for the aesthetic and laid great stress on proper appearance. Of delicate constitution, he rarely enjoyed perfect health. He was a lonely man who did not make friends very easily and, being an intellectual aristocrat, had a high standard for those he considered worthy of his friendship. In many respects he was a man of strong convictions, with a pronounced feeling for justice. On the other hand, he also had strong prejudices which he took no trouble to hide. "I regard it as worthy of little men," he says in one of his articles, "to advocate the golden mean, this travelling in the middle of the road, which as everybody knows is reserved for beasts of burden, when the pavement on either side is intended for men." He never left people in doubt as to which side he favored. It was not easy for him to adapt himself to his surroundings. His nature was not a very happy one, but in a congenial circle he would show the whole charm of his attractive personality. With a whimsically ironical, yet good-humored smile, he would give amusing characterizations of persons as well as of books and events and he could be a most entertaining conversationalist. To those to whom he gave his wholehearted friendship this was a rare and highly appreciated gift, and they could count on him in every respect. Altogether he was a marked individuality who exerted a strong influence on the scholars, and the few laymen who cared for scholarship, with whom he came in contact.

11

Max Leopold Margolis

MAX LEOPOLD MARGOLIS was born on October 15, 1866, in Meretz, Government of Vilna, a descendant of a family of rabbis and scholars who were proud to count R. Lipmann Heller among their forefathers. His father, R. Isaac Margolis, was a man of unusual attainments. He had devoted his youth exclusively to the study of the Talmud, but, instead of looking for a rabbinical position, he first tried his luck as a businessman. Failing in this, he was later compelled to accept the professional rabbinate and made a name for himself by some apologetic pamphlets in defense of the Talmud and *Shulhan Aruk*, as well as by a volume of tales from the Talmud written in simple and attractive Hebrew style. But his interests were not entirely limited to ancient Jewish literature. Self-taught, he acquired a knowledge of the classical languages, mathematics and science, and some of his contributions to Hebrew periodicals gave evidence of broad knowledge.

The son received his earliest instruction from his father. When, at the age of five, he was brought to a *heder* in the customary way, the experiment did not work. The little boy stayed for only an hour and, calling the *melamed* an *'Am ha-Aretz*, he walked home, to have his father continue his education personally. The gifted youngster somehow attracted the attention of the Greek-Orthodox priest of the village, who taught him Russian, arithmetic and other elementary subjects.

By the age of eleven the boy had already learned to read the weekly portion from the *Sepher Torah* as well as the prophetic lessons and the Book of Esther; he also was on the way towards becoming an expert Torah-scribe. As a matter of fact, once, when he was about seven years old, his father having been called up to the Torah, the young lad trailed after him and insisted on reading the *parasha*; in order to avoid disorder, he was placed on a footstool and he actually read from the Scroll. His eagerness for study, however, did not prevent him from taking an active part in boyish games. His home town was situated on the Niemen, and Max enjoyed swimming in the river in the summer and skating on it in the winter; he became an expert in both arts. The thoroughness and strong will power so characteristic of the man were evident in his early youth, as was his brusque way of speaking his mind, which, as we have seen, he already showed in the *heder*. Strong-willed as he was, he decided, after having attained the age of *bar mitsva*, to leave the little town which offered so few possibilities for satisfying his thirst for knowledge. He ran away from home. The attempt was naturally unsuccessful, but his father thereupon decided to send him to Berlin to his father-in-law, David Bernstein. After a few weeks the boy returned home. The father now tried to transmit to his ambitious son the knowledge he had himself acquired with such great difficulty, and for the next few years he took entire charge of the boy's education. When he went to Warsaw, where he gave private instruction, he took Max with him. Thus Max was there at the time of the first pogrom, in December, 1881. The anxious days spent in a cellar under the protection of gentile friends left an indelible impression on the boy's mind, so that under no conditions did he ever want to go back to Russia.

During those years his father not only continued his Hebrew instruction, but also taught him the rudiments of Latin, Greek and mathematics. His brother Elias, to whom I am indebted for the information on Max Margolis' early history, had a Hebrew textbook on trigonometry and logarithms prepared by his father for Max's instruction.

The father realized that this training could not lead to a rounded-out education such as this ambitious and precocious lad required. In 1885, when Max had reached the age of seventeen, his father again took him to Berlin, had him matriculated in the Leibnitz Gymnasium and left him in the house of his grandfather where Max now felt happier than on his previous visit. In the Gymnasium, Max distinguished himself in Greek, Latin and mathematics and, during the last three years of his stay there, was considered the best student of Greek. He always retained a special predilection for that language, as is evident from so many of his later publications. At the same time he kept up his Hebrew studies and corresponded with his father in the holy tongue. There are still extant two congratulatory poems with an acrostic, upon his grandfather's birthday, written in his clear and beautiful hand which was quite remarkable. His Hebrew knowledge stood him in good stead, as it enabled him to earn his expenses by giving Hebrew lessons. Among his pupils were three sons of the well-known Cassierer family in Berlin, with whom he always kept up friendly relations in later years.

A year after his father had brought Max to Berlin, he with his family visited him there on his way to New York; it was the last time that Max was to see his father, who died at the age of forty-five, only a year after he had made a new home for himself and had become the rabbi of the Kalvarier Schul in New York. Max remained in Berlin to complete his course at the Gymnasium from which he graduated after only four years of study, in 1889 — clear evidence of the excellence of the preparation he had received from his father. The years of his attendance at the Leibnitz Gymnasium left an indelible impress on Max Margolis' entire life. Here he acquired the mastery of

Greek and Latin, and also the sure method which was so characteristic of his whole scientific activity. In his biographical note at the end of his doctoral dissertation, he stated that he was imbued with German culture when, after finishing school, he decided to follow his family to the New World.

In the fall of 1889, he entered Columbia University, studying Semitics under Professor Gottheil, Latin under Professor Peck and Philosophy under Professors Butler and Catell. In 1890, he attained the degree of M. A. and in 1891 that of Doctor of Philosophy for a dissertation written in excellent Latin. His subject was a discussion of the value of Rashi's commentary for the preparation of a critical edition of the text of the Talmud. He chose the treatise of Erubin, probably because for this treatise he had access to the very rare first edition, Pesaro 1514, and to readings from other important texts incorporated in the notes of the *Variae Lectiones* of Rabbinovicz. In the introduction he emphasizes the necessity for a critical edition of the talmudic text and the inadequacy of the then recent specimen published by Friedmann. He discusses the early efforts to correct the text by conjecture and intuition and states that it is time to stop building from the top and to begin by laying the proper foundation. Turning to his special subject, he gives a list of Rashi manuscripts known to him and then shows in detail how Rashi's commentary may be used to evolve the underlying talmudic text which antedates the existing manuscripts considerably. His treatment is a model of such work and shows the young man to have mastered all the intricacies of the complicated problems of textual criticism and to have a special flair for that kind of research. He tries to establish the relationship of the various Rashi texts to one another and to the manuscripts of the Talmud as far as their readings were gathered by Rabbinovicz.

After his graduation, Doctor Margolis was given a fellowship in Semitics by his Alma Mater for a year, during which he published a description of *The Columbia College Manuscript of Meghilla*, establishing its relationship to the other Talmud manuscripts on the basis of a minute collation of several leaves.

He wrote, many years later, that he had then conceived the ambitious plan of a critical edition of the Talmud "based not only on the direct evidence of the manuscripts, but also on such secondary sources as the gaonic responsa, Nissim, Hananel, Alfasi, the *Aruk*, Rashi, and so on." He goes on, however, "Not only did America prove to be the wrong place for such an undertaking, but the circumstances were not lacking to lead me away from my proposed plan into entirely different work." The task of preparing a *Manual of the Aramaic language of the Babylonian Talmud with Chrestomathy and Glossary*, which was entrusted to him by the Berlin theologian and orientalist, Professor Strack, in 1894, was dropped after a time, when Margolis realized that in this country he could not have access to the helps indispensable for giving satisfactory texts for his selections in a chrestomathy. Only thirteen years later, when he had gone to Europe after giving up his position at the Hebrew Union College, did he once more turn to the first field of his studies. Then, after careful perusal of all the Talmud codices found in German libraries, he wrote his grammar which is based entirely on passages compared with the manuscripts and thus reliable in every detail, not to speak of the texts of the chrestomathy. Even for the paradigms he did not choose, as is customary, a certain verbal root and give it in every form no matter whether it occurs in the Talmud or not, but he selected only forms of verbs which are actually found there. Thus we are always on safe ground in this short but comprehensive grammatical treatise, which includes the first attempt at a systematic presentation of the syntax, lacking in the works of all his predecessors. While engaged in the preparation of this work, he wrote an appeal in a Baltimore weekly that the only complete Talmud manuscript be made accessible through photographic reproduction. In this appeal he informs us of his old comprehensive plan.

But I have anticipated. In 1892 Margolis was appointed instructor in Hebrew and Biblical Exegesis at the Hebrew Union College; and he later became Assistant Professor. The young instructor found the elementary Hebrew grammars unsuitable for the classroom, as they did not sufficiently reflect the recent advances of research in that field, and he therefore published, in 1893, *An Elementary Text Book of Hebrew Accidence* based on the most recent and authoritative works. Even here he gave some results of his own research. The little book is characterized by a conciseness of statement which prevails in most of his publications. His *Notes on Semitic Grammar* published during this period, 1894–96, shows his fine philological sense and his thorough familiarity with the grammatical phenomena of the various Semitic languages. That he also had become interested in theological questions in his new surroundings is evidenced by his paper on "The Theology of the Old Prayerbook," published in the *Yearbook of the Central Conference of American Rabbis*, 1897. In the same place there appeared in 1903 his "The Theological Aspect of Reformed Judaism." The radical attitude expressed in this paper was not maintained by the author in his later years.

In 1897 he left Cincinnati to accept a call to the University of California as Assistant Professor of Semitic languages. In the following year he became Associate Professor. He remained there till 1905.

During that period he was engaged in a most important plan to revise the Hebrew and Aramaic equivalents in the concordance of the Septuagint, several specimens of which he published in 1905 and 1906. It was his intention to arrange these equivalents in such a way that it would be possible to reconstruct the original text underlying the Septuagint with absolute certainty, or, as he expressed it, "in place of the brilliant but uncertain guesses [it would lead to] results which may be predicted with almost mathematical accuracy."

This plan of Doctor Margolis' was received with general approval by the most eminent scholars in the field, and in 1908 men like Adolf Deissmann, Driver, Kautzsch, Nestle and Strack issued an appeal to raise a fund to enable Margolis, whom they state to be "admirably qualified to execute the work," to devote two years to its execution. After careful examination they enthusiastically endorsed the plan as "of the utmost importance, both for the scientific study of the Old Testament and also for checking the unscientific and hazardous use often made of the Septuagint. It will be a work that can never become antiquated, but will simply be indispensable to every student of the Old Testament."

In September, 1905, Margolis returned to the Hebrew Union College as Professor of Biblical Exegesis. In March, 1907, he resigned because of a controversy on Zionism between him and Doctor Kaufmann Kohler, then President of the College. After his resignation, Margolis left the United States for an extended European trip, visiting libraries and meeting many scholars. He used this opportunity to prepare the material for his *Manual of the Aramaic Language of the Babylonian Talmud*, which he wrote in English and German, and which appeared in both languages in 1910; but of this I have already spoken.

In 1908, an agreement was reached between the Jewish Publication Society and the Central Conference of American Rabbis to cooperate in bringing out a new revised English translation of the Bible. The board appointed

by the two bodies immediately and unanimously chose
Margolis as editor-in-chief and secretary to the editorial
board, for he had by that time made for himself a name
as one of the foremost Jewish scholars in the biblical field.
Naturally, he had to carry the lion's share of the work
which covered a period of seven years. The notes on the
whole Bible which he prepared for this translation form a
gigantic work and are a most useful aid for textual criticism and exegesis of the Bible. They have been published
only in typewritten form for private circulation. Attention
was paid by him to the ancient versions, to talmudic and
midrashic allusions and to all available Jewish commentators from the Middle Ages to modern times, as well as
to the important non-Jewish commentaries.

The Dropsie College had been opened in the meantime,
in 1909, and Margolis was appointed Professor of Biblical
Philology, a chair which he held with distinction from that
date until his death.

In an institution of higher learning like Dropsie College,
which does not train rabbis but is devoted to general
scholarly education, a wide scope is granted to the prefer-
ences of the individual professors; the courses, accordingly,
give a clear indication of their particular interests, though
due attention is naturally paid to the wishes and the
ability of their special students. Looking at Doctor Margolis' courses from this point of view, we notice his great
interest in every aspect of grammatical study, from the
Masora and the earliest Jewish writings in this field to the
most modern publications. Courses extending over several
years must have given his pupils a rare training in the whole
of Hebrew and Aramaic grammar. Some twenty years
previously, Dr. Margolis had undertaken to write a scientific Hebrew grammar for the *Grundriss* published by the
Gesellschaft zur Förderung der Wissenschaft des Judentums. He started on this work and intended to take it up

seriously after his edition of the Septuagint on Joshua should have appeared. Courses in the Greek and Coptic languages were to introduce his students to the ancient versions in these languages. Topographical studies in Palestinian geography embraced tannaitic literature and Eusebius' *Onomasticon*.

Aside from the interpretation of the books of the Bible, Margolis lectured on Ben Sira and the Fourth Book of Ezra, which he planned to edit for the Classics Series of the Jewish Publication Society. A general course which he gave on the technique of editing texts must have been illuminating. The first course he ever announced, "Scope and Methodology of Biblical Philology," an abstract of which is the first article in the New Series of the *Jewish Quarterly Review*, was meant to be elaborated into a comprehensive volume in the style of Böckh — one of the many plans which, alas, were not destined to be executed.

Naturally the master's interests also found expression in the theses of many of his pupils; thus three of them, dealing with the language of the Bible translations of Aquila, Symmachus and Theodotion, are connected with his work on the Septuagint-Concordance; one, on the pronunciation of Hebrew according to the transliterations in the Hexapla, goes back to the studies which led him to the Greek Joshua and of which I shall speak later, while his work on that book caused him to have the Aldine Joshua as well as the variants of the Hebrew manuscripts of Joshua subjected to a critical inquiry. A subject like "The Relationship between God and Israel in the Bible," on the other hand, shows that he readily permitted some pronounced interests of his students to have free play.

We can see how widely Margolis' eminence in his field was recognized from the fact that in 1914 he was appointed by the Society of Biblical Literature and Exegesis as editor of its *Journal* — a task which he gave up in 1922 in order to take over the editorship of the *Journal of the American Oriental Society*. For the academic year 1924–5 he was appointed Annual Professor at the American School of Oriental Research in Jerusalem, serving at the same time as one of the first visiting professors at the newly established Hebrew University.

His stay in Jerusalem gave him the long-desired opportunity to visit the scenes of biblical history, to obtain first-hand acquaintance with the new excavations and to watch the growth of the new Jewish center in Palestine, in which he fervently believed.

But his stay in the Holy Land, to which he had looked forward with so much hope and anticipation, was to be marred by a tragedy. He lost there one of his two young sons, and this misfortune left an indelible scar on the rest of his life.

Although I first met Doctor Margolis in 1906, I saw him more frequently after I became a member of the Publication Committee of the Jewish Publication Society, about 1916. He had then been a member of that Committee for many years. The monthly meetings, which he attended most conscientiously, gave me an opportunity to appreciate his critical judgment, his vast learning and his deep interest in anything Jewish. He frequently reported on manuscripts which he had read for the Society, and these were by no means limited to scholarly books. He read novels, dramas and other manuscripts, and his caustic criticism was always the result of careful thought. We especially turned to him in anything that concerned the Bible.

Hand in hand with the preparation of the new Bible translation, the Publication Society planned a popular commentary on the Bible, intended primarily for the teacher, the inquiring pupil and the general reader, which was to be both reliable and Jewish.

In 1908 Margolis published his commentary on Micah

as a specimen for this series. After the completion and the publication of the Bible translation, this plan was taken up again, and in 1920 an announcement was published by a committee of which Margolis was the secretary. He was to be editor-in-chief of the series, and he undertook personally to comment on the first two books of the Pentateuch. He began this task, but the lack of means at that time prevented the Society from proceeding with the plan.

To another series of popular books on the Bible, connected with the new translation, Margolis contributed two little volumes: *The Story of the Bible Translations* (1917), and *The Hebrew Scriptures in the Making* (1922). These books, while strictly popular, are based on an exhaustive study of all the questions involved.

Another undertaking of the Publication Society was to bring us into more intimate association. An offer was made to the Society to finance a one-volume *History of the Jewish People*, and Margolis and I were asked to write it. Margolis was to carry the main burden of this task. He did the writing of the book, using my notes for the talmudic and mediaeval periods. He frequently came to New York to discuss various problems in connection with this work. While our opinions naturally differed on many points, no difficulty or misunderstanding ever arose, and both of us enjoyed the collaboration which brought us closer to one another. I learned to admire his sound judgment, his untiring industry and his unusual powers of concentrating on his work. Besides all his other duties, he would generally devote eight hours a day to the *History*, which progressed very rapidly, in spite of the fact that the year he spent in Palestine fell within that period. Although the biblical period was his main field, and he enjoyed the opportunity to present his view of biblical history in comprehensive fashion, he showed a thorough acquaintance with the later periods of Jewish history and literature as well. The arrangement of the chronological tables at the end of the volume, placing the events in different countries in parallel columns, gives evidence of his practical and methodical mind.

During all that time he never neglected his work on the Septuagint. In connection with his plan for a revision of the Hebrew equivalents of the Septuagint Concordance, he made all kinds of observations on the methods of the translators as well as on the changes in transmission due to revisors and copyists. His *Studien im griechischen Alten Testament* (1907) sum up in sixty pages a great many of his results under various topics. It seems that in the course of these studies he began to examine the transliterations, mostly proper names, found in the Septuagint. He gathered about twelve hundred and, in 1910, according to his own statement, they were almost ready for publication.

In the course of these researches he observed that the numerous proper names in the Greek Joshua offered a key for grouping the manuscripts of the Septuagint. He then began to concentrate his studies on this book, and Dropsie College readily provided him with the necessary photographs of Greek Joshua manuscripts. Originally he intended to publish an edition of a small group of manuscripts showing a particular recension. "The K Text of Joshua" (1911), was meant to be preparatory to this larger work. Professor G. F. Moore said: "As a specimen of text-critical study, it would be difficult to praise this work beyond its desert." But in time his plan expanded to a critical and final edition of *The Book of Joshua in Greek, According to the Critically Restored Text, with an Apparatus Containing the Variants of the Principal Recensions and of the Individual Witnesses*. A specimen containing chapter VI, 1–12, appeared in the *Israel Abrahams Memorial Volume* in 1927. The printing of the text with its various types and sigla proved an almost impossible task, and it was found advisable to reproduce the author's manuscript by a photographic process. Margolis thereupon recopied in his beautiful, clear handwriting the 400–500 quarto pages of his text with the full apparatus. It is difficult to describe the complicated arrangement of the pages with their eight to nine separate groups of variants and notes under the text. In order to appreciate Margolis' work one has to see this masterpiece of calligraphy, testifying to his inexhaustible patience, industry, methodical planning and meticulous execution.

While heretofore all the editors of the Septuagint were satisfied to reproduce one of the old manuscripts, usually the *Vaticanus* or the *Alexandrinus*, and to add to it the variants in other sources, Margolis realized that the task of an editor is to establish as nearly as possible the original text. His researches showed him that of all the available codices, the *Vaticanus* comes closest to the original; but his edition is no longer a reproduction of this one codex, but a very much revised and improved text. The readings are arranged according to the principal recensions: the Egyptian, Syrian, Palestinian and Constantinopolitan, as well as of a mixed group, while his own notes explain some of the differences and sum up the bearing of the Septuagint on the Hebrew text of the book.

I may mention, in passing, that aside from Greek manuscripts his remarkable linguistic equipment permitted Margolis to refer, at first hand, in his apparatus to the translations from the Greek into Syriac, Ethiopic, Coptic and Bohairic. What an amount of minute collation of photographs, demanding the greatest exactitude and most infinite patience, was required in preparing this *magnum opus* is very difficult to realize, even for those who have worked on critical editions; but Margolis never shirked any labor that would lead to exact results. For a mere review of a new edition of an important Greek manuscript of Ben

Sira he took the trouble to check all the references to this manuscript in the large Septuagint of Holmes and Parsons and to compare them with the new edition.

Some time before his death, the first part of his Joshua appeared under the auspices of the Kohut Foundation. Three more issues appeared till 1938; the continuation was interrupted by the war. The transcription of the text had been entirely finished long ago, and at the time of his death Margolis was engaged in the preparation of the elaborate prolegomena. Two days before illness compelled him to stop his work which he was never to resume, he wrote to me about the present status of the book which he hoped to finish in the course of the year.

In connection with the work on Joshua, and in order to simplify his introduction, Margolis prepared an exhaustive paper of about 200–300 pages, as far as I recollect, on the lost Codex of the Dutch scholar, Masius, and the latter's work on Joshua. On the recommendation of the late Professor Moore, this volume was accepted for publication in the Harvard Theological Series. But Margolis was not fortunate enough to see even a beginning of its printing.

When his work on Joshua was approaching completion, new plans occupied his fertile mind, and in a paper read before the American Academy for Jewish Research he proposed a cooperative edition of the Masoretic text, according to scientific principles. Many an unfinished work and many a plan died with him! Only some of his smaller publications — the by-products of his larger schemes — and the first issues of his life-work give some idea of his great power and his tremendous learning.

His untimely death, April 2, 1932, removed from our midst one of the few outstanding Jewish scholars and one of the greatest philologians and students of the Bible. He was an inspiring teacher who brought out the best in his pupils and gave them rare training in method and true scholarship. He permitted no sham or superficiality. His criticism was always severe, but based on careful deliberation.

I have spoken at length about the great achievements of Margolis as a scholar. I can only mention in conclusion that much could be said about Margolis as a man and as a Jew. His ardent belief in Zionism, for which he brought great sacrifices, is well known. Anything pertaining to the fate of the Jews concerned him personally. Margolis was by no means a scholar who, secluded in the four walls of his study, lived merely in the past; the complicated problems of present-day life were of great interest to him. There was no topic which one could not discuss with him and to which he could not contribute out of his lucid mind and the rich store of his information.

12

Israel Friedlaender the Scholar

I SHALL try in this brief sketch of Dr. Friedlaender's scientific activity to point out his accomplishments in Jewish and oriental learning of which many, who appreciate his public activities, are not fully aware. He was one of the greatest Arabists in this country, thoroughly familiar not only with the Arabic language but with Arabic thought and culture, an excellent Hebrew philologian, a Bible exegete with original ideas, an historian of deep insight and remarkable powers of presentation, a teacher of mediaeval Jewish philosophy, a gifted publicist and objective reviewer, a rare linguist and a master of style in Hebrew, German and English, both in writing and in speaking.

When Israel Friedlaender came to Berlin, in his eighteenth year, he intended to acquaint himself with the advances of Western education and culture, but he was so thoroughly imbued with Jewish learning through the education he had received at home and so familiar with Jewish literature as it had developed in Russia and Poland that from the very beginning he could give as well as receive. He found that some of the Hebrew and Russian writers had much to offer even to the Western Jews, and his exceptional gift for languages and style made him especially fit to act as mediator. In 1898 he translated from Russian into German Dubnow's *Jewish History*, an essay on the philosophy of history, now familiar to most of us in Miss Szold's English re-translation. Friedlaender was a student at the time and he signed the book only with his initials.

Seven years later his translation of S. M. Dubnow's *Die Grundlagen des Nationaljudentums* made another work of the same writer accessible to the German reading public. An English lecture included in his collected essays presents the substance of Dubnow's "Theory of Jewish Nationalism" to the English reader.

But much more than by Dubnow, Friedlaender was influenced by the ideas of Ahad Ha'Am, a writer upon whom he always looked with special admiration and reverence. His German translation of Ahad Ha'Am's Hebrew essays introduced this Jewish thinker to the Western world. A few separate essays were received with so much interest that, in 1904, he undertook the publication of a considerable volume which had the distinction of appearing in a second edition in 1913, together with a second volume translated by another hand. Since then an English translation has appeared too, but I think we are justified in stating that it is due to Dr. Friedlaender that Ahad Ha'Am and his theories became so well known among the Western Jews who do not read Hebrew.

Friedlaender frequently returned to this favorite author of his, and tried to popularize Ahad Ha'Am's ideas. He delivered a public lecture on him at the Jewish Theological Seminary in 1906 which is now included in his collected essays. These German translations of Friedlaender show his remarkable skill in rendering the words of the Hebrew and Russian writers into such an excellent, idiomatic German that the reader would never guess the translator had acquired this language only two or three years previously.

When Friedlaender came to Berlin with the intention of acquiring the rabbinical degree at the Seminary, he began at the same time to study Semitic languages at the University of Berlin, and in order to get the Doctor's degree he went a few years later to Strasbourg University where he enjoyed the instruction of the greatest master in Semitic studies, Theodor Nöldeke. The latter soon became very fond of his unusually gifted pupil and greatly encouraged him in his work. Friedlaender became so deeply interested in his subject that he decided to change his career and to devote himself wholly to Semitics, with a natural preference for subjects which had some bearing on Jewish matters. For his Doctor's dissertation he selected an investigation of the Arabic language of Maimonides. His researches led him to the conclusion that the common idea of a special Judeo-Arabic dialect had no real foundation. Maimonides, he showed, wrote the same Arabic as his most cultured Mohammedan contemporaries, only that he was more free from the literary influence of the language of the Koran, which restricted the Mohammedans in their literary expression. Accordingly, he maintained that Maimonides' works represent the Arabic of his time in a purer form than the works of Mohammedan writers possibly could. While the Hebrew of Maimonides, as of all Judeo-Spanish writers, is not free from Arabisms, no traces of Hebraic influence can be discovered in his Arabic style. This Friedlaender pointed out in the introduction to the first part of his *Der Sprachgebrauch des Maimonides*, his first scientific production, containing an Arabic-German dictionary of all the words not found or insufficiently supported by evidence in the ordinary Arabic dictionaries. This book is far superior to the common run of doctoral dissertations and exhibits the author's thorough equipment in Arabic philology as well as his great industry and exactness. It showed the orientalists the importance of the Judeo-Arabic texts for their field of studies; it was received very favorably by competent critics and proved to be a great help to succeeding editors of Maimonidean texts. The grammatical part, for which Friedlaender collected very rich materials, was unfortunately never worked out, and only a few gleanings of it can be found in the introduction to Friedlaender's *Selections from the Arabic Writings of Maimonides,* which appeared in 1909 in the Semitic Study Series.

Maimonides remained the favorite subject of Friedlaender's studies. In 1904, a year after his arrival in this country, he delivered a public lecture on the seven hundredth anniversary of the death of this great thinker. Besides this general essay, which was translated into German, his *Past and Present* also includes a lecture on "Maimonides as an Exegete" and a paper on "Maimonides as a Master of Style." He published in different periodicals several responsa of Maimonides in the Arabic original with interesting notes and introductions. These were taken chiefly from manuscripts of the *Geniza.* From the same source he published a letter congratulating Maimonides, probably on his appointment as *Nagid, i. e.,* the official head of Egyptian Jewry. This letter makes an interesting contribution to the characterizations of the philosopher.

For several years, Friedlaender labored on an edition of a larger text of Maimonides which, at the time of his death, was nearly ready for publication. He intended to edit the famous letter to Yemen (on the question whether they should believe in a man who claimed to be the Messiah) from the manuscript of the Arabic original in the Library of the Jewish Theological Seminary and the three extant Hebrew translations of it. In the Arabic text Friedlaender found a lengthy historical statement on some false messiahs which all the translators curiously had omitted. Together with this he wanted to publish two other cognate treatises of Maimonides — on "Resurrection" and on "Conversion under Compulsion" — as well as a few Arabic letters found in our manuscript. In this connection the edition of some further Judeo-Arabic texts from *Geniza* manuscripts may be mentioned. The most interesting of them is the fragment of a curious "Mohammedan Book on

Augury in Hebrew Characters," an almost unique specimen of the fusion of Islam with Judaism, which aptly illustrates the fact that popular superstition does not hesitate to transgress confessional barriers. Two others represent halakic treatises by Samuel ibn Hofni and Isaac bar Ruben. Many more such texts were copied by Friedlaender for inclusion in the Schechter Studies. Friedlaender accompanied these as well as some of the responsa of Maimonides with an excellent Hebrew translation of his own.

When Friedlaender made up his mind to follow a university career and to become a Semitic scholar, he selected Arabic as his main field. He could not, of course, limit himself to Jewish studies, but had to devote himself to Mohammedan history and literature as well. Wellhausen had just started his fundamental researches into early Arabic history and had shown how the different schools of tradition had influenced the Arabic historians. These investigations seem to have greatly attracted Friedlaender, who treated the same subject from different angles. In his *Probevortrag* preceding his admission as lecturer (*Privatdocent*) at Strasbourg University, he discussed the tendency of the various historical constructions of the Mohammedan sources and showed that there were religious reasons for their falsifications. The murder, for example, of the third khalif, Othman, by some of Mohammed's most trusted companions whom the prophet had promised a place in Paradise, deeply hurt the religious feelings of orthodox Moslems. They maintained that, since the act was absolutely against all religious prescriptions, it could not have been committed by such pious men. They accordingly shifted the blame to an enigmatic person, Abdallah ben Saba, a converted Jew reputed to be the founder of the Shiitic heresy. In his inaugural lecture on "The Messianic Idea in Islam," Friedlaender pointed to the strong influence of Jewish Messianism and the Christian heterodox doctrine of Docetism on the development of the Mohammedan heresies. To the study of these heresies and especially that of the Shiites, Friedlaender devoted considerable time. He based his researches on the manuscript account of a prominent Mohammedan theologian of the 11th century — Ibn Hazm. This and other investigations were interrupted by his acceptance of Doctor Schechter's call to the Jewish Theological Seminary. But Friedlaender never gave them up and, during his repeated visits to England, continued them in the British Museum.

The large use which Friedlaender made of manuscripts even for texts of which printed editions are available, like Shahrastani, is a characteristic indication of his painstaking exactness in scholarly work. Before Friedlaender had a chance to publish this work, the text of Ibn Hazm was printed in Cairo. The rich material on the Shiites which Friedlaender had collected appeared in 1909 as a reprint from volumes 28–29 of the *Journal of the American Oriental Society*. The first portion contains an English rendering of the parts of Ibn Hazm's book relating to this subject. He corrected the printed text in many instances from the manuscripts he had consulted. The second part gives the commentary, with considerable cognate material gathered from other sources. This work did not possess the finished form which he always liked to give to his literary productions. The material had grown much under his hands and recasting would have entailed more time than he could devote to the subject. In order to make the results of his investigations accessible he finally decided, distasteful as it was to him, to publish it in this fragmentary form. The work found the warmest approval among competent scholars like Nöldeke and Goldziher and caused a scientific body in far-away India, the Indian Research Society of Calcutta, to appoint its author to corresponding membership.

His occupation with these Mohammedan heresies suggested to Friedlaender close relations with similar Jewish movements in Arabic speaking countries; and considerable reading in Jewish sources on earlier and later sects, down to the movement of Shabbetai Zebi, convinced him of the existence of such influences. His "Jewish-Arabic Studies," which he published in the first three volumes of the new series of the *Jewish Quarterly Review*, are mainly devoted to this subject and throw light on many of the strange theories which we meet in our Hebrew sources. To Abdallah ben Saba, the founder of Shiitism, and his Jewish origin, Friedlaender devoted a monograph in which he pointed out the Jewish elements and influences in Shiitism which most of the modern scholars who had studied the subject, and tried to explain it from Persian or other sources, had not realized. Here Wellhausen had been his predecessor, but Friedlaender with his thorough acquaintance with Jewish literature could in many points correct Wellhausen, prove his thesis more convincingly and adduce more striking evidence of the correlation between the Shiites and Jews. He especially pointed to relations with the theology of the Falashas, but he emphasized from the outset that he could not very well reach satisfactory results and had to leave many questions and problems open.

Once more Friedlaender returned to his Strasbourg studies in his book *Die Chadhirlegende und der Alexanderroman*, in which he discussed some complicated problems of folklore and literary history. His investigations extending to stories of Alexander the Great in Greek, Syriac, Arabic, Persian and Ethiopic, include a fascinating chapter on the traces of the Alexander stories in the Babylonian Talmud.

When World War I brought the problem of the Jews of Russia and Poland once more to the foreground of general interest, the need for reliable information, in order to understand their situation and to take the right steps for

their protection, induced Friedlaender to write, in 1915, a
book offering a bird's-eye view of their history and their
culture. It is based on a series of lectures he had delivered
in Dropsie College and presents in a popular form a comprehensive picture of the history of the Jews in Eastern
Europe. His description of their spiritual development
helps the westerner to appreciate their mental outlook.
This was the first book to treat of this subject in English
and filled a distinct gap. It was translated into German.
A popular edition of this book, the third, appeared in 1920.
At the same time he undertook an English translation of
Dubnow's comprehensive *History of the Jews in Russia and
Poland from the Earliest Times until the Present Day*, the first
volume of which appeared in 1916, while the text of the
third volume was issued for private circulation before the
Versailles Conference in 1919. This final volume appeared
in 1920, completed by an elaborate index making the rich
information contained in the work easily accessible for
reference. When approaching this task, Friedlaender found
that he could not limit himself to a mere translation, but
that the Russian original had to be recast to a considerable
extent in order to make it acceptable to the American
public.

Friedlaender's historical studies maintained a close relationship with the present, as he was always earnestly
concerned with the well-being of his people. His last published book, *Past and Present*, a selection from his Jewish
essays, contains many of his contributions to the discussion
of Jewish problems of the day, especially of American
Jewry. Here we find the best thought of the mature, sympathetic observer who since his youth had carefully followed the Jewish problems on two continents with rare
understanding and who was at least as much concerned
with the spiritual and national revival of his people as he
was with his scientific pursuits. It is obvious from his

contributions to the study of the Bible, with which the volume opens, that "biblical science with its bewildering divergence of opinion" did not overmuch appeal to him, and that he was too conscientious a scholar to accept its critical dicta uncritically. *Ignorabimus*, he was convinced, must remain the answer to many of the mooted problems of biblical criticism and he did not feel a call to add new hypotheses to the large number of those propounded by the biblical students of our generation. Altogether, he felt that we are much more Talmud Jews than Bible Jews. The later literature attracted him more as a subject of study, much as he loved the Bible (indeed, he knew the Hebrew original by heart and had actually every word of it at his fingertips). There was one task, however, which Dr. Friedlaender eagerly hoped to accomplish some day — a commentary on Isaiah and perhaps on some other prophetical books. He felt that a modern interpretation from a Jewish point of view, in contradiction to recent work in this field, would constitute a contribution of real value.

In estimating the scientific work of Dr. Friedlaender we must admire his many-sidedness and brilliance as well as the minute exactness of his research. He had an unfailing eye for the essential and was quick to grasp a problem in its entirety. He intuitively formed a mental picture which enabled him to put all the details in their proper place and proportion. He understood how to make his presentation clear and interesting, however complicated and foreign to the reader the subject matter might be. His striving for accomplished literary form was never permitted to interfere with the scientific accuracy of his research. As a characteristic, one may point here to the elaborate indices which he added to some of his later books and on which he spent as much time and effort as he did on the clearness of his presentation.

Dr. Friedlaender can serve us as a model of the true,

objective scholar who combined to a remarkable degree thoroughness and lucidity. The rare blending of the East and the West which did not cause the slightest break in his personality made his collaboration so precious in our country and in our time of transition, and makes us feel his loss the more poignantly. We can realize how much he would have contributed to our life and to our knowledge if he had been granted a longer life.

BIBLIOGRAPHY

Bibliography

1. Saadia

First published in *Rab Saadia Gaon: Studies in his Honor*, edited by Louis Finkelstein, New York, 1944, 53–95, with footnotes which are omitted here.

The standard biography of Saadia is that by H. Malter, *Saadia Gaon: his Life and Work*, Philadelphia, 1921; reprinted 1942.

Several collective volumes have been published in connection with the millennium of Saadia's death: J. L. Fishman (editor), *Rav Saadya Gaon* (Hebrew), Jerusalem, 1943; American Academy for Jewish Research, *Texts and Studies*, I, *Saadia Anniversary Volume*, New York, 1943, including A. Freimann, "A Saadia Bibliography, 1920–1942," as a supplement to Malter; Edwin J. Rosenthal (editor), *Saadya Studies*, Manchester, 1943; as well as special Saadia numbers in the *Jewish Quarterly Review* (New Series), *Bitzaron, Hadoar*, a. o.

2. Rabbenu Gershom, Light of the Exile

Unpublished.

Naphtali ben Samuel [Simhoni], "Rabbenu Gershom Meor ha-Gola," in *Hashiloah*, 28 (1913), 14–22, 119–128, 201–212 (Hebrew).

A. Epstein, "Der Gerschom Meor ha-Golah zugeschriebene Talmud-Commentar," in *Festschrift zum achtzigsten Geburtstag Moritz Steinschneiders*, Leipzig, 1896, 115–143.

3. Rashi

First published in American Academy for Jewish Research, *Texts and Studies*, II, *Rashi Anniversary Volume*, New York, 1941, 9–30.

293

The fullest biography of Rashi is still that by E. M. Lipschütz, *Rabbi Shelomo Yitzhaki*, Warsaw, 1912 (Hebrew). Other volumes published in connection with the nine-hundredth anniversary of Rashi's birth are: J. L. Fishman (editor), *Sefer Rashi*, Jerusalem, 1941 (Hebrew); Rashi numbers in *Bitzaron, Hadoar*, a. o., and several smaller volumes and essays.

4. MAIMONIDES

First published in *Octocentennial Series*, II, New York, 1935; reprinted in *Studies in Jewish History and Booklore*, New York, 1944, 26–47.

Published in connection with the Octocentennial of Maimonides' birth: S. Zeitlin, *Maimonides, A Biography*, New York, 1935; A. Heschel, *Maimonides, Eine Biographie*, Berlin, 1935; J. L. Fishman (editor), *Rabbenu Moshe ben Maimon*, Jerusalem, 1935 (Hebrew); I. Epstein (editor), *Moses Maimonides, Anglo-Jewish Papers in Connection with the Eighth Centenary of his Birth*, London, 1935; S. W. Baron (editor), *Essays on Maimonides. An Octocentennial Volume*, New York, 1941; as well as special Maimonides numbers in *Ha-Aretz, Jewish Quarterly Review, Monatsschrift für Geschichte und Wissenschaft des Judentums, Moznayim, Revue des Etudes Juives, Tarbiz*, a. o., and numerous essays.

W. Bacher, M. Brann, D. Simonsen, J. Guttmann (editors), *Moses Ben Maimon, Sein Leben, seine Werke und sein Einfluss*, I–II, Leipzig, 1908–1914, is the most important of the earlier publications.

5. MORITZ STEINSCHNEIDER

Unpublished.

As sources for this essay I used in the first place the documents which Miss Goldberg, Steinschneider's devoted secretary, had turned over to the Jewish Theological Seminary together with Steinschneider's correspondence. Some of the most important of these I have published as "Steinschneideriana II" in *Jewish Studies in Memory of George A. Kohut*, New York, 1935, and as an appendix to "Zunz's Letters to Steinschneider," in *Proceedings of the American Academy for Jewish Research*, V, New York, 1934.

Among the others, the most valuable is a *Cassa Buch* for the years 1832–1870, in which, in brief form, all expenses and income for every year are summed up. There is also a complete record of all the cases of "Jewish Oaths" sworn before Steinschneider. It was impossible to go through the entire enormous correspondence, but I read the letters of the bookseller A. Asher of Auerbach, David Cassel and M. A. Levy, his two closest friends, Julius Fürst, Joseph Zedner of the British Museum, Bandinel and Coxe of the Bodleian Library, the correspondence with A. Geiger — Ludwig Geiger had returned the letters addressed to his father after the latter's death — and a few others. Most revealing were the letters to his fiancée. Quotations from these letters are not always indicated by quotation marks, as they had to be translated very freely, on account of Steinschneider's difficult and condensed language, and often had to be shortened.

The autobiographical sketch in Wurzbach, *Biographisches Lexikon des Kaiserthums Oesterreich*, XXVIII, Vienna, 1878, is an invaluable source for the first sixty years of his life. The editor's letters to Steinschneider prove the latter's authorship of this biography. The only effort at a biography of Steinschneider, G. A. Kohut's *Moritz Steinschneider. A Tribute on his Eighty-Fourth Birthday*, Part I, New York, 1900, unfortunately does not go beyond the year 1845. See also Kohut's *Tribute Written on the Occasion of his 90th Birthday*, New York, 1906, and his "Steinschneideriana," in *A. S. Freidus Memorial Volume*, New York, 1929.

For the Zionist episode see N. M. Gelber, *Zur Vorgeschichte des Zionismus*, Vienna, 1927, 202–212, 305–309; S. W. Baron, "Abraham Benisch's Project for Jewish Colonization in Palestine (1842)," in *Jewish Studies in Memory of George A. Kohut*, New York, 1935. See also S. Spiegel's review of the *Jewish Studies* in *Opinion* for April, 1936, 32.

A collection of cuttings and reprints, mostly containing tributes in connection with his ninetieth birthday, necrologies and articles published on the hundredth anniversary of his birth were very helpful. There are among them articles by I. Abrahams and E. N. Adler, W. Bacher, A. Biram, R. Brainin, I. Elbogen, D. Herzog, Joseph Jacobs, H. Malter, J. Pagel, J. Pollak, S·

Schechter, A. Z. Schwarz, a. o. An article by Adeline Goldberg, "Steinschneider als Schulmann" and a "Nachwort" by L. Geiger in the *Allgemeine Zeitung des Judentums*, vol. 80, 1916, were especially instructive. A fuller estimate of Steinschneider by Geiger in the *Berliner Tageblatt*, March 27, 1916, to which he refers, was unfortunately inaccessible to me. If Miss Goldberg had been able, as was her intention, to send me certain papers which she had retained when she turned over the correspondence to the Seminary, it might have been possible to find some additional valuable information.

The exhaustive "Bibliography of the Writings of Professor Dr. Moritz Steinschneider compiled by George Alexander Kohut" fills 34 very closely printed pages in the *Festschrift* for Steinschneider's eightieth birthday. Additions for the last eleven years of his life were published by Miss Goldberg in three instalments in the *Zeitschrift für Hebräische Bibliographie*, 1901, 1905 and 1909; see also F. H. Garrison, "Bibliographie der Arbeiten Moritz Steinschneiders zur Geschichte der Medizin und der Naturwissenschaften," in Sudhoff's *Archiv für Geschichte der Medizin*, 25, 1932 (552 items); see also his "Moritz Steinschneider as a Contributor to the History and Bibliography of Medical Literature," in *Emanuel Libman Anniversary Volumes*, New York, 1932.

6. DAVID HOFFMANN

Unpublished.

L. Ginzberg, *Students, Scholars and Saints*, Philadelphia, 1928, 252–262; E. M. Lipschütz in E. Barischanski's translation of Hoffmann's *Rayot Makhriot neged Wellhausen*, Jerusalem, 1928, VII–XV; J. Neubauer, "Die Bedeutung David Hoffmanns für die Bibelwissenschaft," in *Jeschurun*, IX, 1922, 347–376; Ch. Tschernowitz, *Maseket Zikhronot*, New York, 1945, 244–264; J. Wohlgemuth, *Jeschurun*, IX, 1922, 1–19; O. Wolfsberg, *Sinai*, VII, Jerusalem, 1944, 74–81; L. Fischer, "Bibliographie der Schriften und Aufsätze des Dr. D. Hoffmann," in *Hoffmann Festschrift*, Berlin, 1914.

As sources I used some personal papers of Hoffmann, the

copy in his own hand of the correspondence between R. Hile Wechsler and S. R. Hirsch and a number of letters, some of which were put at my disposal by my brother-in-law, Mr. Mendel Hoffmann.

7. MAYER SULZBERGER

First published in *Publications of the American Jewish Historical Society*, No. 29 (1925), 188–193.

8. SOLOMON SCHECHTER

Partly published in *Publications of the American Jewish Historical Society*, No. 25 (1917), 177–192, and partly in *Memorial Adresses on Doctor Solomon Schechter*, New York, 1917, 2–6; reprinted in *Studies in Jewish History and Booklore*, 377–395.

N. Bentwich, *Solomon Schechter. A Biography*, Philadelphia, 1938; A. S. Oko, *Solomon Schechter. A Bibliography*, Cambridge, England, 1938; Appendix I, 79–86, lists "Studies and Appreciations."

9. THE JEWISH SCHOLARSHIP OF JOSEPH JACOBS

First published in *The American Hebrew*, February 11, 1916, 382; reprinted in *Studies in Jewish History and Booklore*, 396–399.

Mayer Sulzberger, "Joseph Jacobs," in *Publications of the American Jewish Historical Society*, No. 25 (1917); I. Zangwill a. o. in *Transactions of the Jewish Historical Society of England*, VIII, London, 1918, 129–152.

10. HENRY MALTER

First published in the *American Jewish Year Book*, 36 (1926), 261–272; reprinted in *Studies in Jewish History and Booklore*, 409–17.

11. MAX LEOPOLD MARGOLIS

First published in *Proceedings of the Rabbinical Assembly of America*, IV (1933), 368–380; reprinted in *Studies in Jewish History and Booklore*, 418–430.

Cyrus Adler in *American Jewish Year Book*, 35 (1933), 139–144; R. Gottheil, *Journal of the American Oriental Society*, 52 (1932), 105–109.

12. FRIEDLAENDER THE SCHOLAR

First published in *The Menorah Journal*, VI (1920), 344–350, as one of three papers on Friedlaender; reprinted in *Studies in Jewish History and Booklore*, 400–408.

Boaz Cohen, *Israel Friedlaender, A Bibliography of his Writings, With an Appreciation*, New York, 1936. On p. 12, note 3, the more important articles on Friedlaender are listed.